GLOBAL LEADERSHIP, CHANGE, ORGANIZATIONS, AND DEVELOPMENT

Michael Ba Banutu-Gomez,
PhD

iUniverse, Inc.
Bloomington

Global Leadership, Change, Organizations, and Development

iUniverse books may be ordered through booksellers or by contacting:

iUniverse
1663 Liberty Drive
Bloomington, IN 47403
www.iuniverse.com
1-800-Authors (1-800-288-4677)

Because of the dynamic nature of the Internet, any Web addresses or links contained in this book may have changed since publication and may no longer be valid. The views expressed in this work are solely those of the author and do not necessarily reflect the views of the publisher, and the publisher hereby disclaims any responsibility for them.

Any people depicted in stock imagery provided by Thinkstock are models, and such images are being used for illustrative purposes only.

Certain stock imagery © Thinkstock.

ISBN: 978-1-4620-3614-1 (sc)
ISBN: 978-1-4620-3615-8 (hc)
ISBN: 978-1-4620-3616-5 (e)

Library of Congress Control Number: 2011912575

Printed in the United States of America

iUniverse rev. date: 7/21/2011

This book is dedicated to my family and to those who love and care about Organizations positive leadership success.

Acknowledgments

The author would like to thank his wife, Shandra Banutu-Gomez, daughter, Nyima Francine Banutu-Gomez, and friends for their support and encouragement while writing this book.

I hope that this book will contribute in some way to the education and service delivery skills of future dedicated individuals and professionals who care about Organizational success in the 21st century

Contents

Preface

Professor Michael Ba Banutu-Gomez received his Ph.D. at Case Western Reserve University – Wetherhead School of Management, Department of Organizational Behavior in 2001. Professor Michael Ba received his Qualified Teacher Certificate from the Gambia Teacher Training College. He has received his bachelor in Sociology and Applied Social Relations at Eastern Connecticut State University. He received his Masters in Social Work, with concentration in Management from Boston University.

Professor Ba Banutu-Gomez has presented his research work at professional conferences here in the US and in Europe. He worked for Bank of America as well as the Massachusetts Department of Social Services. He also worked for Oxfam America where he was the Coordinator for West Africa Program and Horn of Africa Program. Professor Ba is an Organizational Development Consultant. He has done consulting in the US, Africa, Asia, Middle East and Europe. Professor Ba Banutu-Gomez has conducted consulting for GEM – Global Excellence in Management Innovation and they have conducted leadership and certificate training program for chief executive officers and government offices worldwide. He has also conducted training on sustainable development.

Professor Ba Banutu-Gomez taught at Illinois Institute of Technology – Stuart School of Business. He also taught graduate business courses at Robert Morris College – Business Administration School. Presently Professor Ba Banutu-Gomez is a professor at Rowan University; William G. Rohrer College of Business where he teaches Business Administration, Leadership, Organizational Behavior, Global Leadership and Organizational Culture and International Business for both undergraduate and graduate students. Recently, Professor Ba has completed reviewing Organizational Behavior textbook authored by Schermerhorn, Hunt and Osborn for John Wiley & Sons Inc. Publishing Company and also International Business Textbook: The Challenge of Global Competition by Donald A. Ball, J. Michael Geringer, Michael S. Minor and James M. McNett for McGraw Hill Higher Education. He has recently published a book he wrote about Africa. The title is "Africa We owe it to Our Ancestors, Our Children and Ourselves."

Professor Ba Banutu-Gomez has published his work in academic journals. His work has been published in Journal of Global Business Issues, The Business Renaissance Quarterly, Indian Journal of Economics and Business, The Business Review, Cambridge, The Journal of American Academy of Business, Cambridge, Journal of Global Competitiveness, and Cross Cultural Management: An International Journal, and Business Research Yearbook.

Professor Ba Banutu-Gomez has reviewed papers for International Journal of Business Excellence, Journal of International Business Disciplines, and Journal of Current Research in Global Business, Academy of Management, and Association for Global Business International Conference, Thunderbird International Journal, Journal of Managerial Issues, and Eastern Academy of Management. Professor Ba Banutu-Gomez has presented papers in twenty International Academic Conferences. His current research interest is in Leadership, Global Leadership, Teamwork, International Business, Corporate Social Responsibility, Sustainable Development in Emerging Economy and Cross Cultural Management.

CHAPTER 1
The Author's Philosophy of Leadership

A true leader always has a vision; knows where he or she wants to go and how to get there. The leader values others' skills and experiences and builds teams that make use of them. He or she courageously accepts responsibility for problems and is able to clearly communicate the mission, goals and objectives of his organization. A great leader is willing to challenge the Status Quo while trusting and empowering people. The leader uses obstacles to create a positive future; is consistent: willing to set an example of sacrifice for the good of the next generation. The primary task of Leadership is to establish and maintain "intimacy" (caring) because disciplined unselfishness comes about only through close social relationships. Traditional sources of intimacy such as the family, the club, the neighborhood, life-long friendships and the church are all presently threatened by modern life-styles. Intimacy is essential for healthy individuals and thus, a healthy society. Once a society de-values intimacy, its young people will not develop a sense of community responsibility. These young people will go on to produce the next generation that will have a permanently diminished sense of community. This will soon result in a society solely comprised of individuals with no or only tenuous social ties to each other.

Leadership demands for creating a compelling vision of the desired future and developing motivating judicious strategies for producing the vibrant changes needed to achieve the vision that is not readily available. Vision can be defined as a picture of an ambitious, desirable future for the organization, team or community. Thus, achieving the vision requires effective leaders to share power rather than hoard or control it and find efficient and effective ways to increase an organization's brain power by getting everyone in the organization involved and committed in achieving desired goals or purposes. To sum it up, management can be defined as attainment of organizational goals in an efficient and effective process through organizing, staffing, directing, controlling organizational resources and planning. This means that, leadership cannot replace management; it should be in addition to management to maximize organizational performance. In summary, leadership involves an influence relationship among leaders and followers who intend real positive organizational changes and outcomes that reflect their continued shared purposes.

DISCUSSION QUESTIONS

1. Describe the best leader you have known. How did this leader acquire his or her capability as a leader?

2. What personal traits and skills should a person develop to be a good leader versus those developed to be a good manager in today's organization?

3. What are your strengths and weaknesses for leadership? Discuss your answers.

CHAPTER 2
Great African leaders know that all change must start at the top and at the bottom

For that reason, they take time to first establish understanding and true commitment at the highest levels of their organization. The most important attribute a leader must have is integrity. A leader with integrity provides consistent responses that show a sense of equal respect for everyone. This fosters 'family' type relationships between people. A leader who behaves consistently exhibits the integrity necessary to nurture the growth of trust.

The first task of management is to establish and maintain *trust,* because the success of an organization is determined by the willingness of individuals to make personal sacrifices. Before the objective of commitment to the development of a less selfish, more cooperative approach to working together can be achieved, there must be understanding, which comes from the open expression of opinions, feelings and ideas through a process of public debate and group analysis.

The first step in creating an organizational philosophy is for leaders to conduct a Cultural Profile Audit. Leaders should set an example during these discussions by critically examining the organization's current, actual operating philosophy, business strategy, marketplace goals and the values they place in people. A way to do this is to examine the most recent five key decisions in order to discover what principles were consistently applied.

A sufficient level of trust must be established first, to facilitate honest questioning of assumptions on the part of everyone. The first task for a leader is to set an example by openly disagreeing with others and actively working to create an environment where different opinions are welcomed. Leaders should establish a discussion process that reflects the egalitarianism, openness and participativeness that are the objectives of the change to take place.

Leaders set an example when they facilitate the growth of trust which is needed to implement this type of discussion process by positively accepting criticism. Though it will be painful, any group of people who trust one another to expose their deepest weaknesses is a group that can successfully implement change.

It is only by examining all organizational practices that one can uncover the roots of current organizational behavior. In order to deal with change, everyone must be open; that means being willing to investigate and question each other's work, as well as to appreciate the feedback others give in response when they look into one's own work.

Change requires Leaders to demonstrate a willingness to expose their weaknesses to members; in other words, a willingness to reveal themselves so completely that members may find human weakness there. This teaches members that their leaders are ready to acknowledge that everyone has weaknesses and it proves that all will be accepted in spite of their weaknesses. When nothing needs to be hidden, a tremendous energy is released.

Skillful leaders do more listening than talking; they observe the pattern of interaction in the group and know when to intervene. Skillful leaders utilize frequent periods of silence to give everyone time to process the preceding discussion, which will allow the true issue or conflict to arise in their conscious mind. Good leaders teach group dynamics to all organizational members so they can recognize group interaction patterns. Everyone must learn to see when a group is moving too quickly, how some behaviors interfere with group process, and how to stay on course.

The Best Leaders Teach Leadership

Members should be taught how to provide leadership that facilitates identifying issues, finding the roots of conflicts and creating solutions to problems that everyone can support.

Good leaders communicate with their behavior more than their words and then make sure they recognize and reward positive results of members' efforts immediately. They solicit suggestions from members, as a group, and move quickly to implement helpful ones right away.

Good leaders set an example by being prepared to address tough questions during regular question and answer sessions with members about how the organization is doing, its successes and problems, and other important work-related issues. Good leaders establish mentor-apprentice relationships throughout their organization, which provide frequent one-to-one involvement of members on projects, in order to supply close instruction and guidance to all members.

Leaders can encourage organizational members to transfer to related jobs, in order to expand their skills, by setting up a system of job rotation. Leaders can set an example by participating in the established system of career circulation, themselves. To achieve coordination across functions of an organization, all that is necessary is people who have become experts in several functions, specialties and offices and therefore can knit them together into an integrated whole. Every department should have in it someone who knows the people, problems and procedures of any other area within the organization.

A Self-evaluation of Leaders' Leadership Practices

Feedback from others shows that leaders need to work harder to stay up-to-date and to seek challenging assignments. Leaders need to be continuously aware of what is going on so that they can make strategic plans with others in order to implement changes, which can solve problems. Leaders can speak to supervisors, co-workers, peers, and professors to solicit help in designing challenging assignments for everyone. Leaders need to be more organized in a continuous process to create their vision of the future. Leaders need to more clearly communicate my vision so people can take ownership of it to put it into positive practice. Leaders need to conduct more out-reach in their institutions, organizations and government, where they work, professional organizations and community groups to empower people to feel a sense of identity, take ownership of and participate as a team in their vision. Leaders need to help people feel valued and that they know they can benefit from their knowledge and skills. Leaders must want to continue to allow others to take up responsibility to make their own decisions and to show them that they trust in their judgment and ability to apply their skills and knowledge to create an effective organization. Leaders must want to continue to supply them with constructive feedback so that they can identify their strengths and weaknesses in order to develop strategies to help them improve for the benefit of their own, as well as their organization's future. Evaluation by others shows that leaders need to work on improving how they organize projects into manageable steps and how they communicate their beliefs of how an organization should be run. .Operationalizing projects will allow people they work with to embark on small tasks to facilitate success which will produce the confidence and faith in their ability to solve larger problems. If we tackle smaller issues successfully, then we will win more people to our cause and in that way, we can capitalize and build on our success. Leaders need to continue to be aware to not neglect the need to make sure others are recognized for their contributions; that leader articulate those contributions and take time to celebrate them. Leaders need to continue to learn from others so they can learn how to more successfully implement actions to bring about my vision. Their action plan must include collecting new ideas and informing people through research at school, testing their assumptions by trying to "fix something broken" at their job and developing and trying out a stump speech at conferences they attend. As leaders expand their ability as a leader, they will try to incorporate five exemplary leadership practices into their actions and behavior. They will Challenge the Process by taking risks and experimenting with new ways of doing things. They will Inspire a Shared Vision of how they see the future by communicating it clearly to others. They will Enable Others to Act by fostering collaboration among people. They will Model the Way by setting realistic goals in order to become successful. They will Encourage the Heart by acknowledging the contributions of others with genuine appreciation. In the final analysis, leaders have no choice but to lead by example by influencing the process if they want to be successful and effective in today's global village.

DISCUSSION QUESTIONS

1. Why is it important for leaders to establish trust and commitment in a change process?

2. What skills does a leader need to have to successfully bring positive change in an organization?

3. Do you like change? Discuss your answers.

CHAPTER 3
Kenneth Kaunda, Great Leader

Obstacles and Risks

Kenneth Kaunda started life with several strikes against him. Because his father was a Christian missionary, he was in the religious minority. There was almost nothing from his father's income that his family could live on. His family depended on food from their garden and their flock of chickens. His father maintained strong ties with European Christian Missionaries in the area. Kaunda's background prepared him for his future. His faith gave him an optimistic outlook that carried him through exile and imprisonment; he sang hymns to motivate himself. As an organizer, his own family lived as simply as he had as a boy with a garden and poultry. He had to struggle to see others as adversaries who might want to crush him only because of the color of his skin because he had grown up in a family who had friends of different colors. To compound his disadvantage, Kenneth lived in a British Colony, Northern Rhodesia, where a Black African such as himself had no freedom, who's lifestyle, economic and political aspirations where stunted by widespread discrimination and oppression condoned by a government who offered him no representation.

Moved by a desire to help his neighbors, he developed self-help groups that evolved into a political organization. On a daily basis, he willingly faced the threat of imprisonment, slander and assassination. He traveled long distances by bicycle, alone, constantly in danger of being attacked by wild animals. After frightening off a lion by shaking his bicycle over his head, he sped on. Authorities reacted by exiling Kenneth and his family far from their home in a tiny house with their friends. When that did not succeed in silencing him, Kaunda was imprisoned. During this time, he cleaned the prison, waiting for a chance to see a tree, communing with the birds which brought hope to him. He struggled to maintain ties of communication with his supporters and endured long absences from his family. As his political organization grew, he found it hard to control the reactions of his followers and even himself to malicious efforts on the part of the colonial government to destroy their attempts to acquire dignity, equality and the right to vote; once finding himself on the verge of attacking an official who had insulted him. "I remember saying: if, because of our policy, you are lifted in the air and thrown to the ground, say 'Kill me, but I shall be free.' I was determined to combine Gandhi's policy of non-violence with Nkrumah's positive action. Villagers had been told that these Zambian men were cannibals. They especially liked children since these provided tender meat. Anyone who would go to this extent to telling lies in order to maintain his position I think calls for mental treatment, but this is imperialism at work." (Zambia Shall Be Free, Kenneth Kaunda) When his friend, who had worked side by side with him during many struggles, strayed from principles their organization had been founded upon, Kenneth chose to leave which meant trying to regain his people's trust and loyalty. Denied official permission to publish a newspaper, he created one using his tiny home for an office. After traveling miles to meet with the British government, his willingness to negotiate was met by treachery and a lack of respect for his ideas solely because he was a Black man.

Leadership Qualities and Skills

Kaunda exhibits the qualities and skills of a great leader because he sets a good example without meaning to. His faith gives him dedication; he is willing to take up responsibility to solve problems, no matter how complex or seemingly hopeless because he is possessed by a vision of Zambia with freedom for both Africans and immigrants._ Kaunda was able to mobilize people by getting them to focus on the positive rather than putting blame on anyone. He encourages the skills of others to lead; communicating in a simple, truthful manner with both humble countrymen and supporters from the most educated circles and challenges both his followers and the Status Quo in a positive rather than hostile manner. "One critical role of effective leaders is to be skillful craftsmen of their organization's mission...of equal importance is the ability to communicate their missions in ways that generate great intrinsic appeal." (Inspiring Others, Jay A. Conger)

Leadership Style

Kaunda has a vision of a positive future for his country and a concrete plan of how to reach it. He sets a good example by always being absolutely honest; gladly sacrificing personal comfort and risking his life. Kaunda is consistent in what he says and does; regardless of the situation or the stakes, he never hesitates to follow his principles. "To be persuasive we must be believable; to be believable we must be credible; to be credible, we must be truthful." (Ed R Morrow) "Leaders hold in their minds visions and ideals of what can be. They have a sense of what is uniquely possible if all work together." By appreciating others' skills, Kaunda encourages them to take the initiative. His ability to simplify complex problems allows him to educate by using a communication style that can be understood by all. "Effective framing of an organizational mission will ensure emotional impact particularly in terms of building a sense of confidence and excitement about the future." (The Leadership Challenge, James Kouzes & Barry Posner)

Inspiring Others

Kaunda uses negative experiences to build strength; he reflects on them. A good listener, he respects each of his followers, opponents and enemies; viewing all humans as inherently good, including those who are involved in evil. Kaunda maintains deep faith in his religion and lives by his African cultural values. It is necessary for a leader to have a vision of their organization in the future. They must successfully communicate the mission, goals and objectives of their company in simple, consistent terms to all employees. Setting a good example of sacrifice inspires employees to believe their supervisor lives up to the standards they are required to. This builds trust and creates the organizational strength needed for a foundation to build upon. "Our own self-leadership behaviors serve as a model from which others can learn. As Max DePree, chairman of Herman Miller, the office furniture maker, says, "It's not what you preach, but how you behave."

In contrast, not being a good example causes employees to be reluctant to buy into your ideas, thus, your company will be less productive. Working at the grassroots level, personally taking responsibility for problems will empower your employees. When their problem solving skills are encouraged and appreciated, your employees' self-esteem is built. They will feel confident to take action. Feeling a sense of ownership of the company and a desire to contribute to its wellbeing, they will see themselves as members of a family.

This builds a strong team, which is able to work toward a common goal. Accepting responsibility for crisis is useful for finding ways to improve your company. "The most appropriate leader is one who can lead others to lead themselves. Drucker suggests that the most effective leaders are those not afraid of developing strength in their subordinates. The SuperLeader serves as a source of information and experience, as a sounding board, and as the transmitter of overall organizational goals. For the Super Leader, the essence of the challenge is to lead followers to discover the potentialities that lie within themselves." (SUPERLEADERSHIP, Charles Manz, Henry Sims Jr.)

Lessons Learned

By learning about Kenneth Kaunda, I feel I have a clear idea about the skills and qualities of a great leader. I learned that as a leader, one must possess a vision and be prepared to sacrifice to accomplish it. True leadership requires patience and a willingness to start from where your followers are in order to empower them to use their skills in a positive way. One must be willing to face obstacles and take risks. It is essential that one be consistent and careful to practice what you preach. I have also learned that, as your organization grows, one may find it difficult to control one's followers and for that reason, one must always have a strategy in mind. Negative experiences should not be seen as losses, rather, opportunities for change, growth and learning. Incorporating them can expand one's scope and bring flexibility and strength. If one desires to be a truly great leader, one must strive to trust in the abilities of one's followers and see each of them as equal in importance to oneself, within the organization. I believe it is possible to challenge the Status Quo in one's country using non-violent direct action; Kenneth Kaunda has proven it. Most important of all, is the willingness to listen to what people want and the ability to simplify complex problems in order to educate people by communicating in a way that one will be easily and readily understood.

DISCUSSION QUESTIONS

1. Identify and list five things you have learned from this chapter. Briefly explain how each can help you to become a good leader.

2. What are your leadership qualities and skills and how do you plan to utilize each?

3. How do you inspire people to follow you?

CHAPTER 4
Intergenerational Leadership in Africa

Abstract

With increasing business Globalization and different cultures we have in this world, maintaining and managing cultural differences becomes a challenge for leaders, mangers and supervisors in the twenty-first century. The author explained why it is important to understand traditional African social structure in doing business in Africa. The main goal of this paper is devoted to understanding the concept of intergenerational leadership in Africa and it's importance and role in helping Western leaders and managers to effectively manage and succeed in Africa or developing nations. The paper concludes that organizational leadership in a developing country requires managers and leaders to have a high standard of conduct and being able to design and implement a management system which values innovation and creativity, nurtures flexibility and offers members the freedom to experiment and allow them to become self accountable.

Introduction

The author chose this topic of managing cultural differences in developing countries or in Africa because it is an essential skill all leaders and managers must master if they are to be successful in the global marketplace. As an organizational development consultant in Africa, Asia and Middle East, the author learned that lack of skills in managing cultural differences causes conflict between leaders, managers and staff who originate from different cultures. Thus it can cause serious mis-communication, which can hinder the growth and the productivity of an organization or company. The author is convinced that, for managers, leaders and practitioners to succeed at business in the twenty-first century, they must learn to support, maintain, and welcome cultures different than their own because the workforce who they must now motivate comes from all corners of the planet. Most importantly, Western leaders, managers and practitioners have to understand traditional African social structure as well as practice the concept of intergenerational leadership for them to succeed in Africa.

Defining Organizational Culture

In Africa, the Manjako ethnic group in The Gambia, Guinea-Bissau and Senegal defines culture as "our world of yesterday, our world of today and our world of tomorrow which creates and nurtures cooperation, development and sustainability among our people in our society". The Africans believe that culture is their roots and the foundation of their family, organization, community and society. Therefore ignoring their culture is ignoring their being in this world. When a society ignores its culture that society becomes light as a kite and the wind can blow it into any direction. This is due to the fact that society has no roots to keep it strong and face challenges in this world.

Hill (2003) defines culture as the complex whole that includes knowledge, belief, art, morals, custom, and other capabilities acquired by a person as a member of society. Human beings are social animals. The advent of human culture was an evolutionary leap that initiated the use of culture as a social tool by humans that ensured the survival of their species over time. People understand the meaning of other's behavior because they share understandings about the nature of their purpose in the universe. The safe environment culture enables civilizations to come into being. Cultural artifacts are the outward manifestations of the strong emotions humans feel in response to events that happen to them. People create images, songs, stories and rituals to express their inner climate during significant times in their lives. Therefore organizational culture are sustained by human social interaction through which people develop shared understandings about how to cope with, manage and avoid life's dangers. In addition, these artifacts serve to evoke in others and reinforce those emotions, creating an emotional climate that people can share as a group in their organization. Jones (2000) defines organizational culture as the set of shared values and norms that controls organizational members' interactions with each other and with people outside the organization.

According to Schneider and Barsoux (2003) management scholar Ed Schein borrowing the framework developed by anthropologists Kluckholn and Strodtbeck believes, "Organizational cultures spring from three sources: beliefs, values and assumptions; learning experiences as the organization evolves; and new beliefs, values, and assumptions brought in by new members and leaders". African countries or developing nation's organizational culture can provide the social coherence that will allow the natives to learn from their mistakes as a group and stimulate the innovation they need to discover adaptive strategies for dealing with change.

Understanding Traditional African Social Structure

To lead and manage effectively in Africa requires the understanding of the traditional African social structure. In doing so, we would start with the family. It is important to understand that, the family is one of the most important aspects of traditional African social structures, which Western leaders and managers who care and are concerned about their success in Africa must continue to strengthen. In Africa, the extended family network is responsible for maintaining the status of the family name or lineage. Relationships among husband, wife, and in-laws are strictly prescribed, as are relationships between children and parents. Within the traditional African framework, the family is NOT time limited. In Africa, the concept of the family extends both backward and forward. The individual is seen as the product of all the generation of his or her family from the beginning of the creation of humans in this world. This concept is reinforced by rituals, ceremonies, celebrations and customs, such as stories Elders tell that express reverence for ancestors, and songs Griots sing, which trace family members back over many centuries. Because of this continuity, an African's behavior has a different importance and consequence. This is so crucial in understanding the importance of the interconnectedness of the model that would be described later.

Thus, Western leaders and mangers that want to be successful in Africa must understand that personal actions reflect not only on the individual and nuclear and extended families but also the proceeding generations of the family since the creation of the world. Therefore, individual actions will impact upon all future generations as well. This places a burden of responsibility that transcends the individual's personal concern.

For this endeavor to succeed, one must make sure that power is accompanied by knowledge. They must also be given the power to perform enforcement duties. "If cultures in an organization are integrated in such a way that co-operation and mutual trust can flourish, and this internal strength is used successfully in exploiting environmental opportunities and neutralizing environmental threats, such an organization is likely to gain competitive advantages over other firms were these conditions are not met" (Bijisma,-Frnakema, 2001).

Here are the features of what we will be discussing in the conceptualized model provided below – Traditional African Leadership Practice, Openness and Willingness to Change, Shared Vision, Accountability and Patriotism. The author developed this model based on literature reviewed for this paper. However, it is very important to note why the concept of intergenerational leadership model in Africa is interconnected and that it has traditional African leadership practices in the middle, which then connects all the other categories together. This is important as clearly shown by the model because it is not just enough for a leader or manager to practice traditional African leadership without connecting it with all order categories.

Traditional African Leadership Practice: In Africa, traditional African leadership practices is perceived as the handing down of leadership information, believes, or customs from one generation to another. According to Banutu-Gomez (2002) this traditional African leadership practice has been passed down from generation to generation despite British colonization, the slave trade and current Western influence. In ancient West Africa, the king was the servant and shepherd of the people. His main and most important function was to serve the people. There is long tradition of fair inclusive leadership practice in Africa. Even though the setting has changed, the traditions are similar or the same. According to Africans, these traditional African leadership practices include the commitment and strong relationship of the family, which is the center of life and their existence. Banutu-Gomez (2001) defined Traditional African Leadership Practices as the root and foundation of African people were customs, information and believes are passed from one generation to another. The Africans believe that community is also important for the sustainability of life. This is to say that leadership requires eliciting cooperation and teamwork from a larger network of people and nurturing the people in that network motivated, using all skills of persuasion. Shared Vision:

The process of shared vision in Africa requires that leaders have to be open and flexible in order to share their vision in their organization, community and nation. Visionary leadership is the ability to create and articulate a realistic, credible, attractive vision of the future for an organizational unit that grows out of and improves upon the present (Robbins, 2003). Thus, flexibility and non-compromising is very vital for leaders and managers so that they can nurture their creativity. Thus, it is important that a leader's vision not only be their vision but a shared one that all the employees feel it belongs to them. To bring this to reality leaders must serve as mentor to their people, offer advice, teach new skills and techniques and also encouraged their employees to go to training. Further, the key properties of a vision seem to have inspirational possibilities that are realistic, value centered, culture specific, with high quality imagery and clear articulation. Not only can creative contributions be valuable to a firm, but the ability come up with unique yet appropriate ideas and solutions can be an important advantage for individuals as well (Perry-Smith & Shalley, 2003).

Accountability

The process of accountability here refers to the ability and commitment of the people to take ownership and responsibility of their work. In short if you are confident about your task-related skills, you will get your act together to do the task. This is one reason why you should give people the skills and confidence they need in order to put forth effort (Dubrin, 2001). The assumption here is that it is not as simple as finishing tasks given to the people, but most importantly to show the work belongs to them and that they are responsible and capable of doing it.

Patriotism

Basically, patriotism is referred to in the way people express great love, honor, faith and pride in their country. They want what's best for their country and supported goals and objectives of their organization that support the goals and objectives, which support the sustainability of their nation. In African culture patriotism requires a lot of energy, commitment and willingness to go the extra mile. This means that not only do leaders have a duty to their organization but also a duty to the people of that nation.

Willingness and Openness to Change

It is vital to realize that willingness and openness to change in Africa means that one has to value and cherish the continent's rich and ethnic and religious groups that sees and does things differently. The perception of each ethnic group or religious group is so unique and different that is why it is necessary to embrace the diversity in Africa. Therefore, positive change and encouragement is very important to have in any African organization.

The message here is that African society is interconnected and those leaders and managers in African organizations must value and support the interconnectedness of each level. Through this, they will empower and bring the best out of their employees to become more creative and innovative in their organizations.

Exhibit 1: The concept of Intergenerational Leadership Model

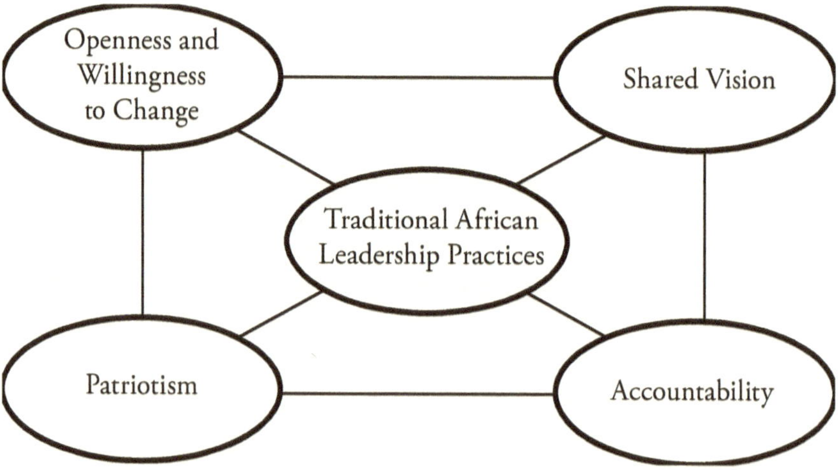

Exhibit one is a representation of Intergenerational Leadership model brought together in an organized framework with traditional African leadership at the core. The logic is that each Intergenerational Leadership component is of central importance to the development and understanding of traditional African leadership system within each employee in the organization or community. The potential payoffs include increased employee or citizen performance, creativity, innovation and consensus decision making process flowing from enhanced commitment, motivation, accountability and employee or citizen capability. Therefore, it seems clear that an essential ingredient to Intergenerational

Leadership is boundless optimism about the potential and ability of ordinary people to accomplish extraordinary things in the world. There are five main categories of the concept of intergenerational leadership model in Africa. The distinct trait of all traditional African leadership practices is consensus decision making in which citizens from one generation to another share a significant degree of decision making power with their leaders, managers, elders and supervisors. It is very important to understand that traditional leaders of African civilizations involved all citizens in the activities of organization via community group dialogue discussion and building consensus of all the important issues in which a decision must be made.

To successfully make this process come true, Western leaders and mangers in Africa must use the concept of intergenerational leadership model. Therefore, the decisions that Western leaders and managers in Africa have to make must address and accommodate the needs of all the stakeholders identified by intergenerational leadership definition. We can define intergenerational leadership as a process that a leader has the ability to practice traditional African leadership, create proactive shared vision, continuously able to nurture accountability, provides and nurtures a great sense of patriotism and begins to adapt to new changes to improve the future of an organization, community or societal level for self–sustainability of a nation. As an example, Africans believe that their ancestors guide their actions and bless them when they make positive choices for their people. This type of belief is ingrained in Africans and is an important aspect of their lives. Due to this Africans will always think about their ancestors when making decisions or taking actions about issues that will affect their families and nations.

This thought process has and will always continue to influence the decision-making process in African nations or developing countries. This is also something that all Western leaders and managers have to respect and adhere to in order to serve to the best interest of the organization, people and society. It is believed that a violation of this process is a disconnection from the ancestors and will not bring blessing to the leaders and managers that ignore it. This belief and thought process helps Africans to feel connected with their ancestors from generation to generation. Therefore, a disconnection of any category shown in the concept of intergenerational leadership model will create a negative gap in the community and organization in a nation. Once the gap has been created, it would be difficult if not impossible for any Western organization leader or manager in African nations to sustain self-sustainability. This is why intergenerational leadership is so deep and important now than ever before because it helps organization and society to become efficient and effective.

This type of interconnectedness in intergenerational leadership helps build in employees and citizens a sense of ownership for their organization self-sustainability. It also helps to build consensus, collaboration, teamwork and team credit and consultation where by each member of the organization has a positive role and purpose. Once this is nurtured, the employees will be motivated and empowered to become creative and innovative in their organizations. Creative thinking enables leaders to contribute novel insights that can open up new opportunities or alternatives for the group or the organization (Dubrin, 2001). This is a challenging circumstance that Western leaders and managers have to face in Africa or developing nations and address through practicing the concept of intergenerational leadership.

When Western leaders and managers in African organization have to make decisions, they are challenged to think and put the needs of families and women as important and valuable criteria in choice making. This is so important to note that the power of women in African society is so strong and eminent that decisions made by Western leaders and managers in African organizations have to consider women's voice. This is very crucial because any decision made by Western leaders and managers in African organizations that do not listen to the voices of the women will affect the lives of the African families. This places consequences to native men when they return back home to their families. This is so crucial in Africa because men usually have private meetings in their homes with their wives and mothers who tell them their choices that they need to be accommodated when making decisions, even if they are not present at public meetings.

Therefore, one has to realize that intergenerational leadership in Africa is deeper than our understanding of leadership talked about in literature or in Western world. The concept of intergenerational leadership is deeper in the sense that it has to do with the community and it's interconnectedness with individuals and all institutions. Therefore, intergenerational leadership in Africa or developing nations requires Western leaders and managers not only lead the organization but also re-build communities. What then does it mean to re-build a community in intergenerational leadership? By this, we mean re-building a society that builds a sustainable nation but building a nation is not like building a house. It is like building a marriage and one must coordinate people not technology in other to achieve productivity.

According to the concept of intergenerational leadership model, Western leaders and managers are required to work with all levels of the employees in the organization and society to ensure productivity is increased through effectively coordinating the efforts of many individuals in that organization. In accomplishing this, a Western leader and manager have to give employees incentives to adopt a cooperative, long-range view of the citizens. This is important because productivity is a problem of social organization. Therefore, in intergenerational leadership, Western leaders and managers have to understand that, in a consensus culture like Africa or developing nations, a community of citizens cooperates with each other to reach common goals through consensus process. Their behavior in this process relies on commitment and trusts fostered by commitment to community mechanisms. Thus the concept of intergenerational leadership requires that, an effective and efficient Western leader and manager in this process have to encourage the growth of informal social networks in their organizations.

Effective intergenerational leaders must communicate openly and honestly, appreciate, value, confront differences and resolve conflicts, and sublimate personal goals for the good of the organization and nation. Leadership effectiveness needs to address the means that a leader uses in trying to achieve goals as well as the content of those goals (Robbins, 2003). They also have to promote cooperation rather than competition. Here is were the advisement by the elders comes in and plays a key role in making things happen in a positive way. In this process, the elders use consensus to practice and nurture-shared vision, accountability, openness and willingness to change and patriotism and serve as spokes person's in all levels of the African societies. Managers and leaders in collectivistic cultures may be particularly motivated to invest in relationship with subordinates who are similar to themselves because the shared attributes provide some assurance that their mutual obligations and understandings will outlast the authority-based relationship (Schaubroeck & Lam, 2002).

By looking at the concept of intergenerational leadership model, one will realize that at one level the elders are bridging the gap between the family, community, ancestors, and generation to generation and organization. At the same time, they are passing on shared vision and connecting the citizens in African societies. They do this process by serving as mentors, motivating and empowering all citizens, from all age groups to be accountable about their societies, nations and organizations. An outstanding advantage of recognition, including praise, as a motivator is that it is no cost or low cost, yet powerful. Recognition thus has an enormous return on investment in comparison to cash bonus (Dubrin, 2001). Furthermore, leaders must recognize that recognition is a strong motivator because craving recognition is a normal human need in this world. Thus, in sustaining the process of accountability and connecting it with traditional African leadership practice, the Western leaders and managers in organizations in Africa must build and nurture a sense of ownership in their employees so that they can maintain efficient, effective organizations and nations.

It is important to understand that leaders, employees and managers in African organizations connect traditional African leadership practice with patriotism through the practice of commitment. Therefore, it is necessary for Western leaders and mangers not to ignore the importance of patriotism in building and sustaining organizations in Africa. This process also requires that Western leaders and managers to be open and willing to change.

However, Western leaders and managers must understand that any change process that would serve to the best interest of the employees in African nations or developing countries must create and sustain trust in all levels of their organization. Therefore trust is very vital for Western leaders and managers in organizations in African nations or developing countries to practice in sustaining intergenerational leadership. Western leaders and managers have to be aware of the fact that, trust takes time to form, building incrementally and accumulating. In fact it will take Western leaders and managers longer to build and sustain trust in Africa or developing nations because the natives view them as an outsider and colonialist. It is necessary to know that trust is not taking risk but it is the willingness to do so. This is what the elders in African societies have been building from generation to generation. An example of the trust that has been referred to here is the relationship between the Western leaders and managers in African organization and the stakeholders of intergenerational leadership such as ancestors, elders, families, women, men, adults, teenagers, children, babies and employees in any decision that has to be taken. Social exchange by means of personal relationships is deeply rooted behavior in most societies. People form relationships in order to give and receive things – both tangible and intangible – of value. Psychological contracts are formed whenever there is a social exchange between people (Eddelston, Kidder & Litzky, 2002).

By considering the needs of the stakeholders in making choices and decisions, Western leaders and managers in African organizations will connect the society in all levels while they maintain stability and trust in African organizations. Trust is a positive expectation that another will not act opportunistically

(Robbins, 2003). Failure to do so will make the native employees to view Western leaders and managers as people who are more interested in their personal gain than the gain of the African people.

However, Western leaders and managers who desire to succeed in Africa or developing nations, have to be aware of the fact that cultural value of individualism is an integral aspect of capitalism as it is practiced by Western countries, is antithetical to the Traditional African values in which "We" is more important than "I". The concept of intergenerational leadership Africa requires that before a society adopts a foreign culture, they must first examine the implications and effects of that culture on their cultural values. By doing this, Western leaders and managers in African nations would be better prepared to understand the economic systems of the African societies or developing nations and how they are interconnected with individuals and community. Thus it is important for Western leaders and managers to understand that economic systems are manifestations of many individual economic transactions within a society. This is so important because people whose behavior is governed by their unique cultural values conduct those transactions. Thus all economic systems display specific value systems. Globalization is not a fashion or temporary development. It is here to stay and most companies or managers have yet to make their accommodation to it (Jeannet, 2000). One of the things that Western leaders and managers in Africa have to be concerned with is that, when Africans set aside their traditional value of community "WE" it begins a psychological conflict. This psychological conflict will then affect their performance as well as their decision-making process. This also creates inner emptiness that cannot be satisfied by the superficial adoption of foreign values. By and large, the inner emptiness becomes a significant psychological weakness, which makes the person vulnerable to dependence. This type of dependence wipes out the creativity and innovation of the employees to compete in the 21st century organizations.

The concept of intergenerational leadership states that, culture is the root of each society, therefore it is vital for Western leaders and managers to preserve the good cultural practices in all African nations or developing nations so that the citizens will be proud of their continent and become self-sustainable. Thus, we have been called by the practice of the concept of intergenerational leadership to serve our communities, organizations, institutions, societies, governments and nations in a more meaningful and productive way.

Managing Business in Africa
or Developing Nations

To manage a business successfully in a developing country one must first find ways to become aware of one's own unique culture. Also drawing on the principles of the concept of intergenerational leadership will be an added asset to one's management skills. Thus being aware of the uniqueness one's particular culture, requires first having a personal experience that reinforces the reality that cultures different than one's own actually exist; in other words, a personal experience of cultural differences. We usually term this personal experience "culture shock" in America. Ethnocentrism is a belief in the superiority of one's own ethnic group or culture. Hand in hand with ethnocentrism goes a disregard or contempt for the culture of other countries. Unfortunately, ethnocentrism is all too prevalent, many Americans are guilty of it, as are many French people, Japanese people, British people, and son on. Ugly as it is, ethnocentrism is a fact of life, one that international business must be on continual guard against (Hill, 2003). This is why; many Americans continue to believe that they can conduct business strictly from an American perspective.

The global economy of today has forced most American companies to no longer consider the United States as only appropriate home base for their operations. According to Harris and Kumra, (2000) the criteria upon which Western managerial competence is based may wholly be inappropriate in an international setting and may indeed be determinants of failure rather than the key to success. The first step in overcoming one's natural parochialism is being able to perceive the need for finding the means to escape from the parochial tyranny of one's particular cultural perspective. First, nations and cultures differ in terms of how they define specific phenomena. Because of this managing cultural difference requires the understanding how objects or events are defined in other cultures. "Intercultural differences influence international business in many ways" (Zakaria, 2000). Thus it is very important to realize that when employees are sensitive to cultural differences in business practices it will help their firm to succeed in international business. "As the move toward the globalization of business continues, companies are establishing operations in overseas countries and markets. Such practices are challenging employees who find themselves suddenly transferred to countries where they are ignorant of the language and culture" (Frey-Ridgway, 1997).

In order to really open our mind's eye we need to acknowledge these truths about what we believe is the truth: 1) That is our perception (of reality) is selective and we only allow selected information through our perceptual screen to our conscious mind. 2) Perceptual patterns are learned. In addition, our personal experiences teach us to perceive the world in a certain way. 3) Perception is culturally determined. This helps us to learn to see the world (and other people) in a certain way based on our cultural background. 4) Perception tends to remain constant. Once we view reality in a certain way, we continue to see it that way. In other words, we perceive what we expect to perceive, according to our cultural mental map. We must be pre-disposed, in order to benefit from situations that might teach us about cultural differences.

Commitment for Self-Evaluation

Thus having an attitude and commitment of self-evaluation is necessary for the person who wants to be successful in managing a business in a culture that is different than the one he or she was brought up in. Therefore, one needs to ask oneself: "How can I transform these American or Western business practices, which I am familiar with and currently feel I need to use, into a form which is congruent with the culture that predominates in the country I am in now?" But, how can one predict outcomes with little knowledge of the culture one finds oneself in? How can one imagine the implications of such outcomes for oneself and the people around one in an unfamiliar society?

Digging deeper into the vast human mystery of culture brings one eventually to diverse complex value systems, the skeletal foundations of all cultures. Therefore, "to be effective in cross-cultural management, expatriate managers need to understand the nature of the culture or the country where they are going to be managing and how to adapt their managerial style accordingly" (Rodrigues, 1998).

Mistakes Foreign Managers and Leaders Make

Thus, lack of commitment for self-evaluation will lead American or Western leaders and managers to make mistakes in Africa or developing countries because the situations appear familiar to them but, in actuality, are quite different. What they do not consider is that the context of the situation determines its meaning. Because they are in a different culture, the context of situations is, in reality, unfamiliar to them. Cultures, which exist in countries in developing areas of the world, such as Africa, are often high-context.

Is it not surprising that, in their interactions with Africans, both at home and on the African continent, Americans or Westerns experience many opportunities that create challenges for people from all works of life? The fact that an American manager's ancestors were originally brought to America from Africa bond by the chains of the slave trade does not make him or her exempt from the negative influences of a cultural bias against Africans in the U.S. According to Peppas (2001) Sanders in 1990 indicated that executives serious about valuing diversity must be willing to take risk and must develop a plan which eliminates stereotypes, explores assumptions about group differences, builds relationships with people regarded as different, and empowers employees.

Below are the five good points, which American or Western business people must remember when doing business in Africa. The author suggested that these points would help anyone from the U.S. or Western who wanted to be accepted by people in many countries with non-Western cultures. 1) The most important thing to do is to be respectful. Don't be suspicious and openly check on something that you have asked you employee to do. 2) Be trustworthy. Always be sure you deliver when and what you promised. 3) It is critical to relax and slow down. Just remember you are not on the same kind of time schedule as you were in the United States or in your own country. 4) In addition learn to be tolerant and don't be overly sensitive to criticism or advice.

Remember, you can learn a lot from the local people. 5) And, most importantly just remember patience is the key to successful business in the 21st century organizations and particularly in Africa or developing nations

The success of negotiations often hinges on non-verbal cues that are often uniquely used by each different culture; consider, for example, the use of silence during bargaining: while "the Japanese silently consider the Americans' offer, the Americans interpret the silence as rejection and respond by making unnecessary concessions (by lowering the price). An example is, Latinos and Africans touch much more than Canadians, who in turn touch more than Swedes do. Arabs maintain much greater eye contact than do Americans, who in turn use more than the Japanese. In addition, Africans do not use eye contact as it is viewed as lack of respect but instead look down as a sign of respect when you talk to them. According to Robbins (2003) the cultural context of the negotiation significantly influences the amount and type of preparation for bargaining, the relative emphasis on task versus interpersonal relationships, the tactics used, and even where the negotiation should be conducted.

The Need to Design a Bottom-up Management System in Africa

Western leaders and managers in Africa need to know and design a bottom-up management system because it will help them to tap on the richness of African culture. This system should provide a two-way exchange of ideas, values innovation and creativity that sustains flexibility and at the same time allows members in the organization the freedom and opportunity to experiment. The process should rely heavily on consensus because this is how decisions are made in Africa or most developing nations. The reason why it should rely on the process of consensus is because consensus is part of the people's culture. Our culture is our comfort zone and so all developing nations should not be exempt from it. In addition, consensus does not recognize problems are either yours or mine because it teaches us that this is we. The mystery that comes in this process is a paradigm that unifies us and beckoning to us, so we can se what we are in our organization, community and nation. This is how creativity and innovation blossoms in a consensus culture. Conversely, the 21st century design, at its core, is about mutual relationships in service of a common goal or visions. It may have many of the elements that appear similar to the 20th century design, but the dynamic is fundamentally different. Internal and external relationships meld together in a common purpose. This design will produce higher energy, less stress and aggression, more innovation and creativity, as well as higher levels of performance (Twomey, 2002).

Therefore, the designing and implementing of systems, mechanisms and whose functions that fulfills the necessary tenets of productive democracy, predictability and stability, within a paradigm that allows people to seek their objectives and goals will be more attractive to developing nations. To sustain the system Western leaders and managers must continuously communicate and build a sustainable partnership with people in their organization about vibrant economic policy and accountable, economic management in a process and principle that builds and nurtures a trusting feeling of appreciation among the citizens. What will the bottom-up management system look like?

The bottom-up management system should be designed in a team centered approach organization because this is not a new concept in Africa or developing nations. It is important to note that collectivism is what dictates people actions in Africa or developing nations so using teams will be the best natural fit for organizational success in these nations.

Although, many people believe there is magic in the team interaction process. They imagine that by working together, members of a team will eventually evolve the structures they need. This is a false assumption. A successful team: 1) engages and sustains member motivation by giving attention to the *meaning* of the team's work, the *autonomy* they have in executing it and on direct *feedback* about results. Also, 2) it is as small as possible (given the work to be done), has clear boundaries, includes members with adequate task and interpersonal skills, and has a high level of diversity. In addition, 3) there are clear specifications regarding the extent and limit of the team's authority and accountability and 4) the team must use consensus in decision making process. No team can be successful unless it has a support system from top management in the organization that believes in teamwork. An adequate support system provides: 1) rewards to recognize and reinforce excellent team performance, 2) training and technical consultation as needed to develop members' knowledge and expertise, 3) a feedback system to provide data members can use to manage their work, and 4) a source of materials, such as equipment, tools, space, and money. However, to sustain a type of organization that uses consensus in decision making process, Western leaders and managers must accept that it will take employees longer time to make decision. The key to a successful consensus team decision-making process is patience.

According to Robbins (2003) teams are more flexible and responsive to changing events than are traditional departments or other forms of structure in organization. Therefore to perform well as team members, individuals must be able to communicate openly and honestly to confront differences. In this way team members will be able to resolve conflicts and to sublimate personal goals for the good of the team and organization. In other words, Western leaders and managers are required to give employees the encouragement to share skills and ideas and act on what they suggest to improve the organization. The emphasis on individualism may also make it difficult to build teams within an organization to perform collective task. If individuals are always competing with each other on the bases of individual performance, it may be difficult for them to cooperate (Hill, 2003). Above all, teams in Africa or developing nations should be encouraged to treat their development as a constant learning experience and should look for ways to improve, to confront member fears, and frustrations, and to use conflict as a learning opportunity and growth in the organization.

Conclusion

In summary, to be effective, Western leaders and managers must play a key role in the creation and maintenance of organizational culture in developing countries by creating and influencing legends, rituals and celebrations, as well as, visual images which represent their vision for that nation. As their employees are socialized to this organizational culture, a sense of belonging stimulates them to pass on these traditions to their children, thus providing them with an identity within this organizational culture.

It is also important to commit to the use of community teambuilding: group problem solving, task autonomy, accountability and responsibility, because one is in a consensus culture. This is one of the best ways to lead and manage in Africa or a developing country because one is in a high-context situation. Leading and managing in this kind of situation requires being able to design and implement a bottom-up management system, which includes a two-way exchange of ideas, sustains the concept of traditional African social structure, values innovation, nurtures flexibility, sustains diversity and offers members the freedom to experiment. In this way, people in developing countries around the world will soon be able to independently sustain them in the global marketplace. Above all, it is more urgent today than ever before for Western leaders, managers and practitioners to be willingly embrace, nurture and practice the concept of intergenerational leadership in Africa to compete in global economy and to be successful in 21st century organizations.

DISCUSSION QUESTIONS

1. What is intergenerational leadership?
2. What are the challenges one is likely to encounter in conducting business in Africa or developing nations?
3. What are the lessons you have learned from reading this chapter about business conduct in Africa and developing nations?

CHAPTER 5
Great Leaders Teach Exemplary Followership and Serve as Servant Leaders

Abstract

This chapter focuses on the impact of exemplary follower and servant leader. Thus it examined their relationship and the roles they play in the creation of the "Learning Organization" of the future. The first part of this framework addressed the process of a good follower. This process include leaders alienating followers, leaders face problems in teaching leadership, skills of exemplary followers, exemplary followers and team, organizations of the future, leaders transforming people and leaders measured by the quality of their followers. The second part of the paper deals with servant leader. Thus its process include servant leaders elicit trust in followers, modern western societies, community provide love for humans, business organizations are expected to serve and modern organizations searching for new mission. Together, the two frameworks provide insights and guidelines for managers and leaders in leading organizations of the future.

Exemplary Followership

To succeed, leaders must teach their followers not only how to lead: leadership, but more importantly, how to be a good follower: followership. Contrary to popular negative ideas regarding what it means to be a follower, positive followership requires several important skills, such as, the ability to perform independent, critical thinking, give and receive constructive criticism and to be innovative and creative. Furthermore, we believe that Great Leader is a process that can be learned, that is not restricted to a few "chosen or special" individuals that are born with an unusual capability or skill. Though, some seem to have more to learn than others do, but the potential for exemplary follower seems to be universal. Through solicited comments and regular participation, employees shared ownership in determining policies at work (Gilbert & Ivancevich, 2000). Being a follower has a negative connotation because it is usually used to refer to someone who must constantly be told what to do. Regardless of work unit individualism/collectivism, supervisors were more likely to form trusting, high-commitment relationships with subordinates who were similar to them in personality (Schaubroek & Lam, 2002). Most people think of a good follower as someone who can take direction without challenging their leader. In contrast to this definition, exemplary followers take initiative without being prompted, assume ownership of problems, and participate actively in decision-making. Not only can creative contribution be valuable to a firm, but the ability to come up with unique yet appropriate ideas and solutions can be an important advantage for individuals as well (Perry-Smith & Shalley, 2003). They distinguish themselves from ordinary followers by being "self-starters" going above and beyond what people expect of them (Kelley, 1992).

Leaders Alienating Followers

All leaders have at least one follower who has become alienated in relation to authority. This person usually thinks they are right and exhibits a hypercritical attitude toward authority figures. Their hostile feelings toward leaders are often the result of unmet expectations and broken trust. If these experiences turn us off, they shape our subsequent response to the culture. For example, too much certainty leads to complacency and not enough predictability can result in alienating workers. A leader's actions, therefore, can create either alienated or committed workers (Fairholm & Fairholm, G, 2000). They may be people who were not recognized for their contributions in the past. An outstanding advantage of recognition, including praise, as a motivator is that it is no cost or low cost, yet powerful. Recognition thus has an enormous return on investment in comparison to cash bonus (Dubrin, 2001). Leaders must first confront the hostility expressed by alienated followers in order to replace it with something more positive.

To address the complaints of an alienated follower, a leader must confront the perceived inequality and re-establish trust. If goals have diverged, an overarching goal, which both leader and followers accept must be found. When this has been accomplished, leaders can continue to work with alienated followers to help them accept that setbacks are part of reaching any goal. Consequently, people understand each other, they share the same concepts, and they have the same vision (Deneire & Segalla, 2002). Leaders need to remind followers that if you belong to a community or organization, you have a responsibility to contribute to making it better for everyone, not just yourself. This is why the leader is required to go beyond reminding followers and instead lead by example. In other words, leaders must help their followers relinquish a typically Western credo: "I am free to do whatever I want, so long as it does not harm anyone", and substitute instead, "I am free to do whatever I want, so long as it benefits more than just myself". Leaders must convince their alienated followers that they want to achieve more than just a mutually satisfactory resolution of past grievances, rather, a mutual acceptance, understanding and appreciation of a shared dream or goal (Kelley, 1992).

Exhibit 1
Exemplary Followership Model

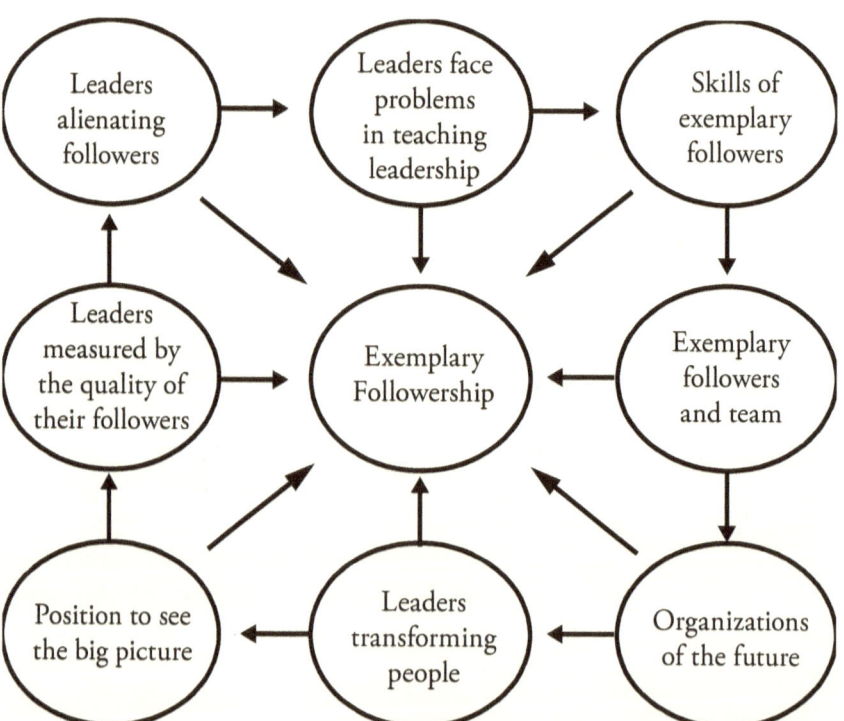

Exhibit one is a representation of Great Leader model brought together in an organized framework with exemplary followership at the core. The logic is that each Great Leader component is of central importance to the development of exemplary followers system within each employee in the organization or community. The potential payoffs include increased employee or citizen performance and innovation flowing from enhanced commitment, motivation, and employee or citizen capability. Thus, it seems clear that an essential ingredient to Great Leader is boundless optimism about the potential of ordinary people to accomplish extraordinary things in the world.

Leaders Face Problem(s) in Teaching Leadership

The problem leader's face, in trying to teach leadership to their followers, is that many people actually find freedom terrifying because it poses too many choices and too much uncertainty. Thus, knowledge transfers take place more efficiently when an activity is internalized because a shared culture and language help firm members transfer and combine knowledge to develop organizational capabilities (Coff, 2003). People need structure, order and predictability. Being given too much freedom makes people feel powerless and afraid so they often turn to anyone, usually a dictator, who offers to remove from them the burden of responsibility which freedom brings. The reality is, the world is far too complex for leaders, alone, to coordinate it. In times of stability, conformity may be an appropriate response by a follower toward a leader if it can contribute to efficiency. But, in times of chaotic change and social and economic fragmentation, only the clash of conflicting views provides the diversity needed to create the innovation which can adequately meet the challenges that impinge on a group or an organization. During these times, leaders desperately need someone who can challenge their belief system rather than reinforce it because conformity imposes a false sense of order and keeps leaders from confronting the reality of the need for change. By trying to avoid conflict, many followers actually open themselves up to being exploited by unscrupulous leaders.

Though it may sound paradoxical, to successfully lead, leaders must cultivate independent, critical thinking in their followers. Super Leaders offers the most viable mechanism for establishing exceptional self-leading followers. True excellence can be achieved by facilitating the self-leadership system that operates within each person – by challenging each person to reach deep inside for the best each has to offer. Employee compliance is not enough. Leading others to lead themselves is the key to tapping the intelligence, the spirit, the creativity, the commitment, and most of all the tremendous unique potential of each individual (Osland, Kolb & Rubin, 2001). Leaders need followers who can ask tough questions about an idea's feasibility. Leaders and followers both need to confront their fear of conflict because conflict often clears the air so that real progress can be made (Kelley, 1992).

Skills of Exemplary Followers

Exemplary followers possess skills that can be learned such as commitment and initiative and exercising a courageous conscience. An important part of becoming more creative involves understanding the stages involved in creativity, which is generally defined as the production of novel and useful ideas, (Dubrin, 2001). Exemplary followers add value to groups they are members of by focusing on goals, taking initiative and being who they are. Exemplary followers are committed. They figure out all the steps involved in achieving a goal. The creative person looks at problems in a new light and transcends conventional thinking about them (Dubrin, 2001). Commitment and focus are not enough to make a difference. They have to have a sense of direction, drive and intensity. Exemplary followers master skills that make them indispensable to their organization. By knowing what the leader is trying to achieve, they determine what essential skills will help reach those goals the best. After they master the skills needed, they set a work schedule and lay out a plan of action with deadlines to meet. Then, they break the entire work to be done into small sub-projects and write a "to do" list of prioritized activities that will result in sub-goal completion. Exemplary followers review their progress daily, reorganize priorities, analyze their performance and determine the criteria for success. When they have been successful, they go on to develop additional expertise and continue to champion new ideas. This means involving oneself in continuing education. For this reason, the "Learning" organization of the future develops exemplary followers (Kelley, 1992).

When an exemplary follower has a new idea, he or she ties it to organizational goals, documents its costs and benefits, test it out and builds a prototype. Exemplary followers follow through with their ideas. They do not give up ownership of them until they have accomplished a successful handoff to someone else. In other words, the exemplary follower exhibits behaviors commonly associated with leadership, such as initiative and innovation.

The central task in becoming creative is to break down rigid thinking that blocks new ideas (Dubrin, 2001). In actuality, leaders can accomplish very little without at least a few followers who are exemplary. When one looks at both leadership and exemplary followership simultaneously, the distinction between them blurs. What eventually emerges from a steady examination of both of them is one single role, which every member of an organization should be prepared to perform; a role that, depending on circumstances, periodically calls forth the ability to inspire others while most of the time, requires the ability to be inspired by others (Kelley, 1992).

Exemplary Followers and Team

Exemplary followers are able to work together well in a team because they focus on several essential skills required to build an effective team. Thus, teams with unified cultures are likely to perform better than other teams. A unified team culture facilitates internal communication (Earley & Mosakowski, 2000). They start by making sure their entire team members share a common understanding of the team's purpose and goals. A leader who uses supportive communication nurture group members and brings out their best (Dubrin, 2001). At each team meeting, they commit to the timing and specifications of agreed upon output. While working, they seek to maintain an equitable division of labor. If they are having trouble or getting behind in doing their scheduled tasks, they let their teammates know immediately. In addition, they show other members their work before it is due to solicit feedback and constructive criticisms, which they use to go back and improve it.

Exemplary followers are skilled at "assists", a term taken from basketball, where one does not actually score oneself, but rather, one *helps* another teammate do it for the good of the team. Once goals, structures, and norms are established, a group can work more effectively. Members share the group goals and conform to the group norm of high productivity (Chang, Bordia & Duck, 2003). Exemplary followers help keep their team on track, moving toward group goals by making sure each team member is actively involved in the process. Creative thinking enables leaders to contribute novel insights that can open up new opportunities or alternatives for the group or organization. The role of creative leader is to bring into existence ideas and things that did not exist previously or that existed in a different form (Dubrin, 2001). They are always on the lookout for anything that may be useful, not just for them, but instead, their focus is on what other teammates might find useful in their work. Here again, the line between which behaviors are appropriate for a leader and which are more appropriate for a follower is obliterated. The fact of the matter is that the best leaders are the kind of people who are most comfortable as an exemplary follower and usually have been one for quite a while. For this reason, this kind of leader is especially sensitive to the needs and feelings of their followers. Leaders understand that the successful articulation of vision relies on using language and symbols to create new, and special, meanings for organization members (Kelly, 2000). Instead of a figurehead, they are a leader among equals, like the leader of a flock of migrating birds. He or she shares in their dangers and struggles, as well as their enjoyment of tranquil meadows. One can easily identify them in a group because they are quick to laugh at their own mistakes and predicaments. Leadership deals with change, inspiration, motivation and influence (Dubrin, 2001). They frequently acknowledge other team members' contributions and use "we" rather than "I" when they speak (Kelley, 1992).

Organizations of the Future

In the organizations of the future, competent people will join together to achieve what they could not achieve alone. Both individually and collectively, they will be accountable for their actions. Equitable exchange is simply about helping a partner when he or she requires it and receiving help when you need it (Bouty, 2000). They will share information and power because in the near future, information will BE power. By sharing the bottom line and the details of organizational expenses, they will also be sharing the responsibility to take action and will not need to be protected from clearly understanding the reality of their own performance. "First, they always articulate the organization's vision in a manner that stresses the values of the audience they are addressing. Leaders regularly involve people in deciding how to achieve the organization's vision (or the part most relevant to a particular individual). This gives people a sense of control. Another important motivational technique is to support employee efforts to realize the vision by providing coaching, feedback, and role modeling, thereby helping people to grow professionally and enhancing their self-esteem. Furthermore, good leaders recognize and reward success, which not only gives people a sense of accomplishment but also makes them feel like they belong to an organization that cares about them. When all this is done, the work itself becomes intrinsically motivating" (Kotter 1990). Each and every person will be responsible for his or her OWN motivation. In short, if you are confident about your task-related skills, you will get your act together o do the task. This is one reason why you should give people the skills and confidence they need in order to put forth effort (Dubrin, 2001). In this way, each will know how valuable they are in relationship to everyone else so as their contributions increase; they will see this reflected in the compensation they receive. If everyone stands a chance to gain or lose then all will see the significance of a unified effort (Kelley, 1992).

Leaders Transforming People

How can leaders transform people who are ordinary or even mediocre followers into exemplary followers? First, they must create organizational environments, which nourish the growth of exemplary followers. One way is to become less of a hero and more of a hero maker; in other words, share the limelight! Social exchange by means of personal relationships is a deeply rooted behavior in most societies. People form relationships in order to give and receive things – both tangible and intangible – of value. Psychological contracts are formed whenever there is a social exchange between people (Edleston, Kidder & Litzky, 2002). A leader's role is to sell the group's ideas in order to obtain the necessary resources. Leaders should represent their group to larger organizational units, including government and the society at large. The role of leaders should be to remove obstacles to the group's productivity and shield them from bureaucracy's tentacles. The main task of leaders is to step out of their followers' way. The leader's job is to overcome internal resistance, to help followers accept new beliefs, to build new frames of reference, and to seek alignment with the organization's environment by providing a dynamic vision (Egri & Herman, 2000). Many leaders haven't realized that the most common hindrance to productivity is their own constant interruption! To avoid this, leaders should encourage self-management in their followers. Organizational members can identify critical issues and suggest steps to resolve them. They should be encouraged to gather their own data so they can solve problems. Followers should be involved in decisions, which may affect them (Kelley, 1992).

Position to see the Big Picture

Because they are in position to see the big picture, leaders can integrate the flow of work and create networks among members of their organization. Another name for leader could be "synergy catalyst". Drucker believes "a leader's actions and a leader's professed beliefs must be congruent. Effective leadership is primarily based on being consistent" (Drucker 1988). When workers have a plan that will work just as well as the leaders plan to reach a goal, the workers' plan should be adopted by leadership, since the workers are the ones who must devote the energy to make any plan, which is adopted, work. Feedback-intensive development programs help leaders develop by seeing more clearly their patterns of behavior, the reasons for such behaviors, and the impact of these behaviors and attitudes on their effectiveness (Dubrin, 2001). Leaders must be sensitive to the personal dreams of their followers so they can mesh the personal goals of their followers with organizational needs. However, research in organizational transformation has repeatedly suggested that strong emotions are involved in transformational learning and change (Seo, 2003). Leadership's role is fluid, sometimes in the foreground, sometimes fading into the background. Leaders must know *when* it is appropriate to lead and *not lead* when it is more appropriate to follow their followers' *lead*! Leaders can take an active role in assisting effective goal setting, work distribution, resource gathering and the establishment and maintenance of organizational interfaces. They can advocate for organizational needs and reinforce the acceptance and understanding of their particular organization's limits. Leaders are people who can play different roles in different situations (Kelley, 1992).

Leaders Measured by the Quality of their Followers

Leaders should be measured by the quality of their followers. Followers provide their leader with power by following his or her lead. To take away this power, they need only to exercise their right to disobey their leader. Although disobedience is often met with ruthless force, eventually, like water wearing down a stone, it will prevail and then the leader who was unreachable will shrink down to nothing. Schein (1992) noted, "When an organization faces a crisis, the manner in which leaders deal with it creates new norms, values and working procedures and reveals important underlying assumptions". Followers can evaporate a leader's mask of power merely by dis-believing in it. Authority does not reside in those who issue orders; rather, authority lies with*in* the *responses* of persons to whom those orders are addressed. In his book, The Power of the Powerless, President of Czechoslovakia, Vaclav Havel states, from personal experience, that even in totalitarian states, followers hold significant power, but only if they are ready to *act* on it. Holocaust and genocide continue to this day despite hand wringing because some of us are unwilling to make the sacrifice to confront it. We turn our eyes away because in some ghastly way it benefits us perhaps by merely creating a distraction for those who would challenge us. We do not have to wait for valid leaders to appear to tell us it is time to offer the gift of our own exemplary followership to each other. There is no need for us to be hypnotized by the myth of leadership created by those who would have us remain passive instead of *active*. We only have our own selfishness to blame for our powerlessness. We willingly gave up our power to buy freedom from risk, responsibility and accountability.

Servant Leadership

If we teach members of organizations to become exemplary followers, we should not be surprised if they begin to respond positively only to able servants who would lead them. The two roles of servant and leader can and should be fused. The servant leader needs to have a sense of the unknowable and be able to foresee the unforeseeable. Therefore, the central role of the servant leader is establishing sustainable strategic vision for the organization or community. The effective leader must articulate the mission of the organization in a convincing and inspiring fashion (Neuschel, 1998). Thus, the most important commitment a leader makes in relation to a vision is the commitment to continuously model the vision through one's own behavior in a visible and consistent manner in the organization or community. In all cultures, great leaders emerge FIRST as servants.

Culture enables humans to develop civilizations and technology by supporting and maintaining shared meanings thus empowering collective action on a scale unheard of in any other species of living being (Banutu-Gomez, 2001). If we teach members of organizations to become exemplary followers, we should expect them to freely respond only to individuals who have been chosen to lead because they have first proven themselves as servants. Leaders embed attributes in their organizational cultures by their actions (Schein, 1992). Thus, in the future, the only truly viable organizations will be those that are servant-led. All great leaders report that they experienced the feeling of wanting to serve FIRST. This experience is what led them to the aspiration to lead. The servant's natural impulse is to make sure that other people's highest priority needs are being served, by asking themselves one question: "Will the least privileged in my society become healthier, wiser, and more autonomous, (in other words, be empowered) as a result of what I do?" Greenleaf (1977) asserted: A new moral principle is emerging which holds that the only authority deserving one's allegiance is that which is freely and knowingly granted by the led to the leader in response to, and in proportion to, the clearly evident servant stature of the leader. They inspire hope and courage in others by living out their convictions, facilitating positive images, and by giving love and encouragement (Kouzes & Posner, 1993). By doing this, their actions will reflect appropriate, unconditional love and caring in the workplace and they will build long last relationships in the organization or community. Showing concern for others and making their needs and interests a priority demonstrates empathy and elicits trust (Bennis, 1997; Block, 1993; Greenleaf, 1997; Kouzes & Posner, 1993).

Exhibit 2
Servant Leaders Model

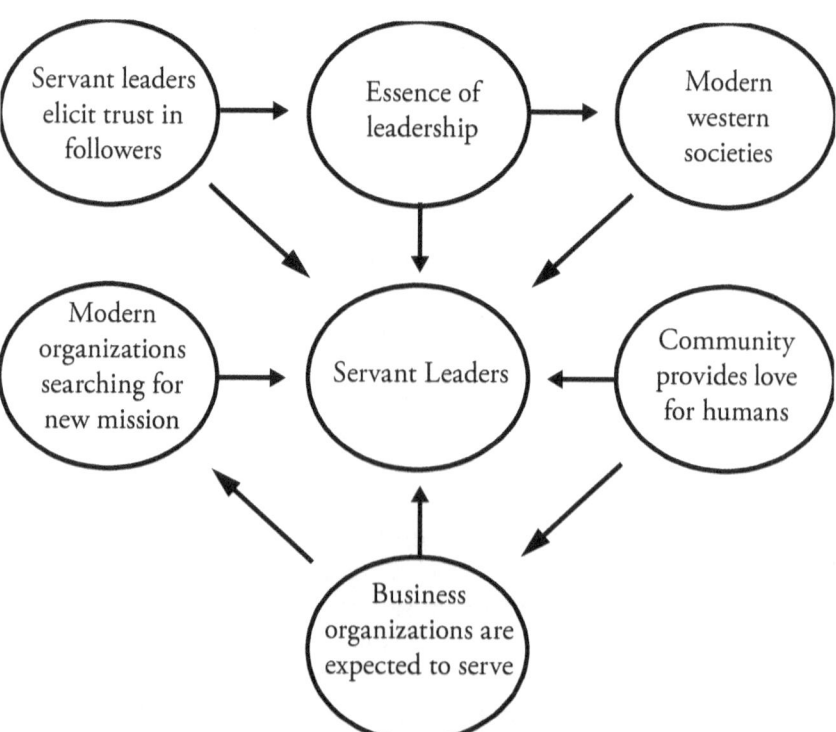

Exhibit two is a representation of Great Leader model brought together in an organized framework with servant leaders at the core. The logic is that each Great Leader component is of central importance to the development of servant leadership system within each employee in the organization or community. The potential payoffs include enhancing and increasing employee or citizen to be able to foresee the unforeseeable and establish a vibrant sustainable strategic vision for the organization or community.

Essence of Leadership

The essence of leadership is to go out in uncharted territory to show the way. A leader sees more clearly than anyone else does the way to go by nurturing a continual inner openness to inspiration and revelation. But this is not all a leader must do. A leader actively recruits people be followers. The openness of leaders to receive input from others influences leader-follower trust (Bennis, 1997; Fairholm, 1998; Nanus, 1992). Servant leaders associate with and listen to those they serve (Roberts, 1987). Knowing the path is uncertain, even dangerous, a leader initiates ideas and structures based on them. A leader need to help individual members achieve their role as a whole/part – to be fully functioning individuals with self worth and skills that make a contribution to the team and organization and as a result, to the wider society (Cacioppe, 2000). This is to say that; leadership key role is to facilitate wisdom and spirituality in the work place. A leader willingly accepts the risk of failure in order to achieve a chance for success. The servant leader is a person who desires to sacrifice themselves out of love for others. The servant leader is more than the leader who can merely articulate a dream and inspire others. In the face of difficulty, most leaders react by trying to pin the problem on someone else. The behaviors of senior leaders also establish the ethical tone in their organizations (Bennis and Nanus, 1997; Kouzes and Posner, 1993). The leader is responsible for the environment and one way to influence it is to demonstrate by their behavior their commitment to set of ethics they are trying to institutionalize (Bennis and Nanus, 1997). Effective leaders instill values through deeds as much as or more than through words (Malphurs, 1996). The servant leader automatically responds by LISTENING FIRST. Leaders benefit from listening because they learn as they listen (Bennis, 1997; Maxwell, 1998; Miller, 1995; Roberts, 1987). Also, listening is a critical aspect of delegating and empowering (Miller, 1995; Roberts, 1987).

Servant Leaders Elicit Trust in Followers

Servant leaders elicit trust in followers because they respond to crisis by owning the problem. Anyone who wants to become a servant leader must submit to the discipline of learning to listen, not only to others, but also, to oneself. Today's leaders must possess new skills, knowledge, and abilities that give them task competence among their followers (Bass, 1990; Fairholm, 1997, 1998). Establishing trust is one of the most essential parts of good leadership, especially servant leadership (Bennis, 1997). Leaders must demonstrate concern for people and practice integrity in order to build trust (Shaw, 1997). Thus, having an attitude and commitment of self-evaluation is necessary for the person who wants to be successful (Banutu-Gomez, 2002). Servant leadership requires frequent withdrawal in order to reorient oneself; to sort out and prioritize. Such withdrawal should be only temporary because all the information needed for a decision rarely appears, regardless of how long one listens. On all-important decisions there exists a significant information gap that must be bridged by intuition, which is an unobservable process. Intuition provides servant leaders with a nonverbal ability to judge based on patterns emerging from what has happened. Servant leaders recognize the need to nurture the conditions that permit the effective operation of intuition in both their work and personal lives. Leaders must trust that employees are committed humans and that they are capable to perform to the best of their ability (Banutu-Gomez, 2003).

Modern Western Societies

In modern Western societies, where laws regulate actions, the incentive to exercise individual conscience is diminished. In contrast to non-Westerners, such as those from ancient cultures in Asia and Africa, Westerners are naïve about what can be done with law. A great judge makes his or her decisions intuitively and afterward, devises fine legal reasoning to justify them. The creative process requires one to withdraw in order to effectively release the pressure of analysis. Bartuneck (1984) states, "Leaders shape the course of second-order change by legitimizing the expression of particular perspectives because they have primary influence over which alternative interpretive schemes, actions and structural changes are expressed."

Leadership intuition provides leaders with the foresight that enables them to see far beyond present circumstances. Organizational development processes need to help align the vision, objectives, structures and actions to fulfil these needs. Thus, servant leadership involves turning the traditional organizational pyramid upside down (Blanchard, 1997; Turner, 2000). Miller (1995) suggests that servant leaders should establish vision and direction, but delegate decisions about how to reach the goals. He cautions, however, delegation is not abdication; rather, it involves both trust and accountability. Encouraging true service to the customer, employees and the community is a key part of the leadership and organization development function (Cacioppe, 2000). Once a leader looses their foresight, they can no longer lead but only react to events. The roots of leadership failure originate in a loss of the ability to foresee what could have been foreseen and a fatal hesitation in the necessary willingness to act it while the opportunity to act is still available.

Community Provides Love for Humans

Humans require the type of love only community can provide. It cannot be provided by organizations that exist apart from the community they profess to serve or by those that seek to solve a particular social problem by removing it from the community. The love of the community involves unlimited liability. Modern Western organizations are designed to limit the liability of those who serve the community through them. Putting people first; caring for people through the development of community, has been the foundation of all great civilizations. Leaders who want to empower must be teachers (Ford, 1991). Leaders are those who bring forth the talents of others (Baggett, 1997). In our modern day and age, caring is no longer provided face-to-face, but instead, is mediated by large, impersonal organizations. Informal networks in large organizations create an organizational culture and community that provides the "glue" to hold the formal organizational structure in place and allow it to operate effectively. People accept a person's leadership as their individual cultural heritage and the organizational culture are in harmony because it is that harmony or "unique common psychology" that engenders confidence, comfort, and trust (Fairholm & Fairholm, G, 2000). In contrast, bureaucracy is an organizational sickness in which community is not nurtured and organizational culture has become destructive.

A large modern organization needs both administration to provide necessary order and consistency and leadership to build team initiative, accountability, and creativity. Empowerment emphasizes teamwork and reflects the values of love and equality. In order to achieve empowerment, a leader's behavior must pull rather push people along; "a pull style of influence works by attracting and energizing people...it motivates by identification"

(Bennis & Nanus, 1997). Leaders, who communicate accurately and honestly, with a commitment to the common values of the organization, develop group trust (Fairholm & Fairholm, G, 2000). The lonely leader at the top of a vast pyramidal structure inevitably becomes corrupt because they are deprived of colleagues. Thus, normal communication patterns become distorted. The tradition Western pyramidal structure creates bureaucracy by weakening informal ties that nourish community. A pyramidal structure precludes leadership by persuasion because the chief has been awarded too much power; whatever they say is viewed as an order. Because the pyramidal structure concentrates power in one individual, it halts personal growth in the person whose behavior should be an example others in the organization follow. Leadership is the behavior of an individual that results in non-coercive influence when that person is directing and co-ordinating the activities of a group toward the accomplishment of a shared goal (Rowden, 2000). Leadership should originate in whoever in the group has the greatest team-building ability; who stimulates the group to move in common purpose toward agreed upon objectives by asking effectively probing questions. A creative person is able to utilize several categories of influence tactics, inspiration, persuasion, bargaining, personal appeals, pressure, consultation, coalition-building, and negotiation. In a field study, Yukl and Tracy (1992) found rational persuasion, inspirational appeal, and consultation the most effective influence tactics. Thus, these types of non-manipulative methods are most appropriate for determined servant leaders. These leaders are influential, but most importantly they gain influence in ways and methods that significantly differ from traditional models and methods that we are most familiar with in our organizations or community.

Business Organizations are expected to serve

Increasingly, business organizations are expected to serve both those who produce goods and services and those who purchase and use them. Our present complex organizations are increasingly expected to provide meaning and significance in individual members' lives. Thus, business achievements depend on success in learning and development (Masalin, 2003). To do that, they must become the "learning organization" of the future; they must begin to transform their emphasis on production to "growing" people. Most educators agreed that individual personality traits provide at least part of the basis upon which leadership skills are built, and such characteristics reach stability by adolescence. (Doh, 2003). In the "learning organization" of the future, leadership's primary task will no longer be to motivate people to be productive. The experience of personal growth will generate individual motivation. Outside input is important for keeping a broad mind and for inspiring out-of –the-box thinking (Masalin, 2003). In the "learning organization of the future, instead of managing people as the solution to organizational problems, leaders will manage *the process* by which the best solution can be found. Unlearning is necessary to make room for new learning (Masalin, 2003).

Modern Organizations
Searching for New Mission

Many modern organizations are searching for a new mission that can enable them to evolve into better servants of human society and drastically reduce their impact as sources of destruction, suffering and injustice on the earth and its inhabitants. The ability to create new organizational forms and processes, to innovate in both the technical and organizational areas, is crucial to remaining competitive in an increasingly turbulent world (Osland, Kolb & Rubin, 2001). The wisest elders among us know that great organizations, which serve humanity, do not build themselves but all that the rest of us want to do is train the technical expert who advises the leader or the scholar who criticizes the leader. No one wants to educate the leader. Creating future leadership capabilities is a constant challenge (Masalin, 2003). As a result, many of our leaders are self-seeking and corrupt. It is a losing battle for us to try to rescue people from "the system". Law can regulate our present organizations but they will never reach true servant status unless strong ethical leadership emerges to lead them to it. The SuperLeader creates productive thought patterns by carefully expressing confidence in the employee's ability to extend his or her present level of competence. Support and encouragement are necessary. In many ways, this expression of confidence is the essence of the "guided-participation" phase in which SuperLeader teach each employee to lead himself or herself (Osland, Kolb & Rubin, 2001). Who is preparing the next generation of leaders to do this?

Plenty of Innovation

There is plenty of innovation to provide us with a bewildering array of choices among trivialities and new gadgets every day while the important organizations that should effectively serve us are seriously impeded by rigid, obsolete organizational assumptions, behaviors, cultures and structures. In successful learning organization cultures, "each individual contributes uniquely from his or her own experience and talents" (Kotter 1990). The leader of a learning organization helps members to listen to each other. In this way, leaders facilitate the learning process. Leaders can use cultural forms such as celebrations to encourage members to share their unique backgrounds as well as their special skills. But, I think leaders need to remember that because of his or her personal needs for attention and affirmation, a strong organizational culture led by a charismatic leader will promote group-think, which discourages honest communication and necessary constructive confrontation with disconfirming data. Whereas, a leader who puts the needs of workers and other constituents before his or her personal needs for fame can use cultural forms to create a strong organizational culture that provides the sense of community members need to willingly face disconfirming information and learn from it, individually and as a group. An employee's success is no longer defined in terms of individual performance. To perform well as team members, individuals must be able to communicate openly and honestly, to confront differences and resolve conflicts, and to sublimate personal goals for the good of the team (Robbins, 2003). Those in power seem to prefer a desperate last binge of self-serving rather than risk adopting organizational innovations which might positively transform the traditional Western pyramidal structure of authority. You may be wondering, "How can I help my organization become a better servant of society?" We all spend the majority of our time following, not leading; even leaders. . "In a learning organization, leaders' roles differ dramatically from that of the charismatic decision maker. These roles require new skills" (Senge 1990).

If we consider ourselves morally competent people, we can be discriminating in whom we choose to follow and thus, illumine by our own example a path for others to follow us. By examining the steps of Dr. Martin Luther King, Jr., one can see the path Gandhi chose to tread.

In conclusion, Great leaders lead best by becoming exemplary followers of great leaders before them; by listening and heeding the same still voice of conscience that spoke to their hearts.

DISCUSSION QUESTIONS

1. What is a learning organization?
2. How can you teach employees to become exemplary followers?
3. What skills does a leader need to possess to nurture innovation?

CHAPTER 6
Leading Complex Change in Organizations

The strategic leadership and management of organizational change in today's global world have challenged all humanity. The goal of all organizational leaders and managers is to maintain the stability of their organization while creatively adapting to changes in the demands on it, as well as to stimulate innovation and to strengthen its culture in order to increase productivity. Organizational leaders and managers face many daunting challenges including increased world-wide competition caused by an expanded global market-place and the explosion of amazing technological break-through. To survive in this new economic environment, most organizations must now swiftly develop effective strategies for establishing an entirely new and fluid niche for themselves which is much broader.

Employees must accept the reality that, because of necessary changes in management's and leadership priorities, there will be a significant change in the way their company, organization, institution and government does business so their work responsibilities will, as a result, change drastically. Workers can look at the bright side of these changes by focusing on the increases in employee ownership options, such as profit sharing, which many companies now offer. Members of modern organizations now find themselves in work environments that exist within down-sized organizational structures where management and leadership is primarily concerned with operating in ways that are more leaner and smarter than ever before. This is to ensure their company, organization, institution or government has the flexibility to respond successfully to changes in the global market-place and to new stakeholder demands. Because most successful companies now utilize mergers to accomplish this, leaders or managers of merged and down-sized organizations must now work harder than ever to nurture their company's organizational culture, the social environment which provides people with meaning in their lives. Companies who want to survive must use information in highly creative ways while they provide increased value and service to stakeholders whose needs have been transformed. Leadership and Management of these organizations will discover that setting priorities for the allocation of organizational resources, and in relation to this, decision-making about organizational structure, has become paramount. Organizational survival now begins with choosing the appropriate organizational structure. Shall the company become a portfolio business, with the ability to jettison subparts if need be, or a conglomerate whose autonomous divisions produce profits symbiotically?

Leaders and managers must find ways to provide their employees wealth of guidance on how to become an effective organizational leader in our modern times. The world will continue to *Thrive on Chaos*. Therefore, the organizations that will succeed in the future are ones that have fourteen important differences, 1) a flat and team oriented, 2) less hierarchical structure, 3) more autonomous units, 4) an orientation toward high-value-added goods and quality services, 5) quality controls, 6) service controls, 7) responsiveness, 8) innovative speed, 9) flexibility, 10) highly trained and skilled workers who use their minds, and 11) leaders at all levels (no managers), 12) positive thinking in look and outlook oriented, 13) strong and vibrant code of ethics, and 14) sustainable social responsibility to the community.

Many companies now utilize the concept of *strategic management* to manage an organization composed of several autonomous sub-units whose interrelationship becomes its most competitive advantage. In companies where employees now own a significant percentage of the stock, everyone is stimulated to own the organization's problems and each worker becomes accountable for the innovation and quality necessary for all to succeed. As the down-sizing trend further reduces numbers of workers within companies, organizational leaders scramble for ways to use human resources in the most effective and efficient manner. Astute organizational leaders realize that they play a pivotal role in their organization's culture. This is referred to that set of artifacts, beliefs, values, norms and ground rules that define and significantly influence how organizations operate. The most effective organizational leaders strive to nurture within their organization's culture these seven important qualities: a vision of what their organization can become, a clear sense of their organization's purpose (mission), an embracing of their organization's interdependence on its environment, the ability to develop strategic plans which include contingency choices and define what their organization should be like at several intermediate points, flexible yet realistic organizational structure designs which they intend to implement, innovative and efficient usage of advanced technology and telecommunication applications, and a popular reward system which socializes their employees to appreciate positive organizational priorities, values and norms while providing them with opportunities to satisfy their need for dignity and growth. Organizational leaders of our day, and for the future, must have extensive skills and knowledge in these five realms: telecommunications technology, organizational culture, social responsibility, gender and diversity, and the global market-place. In today's global village, organizational leaders must courageously ask themselves the following questions: Why has our vision been narrowed? Why has our flexibility been constricted? Why has our strategy become too rigid? The entrepreneur should view strategic planning not as a road map but as a compass. When you are lost in a swamp, or forest a simple compass allows you to use your ingenuity to overcome difficulties. The most valuable quality an organizational leaders need today is the courage to experiment and learn from mistakes.

It is critical and important for all leaders to understand the process of open-systems planning. To assist them in dealing with increased demands from these three extensive arenas, many modern managers now utilize a "seven stage institutional planning process called *open-system planning*": reach consensus on the "core mission of the organization", draw a "map" which displays the entire "demand system", superimpose, upon that map, a map displaying the "current response system", then, predict what will be the "probable demand system" in the near future, and, clearly and specifically describe "the desired state" of the organization in that near future, finally, "list all the activities which will be necessary to achieve this desired state", and then, select and prioritize the most "cost-effective options".

Coming to consensus on a core organizational mission involves setting priorities. This is what is so difficult "in a complex organization with a variety of conflicting demands for allocation of resources". Often, it is the leaders, the executive management, who must be willing and able to take the ultimate decision-making regarding this. To do this successfully, organizational leaders must analyze and prioritize the needs of all organizational stakeholders and then come to consensus regarding their organization's mission because from it will flow goal setting and resource allocation. Then, leaders can go on to create a map listing all stakeholder groups (domains) with their demands, on the organization, in relationship to each other (also called "environmental mapping"). This is followed by management selecting what they predict will be the most relevant "domains" and "a list of their specific demands is developed".

Next, leaders need to strive to "identify their organization's current responses to those demands". They can analyze this response, in general, and decide whether, at this time, it is typically "do as little as you can, just enough" to avoid a bad reputation or just "do what the others do", no more, no less, or is their company's response a proactive stance, setting a positive example for others to follow, out in the forefront? It is important to check closely to see if the organization actually practices what it gives lip service to, and not be swayed by enthusiastic rhetoric. This process of coming to consensus "also provides opportunities for assessing the future consequences of possible organizational responses". During this stage, organizational leaders can superimpose, upon the current response system, their prediction of the future demand system, thus clarifying the "likely future consequences of the current response system". Leaders can then compare these consequences with how they define "the desired state" of their organization in three to four years. This definition should include "clear and specific goals", as well as, "a set of actions for moving toward" the more desired organizational condition. Leaders can "identify the types of activities, organizational forms, investments and projects that will be necessary" to transform their organization from its current demand/response system to this "desired state". The last stage, in this process, involves weighing the social and economic costs of each of the proposed action alternatives in order to select those which will be implemented; those which employees will be encouraged to commit to supporting whole-hearted.

Changing organizational culture should be the focus of any leader that wants to be successful. Though organizations have been viewed, in the past, "as *input-output systems* which **transform** *needs* and *raw materials* into *services* and *products*", what should be of primary interest to organizational leaders is what goes on **inside** their organization which **controls and produces** this transformation. Since organizations are composed of human individuals and what humans create, when they are together, is culture, organizational leaders should concern themselves with their organization's **culture;** this includes "the attitudes, values, beliefs and priorities" of their employees. By definition, a leader's job is to lead by example, giving transcendent meaning to all of their group's social and economic activities. One can describe the relationship between a leader and his or her followers, "A loyal constituency is won when the people's image of the leader is congruent with their inner environment of myth and legend." Modern organizational leaders must face the responsibility to "determine the culture" of their organization. Thus, "common and predictable characteristics" of an effective organization's culture: it is "purposeful and goal-oriented" because leaders have provided "explicit long-term objectives", within it, "power is widely dispersed" because decision-making is dictated exclusively by the requirements of tasks, for this reason, the basis of all decisions is information rather than hierarchy, as well, rewards are related to the tasks performed rather than to the status level of the performer, with the emphasis equally upon intrinsic, as well as, extrinsic rewards, the free expression of differences of opinion is rewarded, as is collaboration, so all conflict is managed instead of suppressed or avoided, the primary role of management being responsive the constant, often contradictory demands of a complex organizational environment, while continuing to nurture each employee's personal growth and human dignity, this organization is always in a "learning mode" and views itself as eternally "in process" as "built-in feedback mechanisms" continually flood all levels of the organization with the results of on-going assessment, evaluation, and planning.

Leaders and managers must explore the in depth change process in their organization and its impact. When leaders plan organizational change, they must keep in mind three things: the "future desired state" of their organization, the "present state" of their organization (where it is right now), and "the transition state, the set of conditions and activities it must go through to move from the present to the future" and finally "the strategy" that will be driving all the states identified. One can say that a leader's role in organizational change involves "*defining* the future state, *assessing* the present, and *managing* the transition", (in that order). Nevertheless, initially, leaders must look at the **need** for change. It is recommend for leaders not allow themselves to be seduced by "symptoms" but rather, seek to "describe the *fundamental* (root causes) condition needing change". Leaders must first allow focus groups to investigate questions such as "*why* - what might be causing the problem". Thus, membership in these focus groups is "developed by a formula involving lateral representation in several areas as well as personnel from different hierarchical levels, meeting in a 'diagonal slice' group". Organizational leader's first job is to "locate and assess the sources of pressure to change the present situation". By first "conducting an analysis to determine both the need for change and the sources of this need", leaders can also assess the "levels of support or resistance to change" that exist at the present time in their organization.

In this process leaders must energetically focus on their vision of the future. In addition to specifying a vision and mission for their organization, leaders need to build several clear descriptions of mid-point goals which represent a sequence of realistic desirable organizational conditions "intermediate between the present state and the achievement of that vision". In other words, they must prepare themselves to take "one day at a time". Being sure where each footstep will be placed enables leaders to envision not just where they want to be but also, doing what it takes to get there! It is best that these interim goals be dated with targeted deadlines to enhance their sense of urgency. By and large, the best way for leaders to provide projected mid-point goals with a sense of reality is to "write a detailed, behaviorally-oriented scenario that describes what one would expect to see, hear, and even feel in the projected situation at the specified point in time". The purpose of these detailed descriptions is to encourage "members of the organization to visualize their role in the change, thus, facilitating employee compliance. Employee worries about their job in the future, after the change has taken place, is a major source of resistance to organizational change. Leaders can significantly reduce these worries by "providing their employees with sufficient information about the end state to provide a more accurate perception about their future role in the organization" - reassuring them that indeed, they will have a valuable role to play in the future of the organization.

Leaders are required to assessing one's organization's readiness for change because this is the most important part of complex change. Successful organizational change requires leaders to "be explicit" about their strategy for managing the transitional period. In order to do this, they must first "take a detailed look at the present system before determining an action plan for achieving future goals". They must understand that what is needed - at this time - is "a detailed behavioral description of the organization", as it is currently, both formal and informally. Because of the leader's first-hand experience, it is best to give focus groups the responsibility of completing this important task. They feel it's appropriate for leaders to utilize a vertical slice of the organizational hierarchy when trying to determine "what needs to be changed and what does not need to be changed". Then leaders can use this information to "identify and set priorities" regarding specific problems, "identify the subsystems" that are impacted directly by those problems, and "assess those subsystems' readiness and capability" for the changes which have been proposed. Since problems often appear to be overlapping or interconnected, it is important for leaders to "write a brief description of each major problem (and) specify the *who* (individuals and groups), *what* (organizational processes), and *how* (consequences) of each problem". Then they suggest looking for "domino effects" which are bound to occur; "if we change X first, will a solution to Y fall into place?" In this challenging process leaders must first ask themselves "what specific parts of the 'people system' are most significantly involved - the minimum number of individuals who must support the change or it won't happen - and what changes in current attitudes, behavior or work will be needed to reach the desired end state". They label this group of individuals "the '*critical mass*' needed for the change to occur".

Determining the readiness of the critical mass for change requires leaders to analyze their *attitudes* toward the change, as well as, their *capability* to make the change occur. This analysis must address this group's "**willingness, motives**, and **aims**", as well as their "**power, influence, authority to allocate resources**, and the **information** and **skills** required to carry out the necessary tasks" which will accomplish the end state.

Next, leaders must consider how they can increase the readiness of their organization, as a whole, for change, "an 'unfreezing' intervention will be needed to break people away from their deeply held attitudes or behaviors and ready them to try something new", "a goal-setting process should be undertaken in order to build consensus", organizational structures should be revised to reflect the change tasks to be done, "temporary structures should be set up if present structures are unable to institute change", educational activities should be implemented which teach the new information, technical knowledge, and skills needed to achieve the change conditions.

Here is an example the change strategies which could be adopted by the top management of two companies which are merging, **delay the physical integration** of the two organizations, "*develop a (temporary) project organization*, with the technical leadership of both institutions *collaborating* on specific areas of technical and product integration, the management structure of this project organization should have as its chief operating officer, the head of the acquired company and the executive function should be performed by a group composed of this person and the vice-president of technical services and the vice-president of operations from the parent company, to clarify goals, "have a significant group of the leadership of the acquired organization attend the parent company's management meetings".

Furthermore leaders must be able to describe the critical aspects of effective transition management. During the transition state, the period during which the actual changes take place, leaders must determine the major tasks and establish the structures needed to accomplish those tasks. Because "it is highly unlikely that the existing hierarchy could directly manage the transition stage" successfully, leadership should set up a transition task force "team which plans the work flow, manages it through the transition stage, and does the final design of the operation and task activities. This team is responsible to come up with "an activity or change plan which specifies the critical activities and events of the transition period. This plan should a. "clarify NEW ROLES, b. specify what information will be communicated to WHOM, on WHAT DAY, and c. WHEN new structures will begin to operate. It should be realistic, effective and clear and include "*contingency plans* for adjusting to unexpected forces".

The critical decisions facing leadership during the transitional stage include **how, where, what and who**; where in the organization should change begin, what kind of temporary structures and tasks will be implemented there to accomplish change and who will manage those structures and tasks so that change occurs and finally how can this change be nurtured and sustained. A successful transition manager needs to have these three personal qualities: **the power** to mobilize the resources needed to implement changes (can successfully compete for resources with "others who have ongoing work to do in the organization"), **the respect** of everyone in the organization (including "the existing operating leadership"), as well as, the wisdom, objectivity and linkage (in order to "make balancing decisions, such as *how many resources* to but into the change activities and *at what pace*"), and **the effective interpersonal skills** (to *persuade* rather than force cooperation). Any alternative structures for managing the transition period must include these seven parts in order to be successful: a *chief executive* who is responsible for coordinating the change effort, *project managers* who work with the executive manager, under each project manager, a hierarchy of regular *operations managers* with "explicit new responsibilities different from their usual operating duties", an oversight board of people who represent *stakeholder constituencies* who advise the chief executive, an advisory panel of *community leaders* who speak for those constituencies to give feedback to the chief executive, focus groups composed of "a *diagonal slice*" of the organizational hierarchy to provides the chief executive with ongoing information about how changes are taking place at all locations and all levels of the organization, and a "kitchen cabinet" of *colleagues* who have high influence in the organization whom the executive manager can consult to obtain objective and candid input to balance any vested interests expressed by the line managers.

In our modern times, most organizational leaders find that they have "no choice in whether or not to make changes in their organizations, but only in **how**" those changes will occur. In deciding how changes will take place, leaders must first define what they would like the future state or the organization to be. After this is accomplished, leaders usually see that there needs to be a "significant **change in the way work is done**, and a reduction in both personnel and other costs will come about as a *corollary* change". When examining the present state of their organization, leaders often find that "operating managers are fairly traditional and set in their ways", especially if they are "financially well off due to the policies of the company". Perceptive leaders "recognize that the *comfortable*, stable character (culture) of an organization can severely undermine their efforts" to give up things and thus, operate leaner, unless the employees are stimulated to "**join** with the management in recognizing a common 'enemy' (threat)". In this situation, the first task of leaders is to **increase employee discomfort** to motivate them to be *willing* to change. All "assistant" roles can be eliminated if workers are expected to do much more "managing" of their own work. Workers will have an incentive to do this if the way they are compensated is based on how their output is evaluated according to set criteria. Leaders can organize a change management structure that is successful if they recruit a group of young, upper-middle managers from various parts of the organization, who are "somewhat *dissatisfied* with the present methods of doing work in the present system", for a full-time "effectiveness **team**". This team's transitional management plan should utilize these activities, in this order: via questionnaires and interviews, team members collect "a list of areas of potential improvement" (suggestions of ways to do things better), the team meets to prioritize the items on this list in order to select a small number to start with, several focus groups are set up, each headed by a member of the team, each with the task to study one of the items from this small number, in order to recommend a design for a new organizational structure which can accomplish their suggested improvement, by the target date assigned to them by team, 4) focus groups report to the team which first, calls for the formation of *transition teams*, headed by people in key positions for those particular functions, whose responsibility is to implement each design change which is approved by the top management of the organization, then, it hands over the management of the transition period to the heads of the transition teams who form the **change implementation task force.**

Strategies for Leaders in Securing Commitment to Change

Thus, one has to found the various strategies for securing commitment to change, to be extremely useful in other to fully utilize them in today's organization. In order for organizational change to actually occur, leaders must first "determine **who** in their organization must be committed" to implementing change. The sum of these people is "the critical mass of individuals whose *active* commitment is necessary to provide the human energy for the change to occur". A leader who wants change needs to create a strategic commitment plan, devised to secure the support of the natural leaders of the organizational subsystems which are vital to the change effort, that includes this sequence of action steps: **target the natural leaders** within the relevant subsystems whose commitment change is needed, **specify the critical mass of these leaders** which is needed to ensure change occurs, develop and **implement a plan for getting their commitment**, and design and implement a feedback system which can **evaluate progress toward obtaining their active commitment.**

Before they enact this strategic commitment plan, wise leaders will know that "it is necessary to get some degree of commitment (from the individuals in the critical mass), or the change will not happen, but the *level* of commitment need not be the same" for all of them. Leaders should assign each individual in the critical mass a letter from this rating scale in order to clarify the level of their commitment which is actually necessary in order to implement change successfully: agree to "**let** it happen" (passive commitment), agree to "**help** it happen" (follower commitment), agree to "**make** it happen" (active commitment). Leaders should be sure to rate these people according to the *minimum* commitment needed for change to occur and then, rate each person as to their present level of commitment.

Usually, leaders find that "when people are not committed to the degree required by the change effort, they are resisting in some way". There are several intervention strategies leaders can use to "create the conditions for commitment", a. group problem finding, b. training, c. role modeling, and d. a change in the reward system. Problem finding is useful when resistance is caused by an attitude or "fixed bias" because it creates a situation "that is neutral - one in which existing attitudes are not challenged but rather clarified, without anyone being forced to take a position on them". In contrast to problem solving, most leaders find that problem finding, the process of clarifying an issue or problem, is "unthreatening enough to encourage commitment". To create a non-threatening problem-solving environment, leaders can "limit the sense of risk" among participants by announcing that this temporary "ad hoc" group is only for the purpose of issue identification; the work of the group will be limited to the *clarification* of problems so there is no need for consensus or agreement. Another way to create a non-threatening environment is to implement a training program where all students are treated equally during class because they are "all there to learn".

Even after implementing these kinds of commitment strategies, leaders may find that some people are "not sufficiently dissatisfied with the present state of affairs". If some individuals in the critical mass are still not "eager to achieve the proposed end state and convinced of the feasibility of the change, then they believe that the personal cost, to them, is too high. An intervention will be needed which "increases their discomfort with their present situation". In order to commitment themselves to change, these type of people need to be able to see how the end state can "further their personal interests". While attempting to attract commitment from employees, leadership must remember to "practice what they preach by clearly demonstrating its own commitment to the change". By incorporating change activity into their *personal* behavior, leaders can provide role models for other members of the organization. This will help them influence their employees rather than dictating them. Dictatorship in any change process makes leaders to become alienated from their employees. If leaders refrain from punishing managers for mistakes that are exposed by problem finding groups and demonstrate, by their *own* behavior, "the value of listening to people in all levels of the organization", they often find that obtaining commitment to change is not as difficult as they expected.

After securing the commitment to change from of a critical mass of people within their organization, successful leaders use a technique called "responsibility charting" to clarify behavior that is needed to "implement important change tasks, actions, or decisions". This is necessary to "reduce the ambiguity, wasted energy and negative emotional reactions" which naturally occur during change. Clarifying the responsibility for change behavior involves taking a list of chosen change actions and for each action, identifying the people involved in that action. Then, each individual is assigned a letter signifying their level of responsibility for that action, "must be consulted" before anything is done, "must approve" anything that is done, "has to provide resources for the action", "has responsibility for the action" (R). There are several important rules that guide responsibility charting. Leaders must first agree on the same individual to be rated with an "R". If they cannot reach consensus on this individual for each action, leaders can break the action into subparts, consider moving the R to someone higher up in the organization or even, agree on someone who will make the decision for them. For real change to occur, it is essential that leaders base these decisions not on organizational hierarchy but on what is most efficient for task accomplishment. The role of leaders in cooperation is to help people realize and believe that they are successful when others succeed so they are oriented toward aiding each other to perform effectively. They accurately disclose their intentions and feelings, offer ideas and resources and openly empower all employees.

Complex Change

To lead their organization through complex change, leaders must have "a clear vision" of their future organization, specific "intermediate checkpoints" in mind, to reach during the transition period, "detailed maps" (scenarios) of how the organization will look, from the inside, at each of those mid-points, "a clear knowledge of the capability of the organization", and the skills to "get the best performance out of that organization". The recent, immense, changes in most modern organizations' environments now require organizational leaders to accept changes in their organization's priorities. Successful changes in organizational priorities require leaders to implement changes in their organization's structure. This usually means that new personnel policies must be designed to change the roles workers perform. Most importantly, leaders must find ways to transform their organization's culture if they want to change the ways work is done in their organization.

DISCUSSION QUESTIONS

1. What skills does a leader need to have to successfully lead complex change in organizations? Discuss your answers.

2. Identify five things you feel are important to you as a leader in this chapter. Briefly explain how the understanding of each can help you be a good leader.

3. What are the challenges involved in bringing effective and efficient change to an organization?

CHAPTER 7
History as a Mode of Inquiry in African Governmental Life

"African Governmental life is a socially created reality" but what people create soon begins to constrain and direct them. Is this good or bad? Perhaps we create them to do this because that is what we want or need. African Governmental, once established, are taken over and utilized by individuals and groups in order to further their aims and goals. "Social arrangements are choices and habits that evolve from previous choices." But, our choices are selected from ones predetermined by our cultural values. "African Governments are open systems that seek to offset threat and uncertainty." We all feel threatened by chaos and want to be able to predict the future. "African Governmental structures are more differentiated or integrated, depending on how stable environmental demands are." We all want a stable environment.

Those who believe in the myth of science attempt to "identify recurring, systematic patterns, predict and control destiny, and explain permanence among flux. We delude ourselves when we think that African governments are made of enduring structures that purposively further a larger order.

We succumb to the temptation to search for enduring patterns which invites passivity and inactivity." But, perhaps this type of research is done in order to give us an excuse to be passive and inactive - it's a lot more comfortable! "Social arrangements become institutionalized over time. Social reality takes on the character of a given, pre-determined, and unalterable structure." People begin to believe in the myths that form the foundation of (support and maintain) African Governments. This makes people feel more secure because it tells them how to act and who they are.

The child encounters a world of pre-established meanings and interprets this as objective reality to which he or she must adapt. The successful achievement of maturity is accomplished when an individual discovers that the social world is a manifestation of human intention and expression and becomes aware of his or her responsibility to positively contribute to it. In cultures where individuality is nurtured people can choose to neglect this responsibility.

In modern African cultures, those who benefit from the opportunity to control the social world in modern African societies promote individuality. By generating false choices, they succeed in distracting people from this responsibility. Our reality grows out of myths, which are already established. This is how we grow - just like a child who clings to its mother. Those who seek to exploit us would distract us forever so we never grow up, but rather remain dependent on them.

In modern Africa we are distracted by their incessant entertainment and constant stimulation of our greed, everywhere we look. We grow lazy like grubs on their numbing, meaningless chatter. While we neglect our responsibility, someone else has taken control. We have been dis-empowered. "In a spatial and temporal world that society has standardized for us, we suspend our doubt and allow it to orient us to everyday life." We begin to believe in myths that echo all around us. We believe what they say about who we are and what our purpose in life should be. As we act out the roles in them, we do not encounter each other face-to face because we are all playing a part, which we wear like a mask. This makes us see each other as stereotypes.

Our predecessors, who originated the social interaction that became an institution/government, faced dilemmas, made choices and lived in a world of contingency. Young people revolt against and question our institutions/governments because they also need to face dilemmas, make choices and live in a world of contingency. For that reason, initiation, which is challenging is needed and proactive strategy to implement is demanded. "When a person's gesture is isolated and given a meaning separate from its source, no longer is the gesture an expression of the person.

Others define the person as the embodiment of an abstract quality of which the gesture is a symbol. Roles are seen as the embodiments of abstractions and theories are built to further harden the abstractions and to explain and legitimize." In this way, myths become more valued than humans, themselves. "Every individual is defined not only by his or her past, but also by the past that persists in the ideas and institutions/governments that shape his or her thoughts and actions.

All understanding is historical and prejudicial." How can one escape the tremendous power of these influences? "Do not reduce complexities by using a single interpretive point of view; stay close to the particularities and retain alternative hypotheses for a long time; entertain conjectures and do not push too quickly for resolution. Remember, there are an infinite number of ways to tell a story, to accent certain events or features and de-emphasize others. All knowledge involves prejudice and bias" because all knowledge is cultural.

"Exploring governmental history in Africa as a human creation is threatening" because we will have to face our responsibility to shape our institutions/governments. "We depend on the existing power structure to provide us with direction and orientation." If we take up our responsibility, those who are now performing it, on our behalf, would no longer be able to control or manipulate us for their gain. For that reason, they encourage us to believe it is **smart** to sit back and complain. Let others look foolish while they expose their fallibility. In modern African culture, it is taboo to take up one's responsibility to create and change institutions/governments. That is why we are afraid to. This taboo is at the center of the myth of individual freedom, placed there by those who continue to benefit from the power we give up. Which Way Daughters and Sons of Africa?

DISCUSSION QUESTIONS

1. What are the implications raised in this chapter about leading an organization in Africa?

2. What is an open system?

3. Why do African institutions depend on the existing power structure to provide them with direction and orientation?

CHAPTER 8
Appreciative Governance and Sustainable Development in Africa

Executive Summary

This chapter focuses on the creation of accountable, productive partners and the nurturing of strong and viable partnership in the pursuit of sustainable development in Africa. In other words, it is an examination of the relationship between the governing and the governed in an effort to establish a public policy framework for an appropriate form of appreciative governance in Africa. This paper argues that effective and efficient appreciative governance within a democratic context is indispensable to the consolidation of the consensual contract between the people and the government. I conclude that the creative ideas and energies of the populace must be harnessed in the search for the kind of sustainable development that does not compromise the ability of future generations to achieve their dreams and desires.

Suffice to say a redesigned type of appreciative governance demands sharing of vision, power, skills and responsibility between the government and all other partners. These are NGOs, grassroots organizations, trade unions, private sector, social organizations and all other political parties in the Gambia and the International organizations. Thus the empowerment of people and partnership building at national, international, sub-national and sectoral levels is vital for appreciative governance and accountability for a viable sustainable development in the Gambia.

Therefore, the government of the Gambia, with the active involvement of partners, must (1) creates and nurtures a sustainable accountable and transparent economic, political and administrative climate for productive partnership building. The government of the Gambia can do this by entrenching new structures, rules, systems, procedures and practices; (2) rekindle the partnerships through appropriate appreciative participatory management approaches to achieve common national objectives and goals; (3) empower the people to participate in the process and practice of appreciative governance through devolution of functions, de-concentration of decision making and change to even decentralization of administration; and (4) continue to build upon and negotiate with the international community the need for a New World Order that recognizes the fundamental reality of international interdependence and not international dependency.

Appreciative Governance

Appreciative governance is very important because it helps groups, people, institutions and nations to understand and learn from each other. No groups, people, institutions and nations can work together without appreciative governance. The process of appreciative governance is the transfer of accountability among its members by looking at the positives in all groups, people, institutions, humans and nations.

Therefore, to practice appreciative governance in the Gambia, Gambian government, opposition parties, citizens, professionals and Gambian intellectuals must begin to look at the positives that each side has to offer. Once this is in place, both sides must use the positives to create a dialogue that will serve the best interest of Gambia and her people. The Gambian government, opposition parties, citizens, professionals and Gambian intellectuals blaming each other about "lack of sustainable development" does not address the issue nor does it stop it. Neither of the blame speeds up development in the Gambia.

Through appreciative governance both sides will create a team, build partnership, build collaboration and positively work together to speed up development in Gambia. This will help each side to understand each other's needs so that positive strategies and creativity blossoms to address the issues confronting development in the Gambia. These positive strategies and creativity will serve to the best interest of Gambia. To nurture sustainable development in the Gambia, appreciative governance must be the practice that glues and brings Gambian government, opposition parties, citizens, Gambian intellectuals and professionals together in developing Gambia for her children and her children's children. The next issue I would like to address in this article is sustainable development.

The Meaning and Significance of Sustainable Development in Africa

It seems to me that The Gambia like any other developing nation finds it difficult if not impossible to learn from the past. By and large, the experience of the past should have served us as bases to understanding the meaning and significance of sustainable development in developing nations. The Gambia like any other young developing nation must halt and examine our development before proceeding otherwise we will jeopardize the future of our children and our children's children. The large accumulation of debt by the Gambia is clear evidence that we are sacrificing the future of our children. Suffice it to say, sustainable development is defined as "Development that meets the needs of present generations without compromising the ability of future generations to meet their own needs" (World Commission on Environment & Development 1987). To my knowledge, experience and understanding, sustainable development implies an efficient, effective, comprehensive and integrated development in which temporal dimensions, from an economic, political, social and ecological point of view, must be simultaneously met. The accountability to serve the citizens must be the principle and the driving force of our development in the Gambia. We must never allow our political interest to distract us from serving our citizens. For the Gambia to be proud of herself, sustainable development must persist and last as a process of positive change without continued external assistance. As Gambians we have to understand that, by receiving assistance from outside source the country's public policy lend itself to be controlled or dictated by the giver or donor. Thus, sustainable development is a holistic approach to development based on the forms and processes of development that do not undermine the integrity of the environment and the citizen. This is to say that; sustainable development contributes and enhances citizen's health, education, food security, self-security and economic development that embody the concept of long-term resource stewardship, self-help initiatives and citizen's participation in the planning process. The guiding principle here is having and sustaining decentralized management system in the Gambia.

If we are really serious and honest, policies for sustainable development must be formulated, implemented and monitored as a contribution to long-term economic development in the Gambia our beloved country. In this way, we will pave a positive future for our children. Thus, one can say the goals of sustainable development in the developing nations or the Gambia ranges from self sufficiency in food production, macroeconomic stability, poverty alleviation, creating an enabling environment for investment, reducing the rate of population growth, initiating and developing a process resource stewardship, encouraging self-help, self-propelled development initiatives, minimizing waste in production processes, improving efficiency, improving effectiveness, improving educational institutions, improving health systems, empowering the citizens, embracing democracy, obeying the rule of law and valuing human rights. The key goal is to put the interest of the citizens first. The next section I would like to address is an instrument of sustainable development.

Appreciative Governance as an Instrument of Sustainable Development in Africa

The author define appreciative governance as "the way in which the government values and protects the life of its citizens, respects human right, respects the rule of law, involves citizens in public policy creation, accounts for its actions and practices, keeps the interest of the people at heart, opens for dialogue, allows freedom of the media and press to prevail, provides the best quality education, provides the best health systems, builds partnerships and effectively and efficiently manages the social and economic resources of a country by creating, nurturing and sustaining a safe and stable nation for sustainable development". Thus the World Bank defines governance as " the manner in which power is exercised in the management of a country's economic and social resources for development" (World Bank 1992a).

We may recall that for the past decade, the emphasis on good governance of a country has become the focal point of discussion in international arenas. This is evident in the developing countries where democracy and good governance are ignored. The lack of these vital elements of the sustainable development process discourages investors and hence jeopardizes a country's sustainable development objectives and goals. However, one may also recall that international development institutions have realized that many development projects in the world have failed because they lack strong political accountability and commitments, regardless if the projects were financially and technically feasible and beneficial to a given nation.

I believe that good and viable governance plays a key role in the design and formulation of an appropriate public policy framework so that stakeholders, private and public sectors can grow, become creative and manage socioeconomic resources efficiently and effectively for sustainable development.

In broad term appreciative governance has four major dimensions: the government values and protects the life of the citizens, and respects human right and the rule of law; the exercise of authority by government; the type of government; and government's ability to design, formulate, and implement national policies. It is my conviction that to successfully manage the social and economic resources of a country efficiently and effectively, the government must create and nurture an appropriate and sustainable legal framework that will ensure the accountability of the president, the ministers, other civil servants, and private and public institutions. In this way they will provide public goods that support social and sustainable economic development in developing nations or the Gambia. Most importantly, all government must respect and safeguard human rights. By and large, these ideals remain neglected or ignored as if they do not exist in many developing nations and thus many development initiative projects and programs did not succeed in achieving their objectives and goals. Another section I would like to address is the need for an appreciative, viable and vibrant Gambian society.

What we need in Africa - Appreciative, Viable and Vibrant Society

The Gambia like any other developing nation is called upon to avoid poor governance that sometimes came to be associated with the state's inability to nurture and sustain the viable growth and to create the healthy conditions for improving productivity and enhancing welfare of the citizens. Thus, the government of the Republic of the Gambia has to come up with new, vibrant and sustainable economic strategies that will create a future for our children. Suffice it to say, strategies for economic resurgence in the Gambia or developing nations based wholly on actions to influence macro economic variables that do not appreciate or totally embrace the underline dynamics of sustainable social and psychological indicators are likely to fail. As you all may agree with me that human society is viable proposition only as a consensual affair were by people strive to be involved in a variety of pursuits. They do so because in their minds, this is what makes their life vivacious and interesting. People either want to positively exercise the normal freedoms in economics, religion, politics, health, and education or at the minimum, want to be assured that they will not be unduly hindered from doing so at anytime they feel like. Let us pause a moment and think about or visualize the whole world, by doing this we will begin to see or realize that the consciousness of the people all over the world including the Gambia is being awakened. The people of the Gambia are no longer sleeping but well and lively awake. Thus, they no longer regard traditional political participation through political parties and periodic elections or campaigns with empty promises as enough. The people of the Gambia deserve more than this and most importantly they are now demanding the natural right to partial and full inclusion and participation in previously sacrosanct areas of vibrant economic, political, educational, health and social life for all.

According to Schlesinger (1992) states that " if people's demands are not met, then they would either peacefully remove themselves from the formal society and engage in any of myriad activities to circumvent existing structures or erupt in violence as presently being witnessed in several parts of the world". I am convinced that the people of the Gambia can no longer afford to be exempted from any form of development that will affect the life of their children and their children's children.

By and large, a successful process of sustainable development involves the drive to restore hope and renew growth in an equitable and sustainable environment in the Gambia or developing nations. Thus, the drives are as follows:

1. Understanding the legitimate fears of oppression and brutality, concerns and will of real citizens;
2. The designing and implementing of systems, mechanisms and whose functions that fulfills the necessary tenets of productive democracy, predictability and stability, within a paradigm that allows people to seek their objectives and goals; and
3. Communicating and building a sustainable partnership with people about vibrant economic policy and accountable economic management in a process and principle that builds and nurtures a trusting feeling of appreciation among the citizens.

It is my conviction that, in other for the Gambia to successfully achieve the goals and objectives of sustainable development it requires a new proactive and sustainable political agenda, a new vibrant political economy of change that demands to embrace all citizens, political parties, professionals and most importantly partners in the development process in the Gambia. The next section addresses appreciative partners and partnership.

Appreciative Partners and Partnerships

By and large, the increasing concern with the lack of social and vivacious economic development has intensified the call for new approaches to appreciative governance in the Gambia or developing nations. Thus, good appreciative governance must come to mean creating valuable investments in human capital and undertaking minimum transfer programs or projects. In other words, social investment programs or projects must not be facilitative of partisan political clienteles and welfares, but must be aimed at eradicating the spread of poverty from one generation to another in the Gambia or developing nations. The truth here is that the Gambia like any other developing nations must be accountable and mobilize the most inherently legitimate instruments of democracy that is based on the principle of inclusive participation and inclusive consensus-building.

It is my conviction that the good appreciative governance in the context of democracy requires the building of linkages with all the partners, national and international, formal and informal, and creation of accountable and sustainable partnerships for our children. Thus, at the domestic level, all the partners represent all the lawful organizations formed by the people to help manage their responsible actions.

Some of these organizations include but not limited to formal governmental structures, sub structures, local government authorities, autonomous and semi autonomous bodies, political parties, NGOs, trade unions, cooperatives, business firms, cultural, rural development societies, religious and other organizations.

Thus, I define partnership as "the practice of appreciative governance and the nurturing of accountable and productive lawful organizations that continues to be involved in the pursuit of the common objectives and goals of achieving vivacious sustainable development for a given nation". I also believe that all of us have to understand that the process of developing vivacious partnership takes longer than we think. It calls for commitment, patient, accountability, tolerance, appreciation, respect and valuing others views and voices.

Above all, it calls for a delicate balancing and appreciating power differences between partners of unequal power and the ability for successfully resolving conflict. To be successful and create and nurture sustainable development in any form of partnership in the Gambia or developing nations, there must exist a clear and accountable action oriented vision, mission and a plan of appreciative collaborative actions that could be used to achieve common goals and objectives that are the most important ingredients necessary to bring the different parties together to serve the society. The next section offers recommendation strategies to be implemented.

Recommendation Strategies

The author defines strategy as "actions people, managers and leaders take to attain an organization, institution and nation goals". The strategies are as follows:

1. Consciousness-raising, Organizing and Capacity Building.
2. Building Partnership with government, NGOs and Business Organizations.
3. Required Internship before Students Graduate from high school, College and University.
4. Each representative of a District or Constituency must be required to implement a project that will serve the people. It should be people-oriented or bottom-up approach to conceptualizing a project.
5. Government building Partnership with Africans in and out of the Africa as well as Africans in Diaspora.
6. Citizens involved in Small Business and Entrepreneurship in Africa.
7. Africans residing out of Africa going back home and investing in their country.
8. The University of the African nations and Teachers College must build sustainable, viable and vibrant partnership with African intellectuals and professionals residing abroad.

9. The Government and the citizens must collaborate and build a campus for the University of African nations that will accommodate local students and attract foreign students as well as foreign faculty.

10. The Government of African nations and the citizens must utilize African intellectuals and professionals to serve as technical advisers for the country.

11. African Presidents must make it their duty to meet with all their citizens in a country that they visit and not just those who support their party.

12. Promotion and development of agriculture so that the country will be self sufficient in food production. This will curtail food imports in the Africa.

13. Promotion and development of tourism and the re-export trade which are among the major sources of revenue to the country.

14. Empowerment of the people and involving them in the projects so that they have the sense of ownership in them.

15. Provide a conducive or an enabling environment that will attract foreign direct investment (FDI) and investors in the country.

16. The government, the citizens and all religious leaders must speak up and fight against female circumcision in Africa.

17. The government, the citizens and all religious leaders must speak up and fight against arranged forced marriages in Africa.

18. The government and the citizens must immediately create and produce a local African product that it must effectively and efficiently market to other countries so that it can offset the Dalasi inflation rate.

19. The government and the citizens must continue to develop and market historic places in their nation for example Juffreh in The Gambia until it is recognized and utilized as one of the great historical and tourist attractions in the world.

20. Each person, institution, organization, Ministry, department, group, religion, political party or community must ask and answer the following important questions: What have I done to effectively and efficiently contribute to the sustainable development of my beloved country and the continent of Africa? What is my next step

to build a better nation and a better continent for our children and our children's children that we all can be proud off?

21. Please add your own.

Conclusion

In conclusion, when the government of the African nations, all political parties and all our citizen become accountable and committed and accept responsibility as well as stop pointing fingers to our nations problems to someone or a particular party or citizen, then we will have a true, viable and vibrant sustainable development that will serve and provide a hopeful future for our children and our children's children. From this we can proclaim that we have a vivacious nation and continent that we all can be proud to be a part of our life. United we can create and produce a viable and vibrant society that is productive. Divided we can create and produce a poor and dependent society that is useless and unproductive. Which way the people of the continent of Africa?

DISCUSSION QUESTIONS

1. What is appreciative governance?

2. What skills does a leader need to have to build an effective partnership in an organization?

3. What is sustainable development?

CHAPTER 9
Understanding Organizations in Action

Introduction

In studying organizations we must also understand one of the great thinkers of organizational studies by the name Thompson who describes complex organizations as "multidisciplinary phenomena". By describing them in this particular way, he hopes to avoid the static type of understanding that the discovery of universals, which are always necessary, usually brings. In his book, he intentionally limits the focus of his attention to "the behavior of instrumental organizations, those that induce or coerce participation." In Part One, Thompson looks deeply into the "forces that generate and guide the behavior of organizations". Because we expect organizations to produce results, they must "establish limits within which organizational action must take place". Thompson reminds us that our ability to find patterns in organizational behavior depends upon the type of conceptual paradigm we use. In other words, "the kinds of answers we get are limited by the kinds of questions we ask". Since what we see is what we get, perhaps it is time to try out "alternative conceptual schemes". According to Thompson, the "rational" model results from using a "closed-system strategy" to study organizations and the "natural" model results from using an "open-system strategy".

STRATEGIES FOR STUDYING ORGANIZATIONS

Closed-System Strategy

The only way we can predict an organization's behavior is to first "determine its present circumstances". Those circumstances, including variables and relationships, must "be few enough for us to comprehend". The organizational system must be closed or "the outside forces acting on it must be **completely** predictable". Thompson believes we will "opt for a closed-system strategy and rational model if we have responsibility for improving the efficiency of an organization". Utilization of this strategy and model will inevitably result in efforts to "maximize efficiency by planning procedures, set standards, and exercise controls to ensure conformity". This point of view "focuses on structural relationships among units of the organization; efficiency is maximized by specializing tasks and grouping them into departments, therefore, responsibility is fixed. Offices are defined according to position in hierarchy; experts, appointed to offices. Rules categorize activities and clients. It is expected that available salaries and patterns for career advancement will motivate expert officials. Is the rational model actually a closed system? Thompson notes that Weber saw three holes in it. "1) Policymakers, at the top of the bureaucracy, can alter organizational goals. 2) The use of rules, salary and career may not be able to sufficiently divorce an individual's private life from his or her life as an expert officeholder. And 3) the effects of clientele (outsiders) might not be completely nullified by depersonalizing categories". It is clear that these three holes can introduce chaos into the system but it also allows for flexibility and a breath of fresh air.

Open-System Strategy

It is more realistic to assume that "a system contains more variables than we can comprehend at one time, or that some of the variables are subject to influences we cannot control or even predict". Given the natural state of affairs in our universe, these tasks, I believe computers will never be able to completely conquer. A complex organization is "a whole made of interdependent parts each of which contribute something and receive something from the whole". Since survival is the ultimate goal, the relationships of parts to one another and to the whole are determined via an evolutionary adaptation process.

The assumption is that "parts will adjust themselves to producing a net positive contribution or be jettisoned, or else the whole will degenerate". It is assumed that "homeostasis spontaneously governs relationships among the parts, keeping the system viable in spite of disturbances in its environment". Such a concept sounds utopian.

The Open-System Strategy proposes that "organizations are NOT autonomous entities and views the organizations as a unit in interaction with its environment. It focuses on variables that are not subject to complete control by the organization and regards the interdependence of the organization and its environment as inevitable or natural".

Choice or Compromise?

Because "complex organizations are used as instruments for achievement that results from planned, controlled action, and yet, there is impressive evidence that they are influenced in significant ways by elements of their environments", a synthesis of both models is needed. Millions of people depend on them everyday to provide purposeful, effective action. Thompson's thesis claims that "neither model alone provides an adequate understanding of complex organizations. What is needed is a synthesis of the two models because their two strategies indicate something fundamental to the actual culture surrounding complex organizations". One step toward the synthesis needed is to view a complex organization as a "problem-facing and problem-solving phenomenon". Use of this paradigm focuses attention on "organizational processes related to the choice of apparent available alternative courses of action rather than the consequences of alternatives. It assumes that the organization has limited capacity to gather and process information or to predict consequences. For this reason, it recommends that organizations develop processes for searching and learning, as well as for **deciding**. Indeed, the development of capacities for learning is crucial for survival in a changing world. Thompson accomplishes synthesis by defining complex organizations as open systems that are therefore constantly faced with uncertainty. Nevertheless, because they are simultaneously "subject to criteria of rationality", they need to somehow manufacture certainty. The creation and maintenance of organizational culture addresses the uncertainty indicative of an open-system by superimposing the certainty of an abstract cultural paradigm onto it. Therefore, the question is no longer what model best facilitates the understanding of complex organizations but rather, what organizational culture best facilitates the accomplishment of purposes expected of them?

The Location of Problems

Thompson refers to Parsons' (1960) suggestion that "Organizations exhibit three distinct levels of responsibility and control - technical, managerial and institutional". Because an organization is subject to criteria of rationality, Thompson believes it is therefore "advantageous to remove as much uncertainty as possible from its technical core by reducing the number of variables operating on it". To what degree should uncertainty be removed from the technical core? If you do that, members would tend to become resistant to change therefore making needed changes difficult. This would introduce an unnecessary rigidity that would hinder an organization's essential need for flexibility. In contrast, creatively dealing with uncertainty is "indispensable at the institutional level of a complex organization. At this level, the organization is open to influence by elements of the environment over which it has no formal authority or control. It is the important task of the managerial level to mediate between these two other levels. To satisfy its rationality criteria, a complex organization must approach certainty at the technical level while remaining flexible enough at the institutional level to be able to adapt to rapid changes in its environment". It is the managerial level's unsavory yet essential task to "press the technical core for modifications as irregularities stemming from external sources alter conditions". The managerial level performs a similar function, at the organizational level, as the adult psyche within an adult human being. To be successful, an adult must find ways to pacify his or her urgent inner childish needs for the certainty of instantaneous gratification so that uncertain, long-term and external social objectives, instilled by past parental directives, can be eventually accomplished. Thompson's synthesis of the complex organization from its technical, managerial and institutional parts parallels the modern psychological synthesis of a mature individual by the operation of an adult self that must mediate between child and parent selves within a single adult individual.

Therefore, the managerial level would do well to search for something that can provide the organization with both an adequate amount of certainty and the necessary amount of flexibility. Organizational culture is the only thing that can provide both of these things because it motivates and guides people toward the achievement of both short-term and long-term goals without resorting to the rigid rationality of rule making. Organizational culture is superior to the rationality of rule making because it causes people to act because of a force originating from within rather than from outside of them. Organizational culture can do this because it harnesses the force of MEANING. Meaning is a more powerful force than the rationality of rule making because it is not uni-dimensional. An individual's private life cannot be divorced from his or her life as an officeholder. Organizational culture is more powerful because it provides meaning that speaks to and motivates people simultaneously on many levels. A human is not an uni-dimensional being. For this reason, humans hunger for meaning communicated on many different levels. Indeed, as we continue to explore differences between humans and their nearest genetic relatives, primates, perhaps it is merely the ability to create and maintain organizational cultures, which distinguishes us from them. How can we be sure of this? If we look back on our history as a species, glimmers, of once-glorious cultures led by leaders who understood this ultimate truth about people, will still shine back at us.

Rationality in Organizations

Since instrumental action is always "rooted on the one hand in desired outcomes and on the other hand in beliefs about cause/effect relationships, the state of man's knowledge at any point in time dictates the variables required and the manner of their manipulation to bring about those desired outcomes. The question of economics is whether these outcomes are obtained with the least necessary expenditure of resources. I would ask, "Is economics always a relevant way to judge the acceptability of outcomes?" That may be the trend in a capitalist society but perhaps not in others. The problem in capitalist societies is that usually the economic dimension of technology takes priority over questions of instrumentality because there is an increasing desire to find ways to create more and more profit. This desire has encouraged the association of instrumentality with the accumulation of capital. The worldwide spread of this belief causes many modern-day problems because many people in capitalist societies do not differentiate between the two. Because men desire outcomes they cannot alone accomplish, "complex organizations are built to operate technologies that are found to be impossible for only a few individuals to operate". For example, the desire for world peace led to the creation of the United Nations.

Variations in Technologies

"Long-linked technology involves serial interdependence that produces a single product at a constant rate and permits the use of clear-cut criteria for the selection of machines and their human operators". An example of this is the mass production assembly line. Mediating technology involves operating in standardized ways in order to link clients, widely distributed in time and space, who wish to be interdependent". Examples of this are insurance companies and utilities, as well as, the postal service. The selection of what standards will be utilized varies according to how particular clients are categorized but belief in the efficacy of standardization to service clients is never questioned. Belief in the efficacy of standardization springs from the desire to apply scientific methods to human needs. Because scientific inquiry seeks to find validation for its hypotheses, it tends to generalize. Scientific generalization encourages the point of view that standardization is useful. "Standardization makes possible the operation of mediating technology over time and through space via the bureaucratic techniques of categorization and the impersonal application of rules". "Intensive technology signifies a variety of techniques used to achieve change. The techniques utilized are "determined by feedback from the object of such change. The particular combination and the order of application of techniques used depend on the nature of the desired change." For this reason, intensive technology is appropriate for "changing circumstances. It's success rests on the availability of the capabilities potentially needed, as well as, the customized combination of those capabilities required by the individual case or project." One example is the use of intensive technology in the hospital.

Although a group often seeks to minimize influences on itself from the outside, completely sealing off the organization's core is counter-productive. It is also impossible and thus, efforts to do that actually draw off some of its valuable resources. Therefore, it is much better use of those valuable resources for the organization to *learn* how to remain flexible, in other words: responsive to and adaptable to the inevitable influence of environmental factors.

The purpose of input and output units is to "meet fluctuating environments and convert them into steady conditions" that the core can easily deal with. An example on the input side is "the stockpiling of materials and supplies acquired in an irregular market, and their steady insertion into the production process. The recruitment of dissimilar personnel and their conversion into reliable performers through training and indoctrination is another". An example on the output side is "maintaining warehouse inventories, which permits the core to produce at a constant rate but, allows distribution to fluctuate with market conditions". Input and output units "bring considerable advantages to the core but it does so with costs to the organization". One problem is how to "maintain sufficient inventories without incurring obsolescence" as demands of the market change. The main challenge to input and output units is to avoid increasing the spread of rigidity outward from the core but instead, extend flexibility and responsiveness to the environment in toward the core.

Organizations can do this by offering incentives to encourage clients to use their services during slow periods. An example of an incentive is reduced airfares to Florida in the summer. Also, they often use communication channels to detect and even prevent high demand in advance. Fire departments promote home and fire safety educational campaigns in order to prevent emergencies that would cause high demand for their services.

The main question facing organizations is "What activities are *appropriate* for the anticipation of environmental fluctuations at this organization?" Remaining flexible demands that one not over-adapt in anticipation of changes which may or may *not* occur.

Because of the popularity of the belief that important environmental fluctuations, such as demand, are patterned, many organizations operate as if it is possible to correctly forecast demand and therefore, they can plan or schedule the operations of their core at a steady rate.

Rationing involves establishing priorities so that the organization can "concentrate its energy on the most challenging problems and cases or on those which appear most likely to yield satisfactory outcomes, thereby, attending to lesser tasks when the priority tasks are completed".

Domains of Organized Action

Because no one is self-sufficient, each organization must establish a niche for itself by delineating specific boundaries around a part of the whole in which this particular organization will take initiative. "An organization's domain consists of claims which it stakes out for itself in terms of population served and services rendered. An organization's domain also identifies how the organization is dependent on the environment. An organization's environment is composed of four main sectors: 1) customers, 2) suppliers, 3) competitors, and 4) regulatory groups". Usually, these four sectors are contained within the specific culture of a particular society. It is believed that "patterns of culture can and do influence organizations in important ways. Because the relationship between an organization and its task environment is one of exchange, unless it is judged as offering something valuable, it will not be able to survive. Exchange agreements rest upon prior consensus regarding an organization's domain". Consensus rests on assumptions shared in common, in other words: culture. Because its foundations originate in a common culture, "domain consensus is able to define a set of expectations about what members of an organization will and will not do. By providing an image of the organization's role in its environment, the domain consensus of a particular organization serves as a guide for the ordering of action in certain directions".

Management of Interdependence

An organization is dependent on its environment in proportion to its need for resources found in its environment. Thompson cites Emerson's statement that "dependence can be seen as the obverse of power. Thus, an organization has power relative to an element of its task environment, to the extent that it can monopolize the capacity to satisfy that element. Thompson proposes that "an organization's net power results from a set of relationships between the organization and the several elements of its pluralistic task environment". He also proposes that "increasing interdependence may result in increased net power. This is the possibility on which coalitions rest".

Organizations attempt to diffuse their dependence on particular elements in their task environments by joining together in sufficient numbers. "Conditions of perfect competition are infrequent and highly unstable over time. For this reason, it becomes advisable to skew the imbalance in the organization's favor". An example of this is the cartel. An organization acquires prestige by the creation and maintenance of a favorable image. By doing this it can "wield informal power in the community".

The Acquisition of Power

To "manage interdependence, organizations employ cooperative strategies by arranging negotiated environments. Organizations are willing to make a commitment to cooperate because agreements reduce uncertainty. Thus, the effective achievement of power rests on the exchange of commitments". In other words, "uncertainty is reduced for the organization through its reduction of uncertainty for others". This type of reciprocity is usually described as a shared culture. Thompson notes, "Coalition not only provides a basis for exchange but also requires a commitment to *future joint* decision making.

Defense of Domain

Organizations "move toward their objectives through compromise, which is inevitable. They often join forces to establish evaluating organizations which develop yardsticks and set standards". Leaders must realize that to compete, organizations must engage in a continuous negotiation process. This will allow organizational systems to compete in a changing global environment. This type of change is inevitable because we all operate in a new world of technology that has made us to become a global village. This new world of technology has challenged all organizational leaders to develop new and proactive ways of leading a diverse workforce as well as employees to develop new skills of becoming vibrant and productive. This domain should take a turn of three hundred and sixty degrees of negotiation process to become effectively functional. All systems must be constantly alive and well in other to become meaningful and significance to serve the whole organization.

Organizational Design

Organizations can remove or reduce contingencies through organizational design.

Vertical integration is "the combination, in one organization, of successive stages of production; each stage uses as its inputs the product of the preceding stage and produces inputs for the following stage.

For organizations that use intensive technologies, "the activity of the client becomes an important contingency so they seek to place their boundaries around them on a temporary basis. Where the intended change in the client is extreme, the placing of boundaries around the client is virtually complete". For the individual thus enclosed, the organization is "a place to live and work where a large number of people, cut off from the wider society, for an appreciable period of time, together lead an enclosed, formally administered life". The organization must develop and maintain a culture, which psychologically encompasses each individual member. To do this, the organizational culture of this type of organization must utilize commitment to community mechanisms such as celebration and mortification, which involve members' emotional, as well as, physical being. Indeed, such organizations are often correctly referred to as communities. Current and past religious communities are organizations which seek to develop their clients' spiritual being and find that the best way to do that is to encompass them in a specific religious culture that is closed off from the materialism and secularism which exists in the wider society.

Balancing Components

As complex organizations extend their boundaries, in order to incorporate sources of contingencies, they find that the problem of balance emerges. The problem of balance is an ongoing one because, as circumstances change, so the right balances changes. If incorporating other organizations, in order to control environmental contingencies, will make the organization too inflexible to adapt to change then what are the correct relationships (for input and output) to maintain with crucial organizations in the task environment? Once those correct relationships have been determined, how should they be changed when circumstances change? "The multiple-component organization inevitably faces problems of balancing the capabilities of its components". Although some resources come only in certain sizes, could this be made more variable through more cooperation with producers of those resources? The root of the problem of balance is the question of size. Therefore, to progress toward finding a beneficial balance, on must pose the problem of balance as one of *"economy of scale"*. Thompson cites Knauth who found that "the advantages of 'bigness' include easier, less expensive financing; more numerous, highly trained experts to attack trouble spots; sustained research; and more accurately tailored and adaptable marketing systems".

Achieving flexibility is so difficult because the costs of acquiring resources are often so great that organizations must make commitments to future use of those resources. It is obvious why organizations constantly strive to grow although unlimited growth will eventually endanger their viability. In the struggle to grow big enough to be successful, many organizations become filled with people who are good at that creating an organizational culture which can support grow best. For that reason, frequently it becomes almost impossible to *see* when the time to limit growth has come and accomplish all the changes necessary to do that. Before they become entirely focused on the need for growth, complex organizations must re-think how to achieve these advantages yet while remaining small and flexible. Most likely, it will take more cooperation with clients, suppliers and competitors. Since circumstances always change, solving the problem of balance and answering the question of balance requires organizations to find ways to be successful and flexible. Finding the best balance requires being able to sacrifice some growth and success in the short-term in order to acquire enough flexibility to remain adaptable to changing circumstances in the long-term. Therefore, balance is in essence a question of perspective. Perspective is maintained and changed by organizational culture or the culture of the wider society.

Organizations controlled by people who can easily transfer their investment in the organization to somewhere else at little cost to themselves tend to demand significant results in the short-term. In contrast, organizations controlled by people who invest large portions of their life and identity in the organization tend to be concerned with the long-term. Both organizations with long and short-term organizational cultures strive for productivity. The problem of balance does not become an issue until those with short-term perspectives discover that productivity depends on levels of *psychological*, as well as, financial investment.

Organizations with excess capacity often re-design the organization by diversification, the development of new products or services. Diversification involves enlargement of domain or development of multiple domains. Organizations seek to enlarge their domain in order to incorporate contingencies caused by the uncertainty generated by competition. They seek to incorporate more and more elements of their task environment within their boundaries because they seek the ability to predict and control their dependency. Organizations compete for market share in order to balance output and demand. As organizations grow, their output increases. To deal with increased output, organizations must find ways to stimulate demand artificially "to the point where it equals capacity".

Nevertheless, Thompson believes "no matter how crucial a contingency or capacity, the organization need *not* incorporate it if the organization can be certain of its availability, when needed, on reasonable terms. Thus, the organization with power relative to another which controls that contingency or capability need not formally incorporate that activity". In reality, power fluctuates with changing circumstances. When organizations accept that certainty is a myth, *and then* they will begin to discover or create new forms of interaction based on shared power and mutual interdependence. As they expand, organizations impinge on the integrity of the market environment in which they originated and that maintains them. Their success becomes a handicap. Initially, it seems to people in the organization that they are better able to predict contingencies and control crucial capacities as their domain increases. Their apparent control of certainty in the short-term blinds them to an increasing distortion of the market environment. Suddenly, their long-term stability and success turns to failure and the survival of their organization is threatened because circumstances, which they did not foresee, are upon them. They cannot see how the expansion of their organization distorted and thus, created changes in, its environment. They are unaware of how their image of themselves as heroic pioneers caused them to imagine an ever expanding frontier, while in reality; their organization had been nurtured within an ecosystem made up of a complex network of interdependencies. It was their desire to escape their organization's dependency that led them to expand their organization until its environmental system could not support it. In the instant the market environment moved in positive self-correction, they realized that because of their organization's present size, it was no longer as adaptable as it needed to be to remain viable. What inner flaw caused this organization's transformation from highly successful to obsolescent? With its capabilities to predict and control, why had no one noticed how changes in the organization, itself, stimulated changes in its environment? Could this process have been changed? What if the organizational culture had promoted an image of the organization as necessarily and positively dependent within the ecosystem of its environment? What if organizational culture had emphasized the value of reciprocity rather than the value of control?

Technology and Structure

What Thompson labels "the synthetic organization" frequently arises naturally in the community, especially in response to an emergency of some kind. Its roots are in basic social behavior which humans have used for millennia. For this reason, one can accurately state that what Thompson terms "the synthetic organization" is the original form of human organization. "In a surprisingly short time, human and material resources being used for other purposes are adapted to disaster-recovery activities. This is not a highly organized effort but rather, a series of efforts". Several things happen to bring about the synthetic organization. "Information regarding needed resources circulates. People bring uncommitted needed resources to an individual or group whose **power rests not on authority but on capacity to coordinate.** The authority to coordinate the use of needed resources is forced upon this individual or group". Often, having capacity to coordinate means merely having found oneself "at the crossroads of resource availability and need" when the need originally emerged. Most often, these people are not experts in any specific field but instead, are individuals or a group of individuals who maintain a specific philosophy about life. "Life is always full of surprises and problems, so when you see something that needs to be done, don't wait, take responsibility for it and get the help you need to take care of it." This philosophy is based on a particular perspective or outlook on life that is nurtured by a culture that places more value on the needs of the community than the individual. Behaving according to this philosophy requires constant contact with others by the utilization of via communication channels. Rarely is anything of lasting significance created by anyone acting alone.

Usually, *ad hoc* organizations dissolve rapidly on their own as the need disappears or is co-opted by formal institutions. The "synthetic organization" has several aspects that are unique to it. Its continued existence relies on consensus regarding goals for action and since it is operating in the interest of and for the benefit of the community, at least on a temporary basis, it has the authority to freely acquire and deploy needed human and material resources. "Men and women leave their normal workplaces without permission (or work there without compensation if their skills are urgently needed) and press into service equipment and materials that may no belong to them. During a disaster, survival needs of the community are determined by consensus while priorities are rearranged to reflect a greater value on the community's well being than on property rights.

"The synthetic organization simultaneously establishes its structure and carries on operations". Under conditions of great **uncertainty**, it researches the nature and extent of the problem, as well as, location of relevant resources. Amazingly, it does all this without pre-established rules or institutionalized channels of communication. Does this prove that organizational structure is sometimes counter-productive? The synthetic organization relies on cultural values for rules and informal channels of communication. Thompson reminds us that "the synthetic organization is considered inefficient by technological or economic standards". Often, in times of disaster, complex technology may not be operable if electricity is unavailable. The purpose of the synthetic organization is to address the needs of the whole community, not generate wealth for a few individuals. For these reasons, the synthetic organization cannot be judged by technological and economic standards. Assuming that "the synthetic organization's headquarters could know *in advance* the extent of the problem and the resources available, (highly unlikely, given the actual conditions in which this type of organization arises) then it could make plans, and establish rules and communication channels between departments as ordinary organizations do. It is the very lack of planning, rules and formal channels of communication that make the synthetic organization uniquely suited to the task of quickly adapting to change. In fact, large, complex organizations facing significant change such as down-sizing and merger are now advised to form at least one *ad hoc* "parallel" organization, on a temporary basis, which is created in order to model forthcoming changes in organizational structure.

Internal Interdependence

Organizations are useful to humans because 'the whole is greater than the sum of the parts'. "The failure of any one part can threaten the whole and thus, all the other parts". Thompson terms this *"pooled interdependence*. Each part renders a discrete contribution and each is supported by the whole. Interdependence may also take a serial form". Part A must act properly before part B can act. Thompson terms this *sequential interdependence* because it is not symmetrical. If the outputs each part are the inputs for the other parts, he terms this *reciprocal interdependence*. In this form, each part is penetrated by the others. Reciprocal independence is unique in that each part is the significant contingency for other parts. Reciprocal interdependence forms a matrix network that is both supportive without being rigid. Thompson believes reciprocal interdependence is the most difficult to coordinate because the actions of each part must be adjusted to the actions of one or more other parts. This requirement is viewed as constraining by people who believe organizations can escape interdependence. People who welcome interdependence as a normal condition of life embrace this requirement because they realize it creates necessary support while offering the most flexibility. They know that to achieving short-term freedom, one must always sacrifice long-term viability.

Regardless of their technology, humans will never escape uncertainty because their particular perspective will always limit their understanding. Therefore, those who succeed, in the long run, are people who put their energy into creating organizations, which maintain ties of reciprocity within them and with many other organizations. Bonds of reciprocity are living lifelines of continuous, beneficial, mutual exchange. Indeed, by the establishment of reciprocal relationships over time, the simplest one-celled organism has been able to evolve into the complex multi-cellular organism each of us call: "myself"!

"*Coordination by standardization* involves the establishment of rules that require that the situations to which they apply remain constant over time". To assume this is to believe in a myth. *Coordination by strategic planning* involves the establishment of schedules, which is more flexible than standardization yet strategic plans designed when conditions were one way are frequently maintained even after conditions change. The reason why rules and plans cause organizations to be rigid is because people become emotionally invested in them. They give rules and plans power by neglecting to view them as agreements which occurred during one period of time under specific conditions.

"*Coordination by mutual adjustment* is unique because "it involves the transmission of NEW information **during** the process of action. It is different because it is coordination in real time instead of coordination by rules and schedules agreed upon in advance. It is more flexible because conditions may have changed since those rules and plans were made. It is more responsive because the information that directs the action is fresh and immediate. Thompson notes that March and Simon called it "coordination by feedback" because it often involves "communication across hierarchical lines".

Departmentalization and Hierarchy

"Costs of planning are minimized when done in the smallest possible cluster". Reciprocal interdependence is so extensive that to simply link all of the involved positions would overburden interpersonal communication channels. For these organizations, the creation of a specific organizational culture provides a particular type of over-arching and pervasive communication using cultural forms, which assists in the formation and maintenance of second-order groups. Thompson defines hierarchy as a "clustering of interdependent groups, to handle those aspects of coordination which are **beyond** the scope of any of its components". Hierarchy has acquired a negative connotation because the availability of power, which the designation of authority provides, tends corrupt humans. Those who have been awarded positions with power attached to them can rarely resist using their power to restrict the scope of small, local units. Gradually, their autonomy becomes more conditional until it disappears as those higher in the hierarchy *extend* their scope of influence to *include* these units. As a result, a morbid organizational rigidity begins to spread because the previously autonomous quality of these units, which enabled them to perform their important function as the organization's adaptable and penetrable 'skin', has been destroyed. The substitution of liaison positions to link organizational groups permitted the growth of much larger organizations by creating the middle management level.

Organizational Rationality and Structure

Thompson believes "the crucial problem for boundary-spanning units of an organization, is not coordination but *adjustment* to environmental contingencies (exogenous variables). He cites March, Simon and Dill, who "distinguish task environments as homogeneous or heterogeneous, stable or rapidly shifting, and unified or segmented.

Boundary-Spanning Structures

Adaptation by rule is the least costly form, in the short-term; therefore, it is preferred by organizations, which are under pressure to be *economically* efficient.

Management retains its position in the organization as long as it is able to persuade members that this range exists in reality and that management comprehends it adequately to predict its variations. People follow rules and plans set by management because they believe in the mental construct of a limited range of environmental variations. It comforts them to imagine that environmental variation is limited and thus, knowable. Agreeing to follow rules displays one's commitment to this shared assumption. At first, "bureaucratic procedures of categorizing events and selecting appropriate response rules become very important. But inevitably, "the range of variations in the task-environment becomes so great that the proliferation of rules places too heavy a burden on the organization's capacity to judge" and the organization becomes paralyzed.

Because the environment is dynamic, rules are inadequate so cues must be taken from the environment; therefore, regional divisions of the organization will be decentralized. "Each boundary-spanning unit is differentiated functionally to correspond to segments of the task environment. In addition, each unit operates on a decentralized basis to monitor" and use consensus to design "responses to fluctuations to its sector of the task environment". The modern-day heterogeneous, dynamic global market environment simply cannot support the large, bureaucratic organizations of the past. For that reason, small, flexible organizations, as well as, large, decentralized organizations composed of many conditionally autonomous, local units, now flourish in this environment. "The more contingencies the organization faces, the more its boundary-spanning aspect will be segmented". To remain viable in this type of environment, a large organization's structure must become like that of the water spider who rests with stillness on legs, which each move separately and seemingly effortlessly as the wave passes under it.

The Organization as a Joint Result

"So long as an organization employs simple technologies and faces s simple task environment, it can be large and still employ a simple structure". A vertically integrated organization will seek to become responsive to changing environmental conditions by dividing into units but subordinate each unit to central planning.

The diversified organization consists of several conditionally autonomous organizations, each corresponding to *one* of the domains of the total organization". In the decentralized version, leadership propagates basic premises for decision-making through the maintenance of a specific organizational culture, as well as, distributes financial resources for research. The ever-present conflict, in organizations under pressure to operate economically, revolves around the temptation to rely on standardization and the need for flexibility. Recently, many have discovered that, because their task environment is undergoing rapid, unpredictable changes, with the creation of the global marketplace, it is necessary to rearrange their priorities and put flexibility first. "The more complex an organization, the more its grass roots will be interdependent, performing coordination through mutual adjustment. As technological change increases, environments become more dynamic so organizations must learn to be more flexible and adaptive. One type of organization designed especially for this has been labeled task force or project management, which is very similar to the synthetic organization.

The Assessment of Organizations

Thompson suggests that there exists disagreement whether organizations should be evaluated in terms or their "maximum attainment of purposes (*maximize*) or their acceptable attainment of desired states (*satisfies*)". This is because some people focus on "the *results* they believe the organization should actually accomplish while others focus on *motivation*, what they believe the organization should try to accomplish".

Variables of Assessment

Assessment always involves creating or choosing a standard of desirability against which actual effects of actions can be evaluated. Standards of desirability originate in cultural values of a particular society. The tradition in Western culture, which utilizes an economic model of rationality rooted in capitalism, supports the belief that "utility is profit. The cultural assumption is, therefore, that profit should be maximized". Thompson believes that people in Western societies are constantly asked to "choose between health and wealth because they are expected to compare all possible effects of their actions in terms of one common denominator: *money*". The individual involved in assessment may believe their understanding of cause/effect is either complete or incomplete.

"Where cause/effect understanding is believed complete and a standard of desirability is clearly established, as is the case in the Western secular and scientific traditional, the *maximizing* approach to assessment uses the efficiency test to measure the degree to which a given amount of resources was used in a way to achieve the greatest result. Where a standard of desirability is clearly established but the assessor believes his or her knowledge of cause/effect may be incomplete, as is common in non-Western societies believe in a spiritual realm, the appropriate test is the *instrumental* one, which measures to what degree a desired state of affairs has been achieved. When standards of desirability are ambiguous and when cause/effect knowledge is believed incomplete, as is the case for many peoples around the earth today, as technology intermeshes diverse cultures, organizations turn to social reference groups. That is why each organization today must create a specific organizational culture to clearly establish standards of desirability with which to assess itself. Without leaders who know how to create and maintain effective organizational cultures, organizations can be paralyzed by differences of opinion. According to Thompson, "The most important question an organization can ask itself is not what it has accomplished in the **past** but whether it is fit for FUTURE action". Since even the near future is unpredictable in a time of massive global change, organizations can best prepare themselves by creating responsive organizational cultures, which take the place of traditional structures based on rigid standardization, and by building flexible networks of cooperation interconnecting them.

The Variable Human

Thompson believes that "organizations abhor uncertainty so if their members behave in unpredictable ways, organizations are in difficulty". Unpredictability has a negative connotation for many people but in some situations, unpredictability enables the accomplishment of innovation. Unpredictability expands alternatives for action for those who learn to embrace and appreciate it. For complex organizations, "the requirements of complicated technologies in complicated task environments cannot be met if the full range of human variations comes into play in the organization". Thus, each organization must select which learned behavior patterns it will support and enhance, in other words, which human variations further the organization's goals. This selection is the basis of the organization's culture. Human action emerges from a view of opportunities and constraints inherent in a situation based on a perspective created by culturally learned aspirations, norms and beliefs. "An individual's decision to participate in an organization and the organization's decision to include him or her rest on a bargained contract which sets expectations and limits regarding the behavior the individual exhibits in the organizational context. The organization defines appropriate member behavior and modifies that definition to meet the changing demands of technology and task environment. Despite initial individual differences, it makes members pliable in the direction of the organization's needs. It defines what is expected of members in terms of their jobs and defines the rewards it pledges for the proper performance of those jobs.

By permitting members to exercise discretion, jobs at contingent boundaries enable them to reduce uncertainty for the organization. To the extent that a member contains contingencies, which are important to the organization, that individual is powerful.

The Exercise of Discretion

Some individuals are more tolerant of risk and ambiguity than others. Thompson claims, "Individuals exercise discretion whenever it is to their advantage and seek to evade discretion on all other occasions". It is possible that this is a learned cultural trait and may not be the case in non-Western societies. Thompson argues that "When uncertainty looms large in comparison with predictive ability, judgment is suspended and other techniques resorted to. Increasing complexity of technology and task environment may call for more flexibility and discretion than the organizational structure established during an earlier period can provide". Nevertheless, in many societies, "the pressures for achievement are strong and achievement is measured by the exercise of discretion. For this reason, individuals are tempted to exercise discretion although the organizational definition of the job permits no discretion. This may be especially true in a bureaucracy where job performance is standardized. The pressure to achieve tempts people in bureaucracies to misappropriate organizational resources, accept bribes and foster favoritism. An individual who has been able to reach a high levels of discretion in the organization often find it hard to resist pushing for a re-arrangement of organizational structures, the installment of new assessment criteria and a revision of resource-allocation procedures, which enable them to enlarge their sphere of action, thus, reducing the autonomy of other members needed to maintain the flexibility of the organization.

The Control of Complex Organizations

Therefore, "we can consider *organizational goals* as the future domains intended by those in the dominant coalition. Interdependent individuals who collectively have sufficient control of organizational resources establish organizational goals. For this reason, individuals in highly discretionary jobs have a strong motivation to avoid decisions, which would end their spheres of action. This motivation contributes to the inflexibility that hinders many organizations. Unfortunately, an expectation of "the emergence of the omnipotent individual is consistent with the Western rational model of organizations, nevertheless, conditions which are compatible with the natural system model may now be occurring as the complexity of technologies exceed the comprehension of any one individual and the organization faces more contingencies than one individual is able to keep under surveillance ".

The basic variables of decision are beliefs about cause/effect and preferences regarding outcomes, determined by societal or organizational culture. "Where there is certainty regarding causation and outcome preferences, as in traditional Western bureaucratic systems, a *computational* strategy is used for decision-making, in other words, decisions are 'programmed' according to a pre-established scientific formula. Where outcome preferences are clear but cause/effect relationships are uncertain, a *judgmental* strategy is used which is most often described as traditionally non-scientific decision-making. When there is certainty regarding cause/effect but uncertainty regarding preferred outcomes because cultural values are in question, as is the case in many modern societies, a *compromise* strategy is used for decision-making. When there is uncertainty in both dimensions because societies are moving toward social chaos, people rely on *inspirational* strategies for decision-making by creating new religions or by returning to old ones.

Organizational change is accomplished by a small committee which meets informally and individually with each member of the organization until the necessary series of compromises appear to mesh. When this has happens, consensus has been achieved. At this point, a vote is not a decision but rather, a formal acknowledgement or ratification of the consensus. In a highly complex organization, a powerful individual can, by the exercise significant leadership, come to symbolize the organization. He or she can only do so with the consent and approval of the dominant coalition. Therefore, leadership rests on consensus, which rests on values inherent in organizational culture.

For the rapid, abrupt adaptation of an organization to a new set of circumstances, a chief executive must first challenge shared assumptions and then substitute one decision premise for another by re-arranging the priority of preferred outcomes. With the modification of organizational culture by the use of cultural forms, he or she is able to indoctrinate and enforce a new organizational paradigm, which will inform discretion and thus, behavior. Thompson views this as being a "superb politician".

Co-Alignment: The Basic Administrative Function

In a living organization such as organism, which is simply a natural system, spontaneous processes such as natural selection handle change. In an artificial organization such as a computer, or any other machine, after it is designed and manufactured, it automatically adjusts to change, given the limitations of its design. In contrast, Thompson claims, "Subtle complications which face complex social organizations call for something more than closed-logic solutions. Organizational survival depends on the co-alignment of technology and task environment with a viable domain, and of organizational design and structure appropriate to that domain. Timing is a crucial administrative matter because as environments change, the administration must deal with not just domain but also, how and how fast to redesign the structure and technology of the organization, in other words, negotiate a revised set of operational rules. Thompson claims, "The configuration necessary for survival does not come from yielding to environmental pressures but rather, from finding the strategic variables, such as organizational culture, available to be manipulated in such a way that interaction with elements in the environment will result in a viable co-alignment."

"The central task of the administrative process is the search for flexibility". To achieve flexibility, the administrative process is not something done at one level in the organization, but spans and links all levels. The administrative process does not simply flows down from one level to the next, but informs the interaction of all levels and units of the organization. Complex organizations must utilize organizational culture principles to accomplish this. Organizational culture is appropriate for this task because "outcome preferences are specified by the "institutional level" of the organization, while specification of cause/effect relationships is provided by the managerial level which controls the kinds of resources inputs obtained and the kinds of interdependence reflected in organizational structure. Organizational culture can provide the managerial level with what it needs to obtain commitments from the institutional level which permit technical achievement while at the same time, obtain commitments from the technical core which provide sufficient capacity and slack to permit administrative discretion and recommitment of resources when organizational change is demanded by the environment.

When administrative processes attempt to solve organizational problems, more often then not they use simple concepts of causality which direct them to 1) search for solutions to symptoms, 2) search for solutions based on currently available alternatives, and 3) search for solutions in organizationally vulnerable areas (finger pointing). Thompson concedes that his propositions regarding organizations in action describe but one of at least two styles of organizational action. He concludes, "It is possible to conceive of monitoring behavior which scans the environment for opportunities - which does not wait to be activated by a problem and which does not therefore stop when a problem solution has been found". Thompson expects "opportunistic surveillance to be found at the institutional level of the organization". Yet, "What accounts for the relative scarcity of opportunistic surveillance?" he puzzles. He believes the answer to this question can be found in the personal attributes of administrators and in the organizational structures they operate. Perhaps, this behavior is not commonly found because it requires the existence of a new type of organizational culture, calling for a different type of leadership and new forms of organizational design.

Thompson blames the "widespread bias toward certainty which shows up as a preference for short-term rather than long-term considerations, quantitative rather than qualitative data, and precedent rather than innovation". Thompson believes that "intolerance for ambiguity causes an administrative bias toward certainty". He notes, "If the powerful inner circle is composed solely of individuals with responsibilities in the managerial level, we would expect problematic search, not opportunistic surveillance to prevail. The conversion of administrators from managerial to institutional responsibilities entails a shift in attention". "Unfortunately", Thompson complains, "the conversion of private insight into sharable, teachable and learnable understanding is not an automatic process".

DISCUSSION QUESTIONS

1. What is a synthetic organization?

2. Why does organizations have to engage in a continuous negotiation process?

3. Compare and contrast open-system strategy and closed-system strategy?

CHAPTER 10
The Role Of Teambuildin In The Creation Of High Performance Organizations

The Social Evolution of Teams

Darwin's theory of evolution has shown that the tendency toward social grouping which is exhibited by many types of living things is beneficial to the survival of those living things. Nevertheless, an instinctual need for a minimum of territorial space limits the density of most living things, including man, according to the size of the area in which a group inhabits and its ability to support the group. An animal does things in the company of its peers that it would not do alone. A society is good if it helps its individual members to survive and they, in response will preserve and promote their society. In this way, human social development is a real evolutionary process.

Rousseau's notion of the General Will was not the will of a ruler, or a group of rulers, or even the will of all the citizens as men. It was a special kind of will, present to some extent in every citizen. It was that part of the will, in an individual or in an assembly of individuals that was directed to the furtherance not of individual private interests, but of the general advantage of the entire group concerned. This is not to say that the citizens cease to think of their own individual advantage - only that there is, in their associative actions, an element, which may be stronger or weaker, of seeking the advantage of the whole association, or of all its members, as distinct from the element which seeks only personal advantage. This element is the individual's contribution, in his associative behavior, to what Rousseau calls the "Moi commun" (group spirit) of the association. Rousseau proposes a society both small and compact enough for the individual citizens to take a direct part in its control in an atmosphere which had an absence of extremes of privilege or inequality that might prevent the citizens from acting sufficiently in a dis-interested (as opposed to self-interested) spirit. Rousseau believed that the "natural man", an ordinary, everyday person, is motivated by a feeling of self-respect which recognizes the equal value of other people, whereas, exclusive self-love is a trait which grows wherever unequal social institutions of privilege exist.

To Weber, the institutional system of the modern Western World is not a 'natural order' which has come about merely by the removal of obstacles to it or by a process of 'natural' social evolution. He believed that it represents only one of several possible lines of social development and that radically different social systems found in Non-Western societies around the world are not simply 'arrested' in stages of development leading in the same direction. In Weber's view, Western civilization is dependent on a 'rationalized' economy in which decisions are made according to a weighing of usefulness and cost. This has given rise, in Weber's opinion, to the modern rational-legal State regulated by a impartial legal system. Weber focuses on the weakness, in the modern Western world, of any social ties which would seriously interfere with the mobility of human resources required by our Capitalistic economy. He compares this to the extended kinship ties and solidarity of local communities, as well as, various kinds of social status groups found in many Non-Western societies.

The role that money plays in our economy is of the greatest importance to Weber. Weber believes money encourages an 'acquisitive orientation' which encourages the measurement of the success of a person based upon their wealth. What money can purchase becomes a new symbol of status and prestige. Weber denies that the modern business man has more 'self-interest' than traditional man. People in Non-Capitalistic social structures are as inherently 'acquisitive' as any Western business person. Prices of goods and services are merely estimates of the chances of success one competitor judges he has over other competitors. This depends entirely on the extent of 'market freedom' which exists, in other words, the degree to which monopolies are discouraged.

Nevertheless, the processes of a competitive market economy themselves influence the distribution of income in ways which fosters the cumulative tendency toward increasing inequality. In our modern society, production is carried out within complex organizations and not by isolated individuals. If an individual has stable unproblematic marketing channels for his or her products, he or she can work largely independently, but the need for a wide market and large-scale organization subject him or her to authority in the organization of production and to dependence on those who control access to the market. Weber sees the only escape from this in the maintenance of a favorable balance of power on the worker's side but dependence on a large-scale worker's organization is merely exchanging one dependence for another.

Marx believed that focusing on the concept of consensus as the basis of a society obscures the fact that conflict and competition, not consensus, is the true basis of all modern societies. Marx argued that there is no General Will but rather, only the imposition of the will of the powerful upon the weak; consensus being a tool used by the powerful to ease their domination. While it is true that conflict is a fact of social life and often consensus reflects the will of some members of a society more than others, most societies evolve a shared vision and, under certain conditions a shared will. Some sociologists subscribe to the popular model of modern society as a mass society in which leaders rely on mass media which they control. This assumes "direct" interaction, actually passive interaction via television, between these leaders and individuals who make up the masses and thus, assumes that previously active intermediary social structures are gone.

Groups in Modern Mass Society

In modern democratic societies, the elites grant legitimacy to certain policies and goals, that serve their interests, and the collectives, in turn, provide political support in the form of votes. In modern Western mass society, the family has lost one of its traditional functions as an organizational unit of production to the corporation. The higher divorce rate of modern families is paralleled by the high turnover in membership of religious groups; a smaller stress on ascription being an accommodation to the vertical and horizontal mobility which modernization requires. Members of modern societies lead lives that are fragmented among several, perhaps incompatible, affiliations. This maintains their individual autonomy.

Etzioni contends that dissensus is the natural state of human society. Consensus is not inherent so must be produced by human efforts and institutions. Normal, ongoing socialization processes prepare the foundation for societal consensus but societal guidance is required to produce it. Once consensus has been established in a society, if efforts to sustain it decrease, that society will move again into the entropic state of dissensus. Consensus will be authentic if it is based upon education rather than persuasion. In his book, Etzioni quotes Simmel who stated that freedom is not the absence of societal guidance but rather guidance that allowed people to be free. He also notes that Mannheim stressed that human freedom should be planned. Etzioni emphasizes that it is not more control that is needed to authentically guide human societies, but rather, what is needed is a qualitative change of control toward an encompassing consensus-building, but not prescriptive, coercive or alienating control. Etzioni warns that this is not important merely in the economic sectors. Democracies, such as the United States, are under planned and under controlled in order to afford narrow freedoms for a few while imposing rigid constraints on the freedom of many citizens. The freedom of American manufacturers to advertise unsafe and unneeded products, such as guns and cigarettes, in ways that glorify the most physical and individualistic impulses of Americans is much more effectively protected than is the health and security of American citizens.

Etzioni does not believe that "natural" democratic processes will be able to correct this. New power relations - those which could exist only under conditions of increased equality - are required to permit societal planning for freedom which would in turn encourage the flourishing of the kind of societal activeness needed to establish and maintain greater freedom from exploitation for individual Americans. In capitalistic democracies, there is a tendency to build up consensus first and then implement a policy. Policies that are not in the self-interests of the more powerful members of these societies often are not implemented until a domestic or environmental crisis demonstrates the overdue need for them. For an example, Keynesian controls of the American economy required the crisis of the Great Depression to be approved and progress on desegregating America only began after African-Americans had been mobilized by serving in the Armed Forces in W.W. II. Because there is a tendency in democracies to delay action that may change the status quo, the pace of social changes usually lags behinds social needs.

Etzioni claims that the important question to ask is not how to maintain a social movement organization permanently, which he characterizes as an utopian effort, but rather, how to maintain a high level of commitment and participation. All societies tend to bureaucratize, decline in responsiveness and give rise to privileged elites. Active societies seek to sustain, strengthen and mobilize the plurality of micro-units which make up the body of human society. The activation of such societies is based on increasing the mobilization of these social units by education and consensus-formation. The transformation to an active society requires much more than the expansion of civil liberties and human rights.

The Role of Small Groups in "The Good Society"

Friedmann advocates a form of human interaction which can only occur within a setting of small groups and operates on the basis of face-to-face relations. As much as possible, these groups (or teams) are self-reliant, independent, and autonomous; creating a free community of individuals. Dialog within the group becomes the medium of transforming action and is the source of its moral power. This kind of radical social practice is always goes beyond the immediate interests of the group itself and is concerned with accomplishing needed tasks in the environment in which it finds its self. For its continued existence, Friedmann's "Good Society" relies on the willing service of individual members to what is held in common trust within the group. The groups in Freidmann's "Good Society" constantly search for effective linkages with other groups who also engage in radical social practice and in this way, mutual support is built. It is important to emphasize here that Freidmann reminds us that these linkages must remain informal because the basic acting unit of such a society should always be the small group.

Friedman disagrees with the idea that the solution to the estrangement of modern life is to abolish private property, the division of labor, social classes, the exchange economy - to dismantle capitalism and substitute for it a social order of perfect communism. Rather, he advocates for radical social practice, in other words, the establishment of small groups who will work for: the equality of women, the humanization of work, the reform of educational systems and the re-structuring of government. Work on each of these takes place at a different level of the hierarchy of our modern society: between men and women at home and at work, among managers, technicians and laborers, among administrators, teachers, parents and students and between politicians and their constituents. The goal of Freidmann's radical social practice is to return to people: control over their minds and bodies, control over the product of their labor, control over their education and, to return to them control over the major instruments of their own governance.

The Individual in a Global Society

Woodiwiss views the emergence of social postmodernity in America in the 1960s as a symptom of a world economy which has become highly competitive; when foreign-made goods began to be dominant in some highly visible domestic markets. During the mid-1980s, an upward trend in the rate of corporate profitability was caused by a substantial restructuring of the American workplace in response to this changed environment. The effect of all these social and economic factors operating since the 1960s, in the U.S., was to intensify the pressures toward 'flexible specialization' and 'post-Fordism'. This has led traditional features of secondary labor markets, such as low wages and reduced levels of social protection, to characterize the primary labor markets; as companies reduce the size of their privileged core labor force and increase the size of their 'contingent' labor force of part-time and temporary employees.

In his book, The Sociology of Social Change, Piotr Sztompka reminds us that what most people term 'modernity' refers to modes of social organization which emerged in the countries of northwestern Europe in the 17th century. The British industrial revolution provided the economic foundation for the rise of modernity: industrial production by a free labor force in urban settings and capitalism as a new form of appropriation and distribution of wealth. Comte lists these traits of the new social order: the concentration of labor in cities, work organized according to efficiency and profit, the application of science and technology to production, the birth of the antagonism between labor and management and an economic system based on free enterprise and market competition. Weber compares the older form of traditional society with the modern capitalist society in six ways: form of ownership, dominant technology, character of labor force, means of distribution, nature of law, and pervasive motivations.

The first principle of modernity is individualism and the triumph of the individual over the community. The individual is emancipated from social bonds and responsible for his/her own actions. This leads to the domination of all social life by economic activities and economic criteria for measuring human achievement. Modern society is primarily concerned with the production, distribution and consumption of material goods; and with money as the common means of exchange. This requires an ever expanding reach into new frontiers, eventually spanning the globe. Modernity is more pervasive than any previous kind of change because it reaches into the most intimate spheres of human life such as religious beliefs, sexual conduct, consumption tastes and patterns of leisure, transforming them into public marketplaces. Changes in the economic system modernity brings create a property-less labor class who must sell their labor like a commodity but do not benefit from the profit such labor provides. Social inequality increases as capitalists reap profits and reinvest them to gain more wealth and power.

The workplace comes to dominate the life of the individual and with it comes an alienation from family life. Families experience isolation from each other and the sense of the community withers and dies as all become possessed with acquiring and consuming material goods as if under a spell. Tonnies noted that modernity severs interpersonal bonds of common locality, ethnicity and religion, resulting in a deterioration of the quality of life for the individual and making them vulnerable to mass movements and totalitarian leaders who promise to provide them with a sense of community. Other negative consequences of modernity listed by Sztompka include: the depletion of natural resources of the earth and the destruction of its natural environment. Lenin predicted that the capitalist system, in its hunger for profits enabled by cheap labor, raw materials and an expanding market, would inevitably become involved in the colonial or neo-colonial exploitation of undeveloped countries, dividing the globe into a minority of haves and a majority of have-nots. In the twentieth century, we have reaped the fruits of capitalist technology, modern weapons, in destructive and viciously inhuman wars; wars caused by the appropriation required to create profit and by a rational, purely instrumental focus which suspends moral considerations, changing living people into dispensable objects - numbers in a book or blips on an electronic screen. Modernity makes holocaust possible and thus, thinkable.

Sztompka focuses on the globalization of modern society when he discusses Immanuel Wallerstein's world-system theory. Small, economically self-sufficient units with complete internal division of labor and a single cultural framework dominated the epoch of hunting and gathering and continued into the epoch of agricultural societies. Then came empires, incorporating many units, based on an agricultural economy and ruled by a ruthless elite which imposed taxation and conscription to fuel their constant imperial conquests. The American and French revolution signaled the end of the epoch of empires but the actual unification and homogenization of global culture did not occur until the 'media imperialism' of tourism and its proxy, television, penetrated the most isolated villages. Ulf Hannerz has researched this evolving global 'ecumene'. Traditional cultures are created by bounded communities and reproduced face-to-face in real-time. By contrast, modern cultures crisscross space and time via the technologies of modern communication and transportation.

Electronic technology has extended the horizon of every human living today. It enables one to compare one's own life with those in other countries. A perception of unjustified disadvantage and relative deprivation leads to a psychological mindframe receptive to social movements. In order to introduce structural innovations, movements must break down or weaken existing social structures first, unfortunately, some movements stop there. A common vision can unite people but not organize them. What is required next is an organizational framework of action. Sztompka agrees with Oberschall that social movement's link micro and macro levels of modern society enabling individuals to exert pressure on social structures, actively choosing the course of human social evolution.

Designing the Workplace of the Future

Recently developed mini-processor-based information technology offers the modern American business executive the advantage of direct access, face to face, to associates, partners, and customers in faraway places and eliminates the need for tiring and expensive air travel. People can now share a common experience, no matter how far away from each other they are; they can 'meet in the same room' in cyberspace, see each other eye to eye and exchange reports and graphs via fax or E-mail. Satellites orbiting the earth forward pictures, voices and graphics to satellite dishes linked to subscribers via telecommunication cables and can simulate the four dimensional space/time of an actual conference room in a business office.

Currently, American executives are asking: "Can we learn valuable management techniques from other countries?" Foreign managers demand more responsibility from their employees, all the way down to the least skilled worker, than do U.S. managers.

Japanese companies are known for their 'quality circles' and 'continuous learning'; employees meet once a week to consider how they can improve on what they are doing.
In German firms, the Meister is more of a teacher than a supervisor. Foreign management structures benefits to fit the individual employee. Companies overseas think in terms of market structure, try to define specific market niches

for their products and design their businesses with a marketing strategy in mind. Instead of saying: "How can I earn a proper profit on what the market wants to buy?", American management still asks: "Which of our products has the highest profit margin - how can we sell it?" When the foreign manager says "market" he is referring to the world economy. Foreign management bases their marketing and innovation strategies on a systematic abandonment of the obsolete and thus, resources are available for innovation - the creation of new products and services. Also, by separating short-term operating budgets from longer-term investment budgets, foreign companies plan for the long haul and control expenditures over the long term.

Managers of large Japanese, German and French corporations see themselves as national leaders who are responsible for the development of positive social policy. One Japanese business leader told Peter Drucker, the author of "The Changing World of the Executive", that the agenda of high level management in Japan is "to postpone discussing economics until we know what the right social policies are; what is right for the individual and for the country as a whole. Who else besides the heads of Japan's largest companies can get a good look at problems from all aspects? Whom else can the country trust for guidance and leadership during times of great change?" Foreign management is merely applying what they learned from American management a half a century ago. Japanese 'quality circles' (teams) were brought to Japan by Edwards Deming and Joseph Juran from N.Y.U. and A.V. Feigenbaum of General Electric in the 1950s and 60s. IBM, first in this country, and then in its European subsidiaries, restructured the role of the first-line supervisor, converting him/her from a foreman to a teacher, the Meister. The distinction between short-term and long-term budget goes back to DuPont and General Motors in the twenties.

Because there is usually two years between the identification of redundancy and the actual closing of a plant or change in processing technology, U.S. management must take responsibility for finding new employment opportunities for redundant employees and then retrain and place them. This has been done by foreign business - not government. After the Russo-Japanese war, Japan needed to make massive changes in its industrial structure. Mitsui, the largest private employer, committed itself to place redundant employees in jobs with other companies and growing Mitsui divisions. Between 1950 and 1970, Sweden needed to change from a preindustrial, raw-material-producing economy to a modern technological economy. Trade union economist, Gosta Rehn, lead groups consisting of labor, management and government, in each region to facilitate the retraining and placement of redundant workers. In this way, Sweden moved almost half its labor force into new jobs, within twenty years, at a fraction of the cost of paying unemployment compensation.

Until W.W.II, for the majority of people who lived in technologically developed countries, land was the true 'means of production' because it provided access to economic effectiveness, social standing and political power. In contrast, in the modern societies of today, the majority of the population are employees - 93% in the U.S. - and therefore, the
'means of production' is a now job. A job is not 'wealth'; it is not 'personal property' but it is a 'right' in the means of production. It is a person's means of access to social status, personal opportunity, achievement, power and most importantly: personal property. In Drucker's opinion, the evolution of the job as a species of property is the only solution to what Marx saw as modern humanity's problem of alienation which results from the worker no longer being able to participate in the ownership and control of the means of production. Drucker sees finding the answer to the question of how American management can cope with the emergence of job property rights and still maintain the flexibility to adapt quickly to changes in the market, as its greatest challenge today.

In 1977, the Bullock Report recommended that the boards of British companies that employ two thousand or more people, including British units of multi-national companies based outside the United Kingdom, provide employees with the same number of representative positions on the board as were held by stockholders.

The "Mental Judo" Style of Management

Traditionally, third world countries exported cheap raw materials to the U.S. who would transform them into finished goods and sell them back, thus ensuring a balance of payments in favor of the U.S. But, by the end of the 1960s, Japan and Korea began to use their cheap labor to do high-quality, technical work. They also created financial and market institutions to favor their goods on the world markets. This change can be attributed to the willingness, on the part of management in those countries, to practice what Mitroff calls: "mental judo". These are the six principles of mental judo which Mitroff has identified: 1) challenge the obvious, 2) question all constraints, 3) challenge assumptions, 4) question the definition of problems, 5) determine whether a problem should be "solved", "resolved" or "dissolved", 6) challenge logic.

The change from reactive to preventative management requires changing the whole reward structure of an organization to enable and motivate people to produce quality products. It also requires giving up the hierarchical principle of task specialization and, in this regard, is a return to the past. All employees must see how their jobs fit together in the final production of quality products. This extends beyond corporate boundaries when management realizes it is important to assist their suppliers to produce quality materials, as well. Corporate goals must become team goals: problems must be solved collectively and individuals rewarded on how well teams meet their goals. Companies are realizing that collaborative relationships can be beneficial. A new organization form is beginning to emerge consisting of small organizations that rely on a network of external suppliers for manufacturing, distribution, marketing and billing. This allows them to reduce costs and obtain the flexibility needed to compete today. The departments of the traditional corporation have been spun off to create "solar system" style companies which are decentralized and lateral. These organizations are fluid and temporary in nature. They forge alliances based on changing needs and strategies. Their boundaries are permeable. Within them, teamwork and communication provide a sense of connectedness. To accomplish the change to the organizational structure of the future, Western societies, such as the United States, must relinquish the myth of the individual who exists independently. For management, this means that both workers and manager must be involved in every phase of design, manufacture and marketing. As Abernathy has stated, labor must be viewed as something to be nurtured, not as something which can be bought or sold.

America is at a disadvantage when competing with countries, such as Japan and Germany, who have an Industrial Policy. Nevertheless, the individual freedom that so many Americans hold dear involves the right to be "left alone", free from the influence and control of anyone and anything which might restrict their choice of thought or action.

In modern America, social institutions which are responsible for promoting links among people, such as the family, are threatened by extreme individualism. In his mid-19th century book: "Habits of The Heart", Alexis de Tocqueville predicted that America's extreme preoccupation with individualism would undermine its democratic freedoms. If each person continues to pursue and guard their individual freedom, who will look out for the common good? Organizations which accomplished social goals in the 19th century: the town meeting, the community church and the family have lost their effectiveness.

Sociologist Robert Bellah warns that when individuals retreat from collective responsibility, a vacuum is created that is filled by those who are NOT motivated by the common social good but by the desire for their own personal gain. The violence which permeates American society today is the expression of this state of affairs.

Television is the strongest force shaping America today. It glorifies individualism. In the past, literature and debate dominated the arenas of politics, religion, business, education and law. Neil Postman has found that in courtrooms, classrooms, operating rooms, board rooms, churches and even airplanes, Americans no longer talk with each other, exchanging and challenging ideas. They passively receive images. In 1946, Albert Einstein warned us: "The unleashed power of the atom has changed everything save our modes of thinking and thus we drift toward unparalleled catastrophe." Robert Reich calls for a new public policy which embraces the reality of the interdependence of economics, foreign affairs and social policy. In his opinion, domestic social policy in education, child nutrition and care, job training and health care services, should be seen as an extension of American economic policies designed for adjustment to global competition.

In the past, it was assumed that the primary purpose of management was to serve the stockholders. Productivity was considered to be whatever positively affected the economic welfare of stockholders and was measured in terms of the ratio of the output, in goods and services, generated, to the input, in capital or energy, invested. The world is now a highly complex system of interconnected elements. In addition to stockholders, STAKEHOLDERS are all those individuals and institutions which affect or are affected by and organization's policies and behavior. Mitroff believes that the world has become an organism in which the heart and eye neither exist nor function separately from the brain or the rest of the body.

The Democratic Workplace

American society prizes its work ethic. In such a society, would it not seem natural that as a corollary of an individual's responsibility to perform useful work, that society would, in turn, guarantee suitable employment at adequate wages to each person who seeks it? Is there not enough work to be done? Isn't there currently a shortage of affordable housing for young couples, the elderly and those previously institutionalized? Is it true that in America, the world's richest nation, health care is not available to all? Despite the facts that over 50 percent of all married mothers return to work within one year of giving birth, there is a tremendous shortage of decent, affordable child care facilities. The infrastructure of the U.S. is crumbling with age, desperately in need of renewal. There is a great need for relevant and affordable education, especially job training. There is a great need for human service workers.

Systems of work may be designed which harmoniously integrate humans into the natural world or, may involve the waste and destruction of natural resources and a disregard for the laws of the earth's ecology. Usually, it is found that an exploitive orientation toward our natural environment brings with it a similar exploitive mode of organizing work and exchange among people. It is important to design work activities which meet the biological, social and emotional needs of all humans while preserving the natural environment of the earth as a resource base for all present and future life on this planet. The organizers of the Conference at The Center for Social Change Practice and Theory, held at Brandeis University in 1985, such as David Gil, believe that the development, preservation and allocation of all productive resources should be controlled democratically by users, consumers, communities and workers via decentralized, horizontally organized institutions. Re-design of work should involve transforming people from "factors" into "masters" of production, enabling them to discover and actualize, during work, their unique innate potential and creativity. There should be an emphasis on high quality and extended durability of goods, shifting from use of non-renewable to renewable natural resources as raw materials. The re-organization of work should transfer actual control of production facilities and processes to the workers involved, to the end users (customers and clients) and to the communities which are impacted by these industries or businesses. Decentralization must occur, allowing industrial settings to be integrated into the countryside and the population to be dispersed from megapoli.

Traditionally, labor, itself, is considered oppressive, only when the worker has lost control of the work process. Proudhon advocates for workers' control to be sought after, not through the state, but at the point of production. Pope John Paul II stated, in his letter, "On Human Work", that the rights of ownership of the means of production are inherent in the act of being a worker. The worth of a person rests not on the work a person does but in the fact that he or she is a worker. The ultimate value of that person resides in the fact that they are a creation of God not a mere factor in the production of a lucrative product. Everyone is needed to work to develop themselves, to create and sustain community, to invent and sustain culture, to build nations and restore human values. In 1982, Catholic Bishops explored several paradoxes in their "Pastoral on the Economy". If the technical solutions for societal problems are available, yet those problems remain unsolved, one can assume that causes of these problems reside within social, political and economic institutions of this society. Liberation Theology sees wealth and power as resources that should be shared in community. Pope John Paul II has stated that, in his opinion, something is wrong with the current organization of work when high global unemployment and extreme hunger co-exist side by side with vast unused natural resources. American Catholic Bishops encourage a new international economic order which ensures that the benefits of global economic growth are shared equitably among all nations of the earth. The Bishops have sent their message to heads of state and transnational corporations as well as to people at the grass roots level, recommending food cooperatives, profit-sharing, worker participation in management and worker-owned industries.

In his book, "Labor and Monopoly Capital", Harry Braverman warns about the dependence of all American social life upon the market place. "No longer is there a reliance on social organization in the form of family, friends, neighbors and community. Not only the material and service needs of Americans, but also, even the emotional patterns of life channeled through the market." Thomas Rice defines Workplace Democracy as an organizational structure which is identified by worker ownership and the democratic control of operations. Fundamental to this arrangement is the expectation that each participant is empowered to have an effective voice in decisions affecting his/her working life. Inherent in this definition is the assumption that the distinction between democratic and hierarchical organizational forms is contained in their structural elements of ownership, authority and compensation, as well as, processes of decision-making and communication. The traditional bias of management ideologies assumes that the only reality is the individual. Recent books about "Corporate Culture" still ignore roles and group-level phenomena. This has led to a futile focus on individual workers and managers with no attention to the contexts of their performance. Bernstein has produced a comprehensive model which contains all of the components necessary for a democratic work-place. These six principles are required: 1) participation in decision-making, 2) economic return to all employees, 3) sharing of management-level information and expertise, 4) guaranteed individual rights, 5) an independent board of appeals, and 6) a heightened democratic consciousness which involves an awareness of rights and responsibilities.

In a democratic workplace culture, shared democratic values are communicated as part of an organizational identity. Norms, such as fairness, responsibility, honesty and consensus, are negotiated and established which create a workplace conducive to democratic relations. Implementation strategies are negotiable and communicated openly. Common dining, social areas, meeting tables, decor, organizational symbols and rituals should reflect a heightened democratic consciousness. A democratically structured organization abides by a legal charter which contains a formal articulation of guaranteed individual rights and responsibilities including the right to an equitable share of any surpluses, the democratic control of investment decisions and a requirement that all contracts contain no privileges or prerogatives not equally available to all employees. It maintains an organizational structure that is decentralized and non-hierarchical, incorporating both autonomy and interdependence.

Leadership of democratically structured organization is based upon knowledge and expertise with the emphasis on self-governance. Responsibility for planning and implementation, as well as, for performing all mental and manual work is equally held by all employees. Educational, training and technical assistance programs are established in order to ensure effective participation, skill transmission, and the democratic distribution of expertise among all employees, regardless of level and role. Conflict-resolution skills are developed in all employees in order that mediation is administered by democratically elected peers with the recognition that conflict is normal and should be managed for the benefit of all, not ignored. Most importantly, self-evaluation is carried on continuously by all work groups within the organization to promote meaningful and ecologically viable growth and development. In addition, systematic impartial external evaluation feedback includes recommendations for follow-up.

We must redefine work so that it no longer exploits the many for the benefit of the few. We must redefine it to mean all which is done to enhance and maintain a positive quality of human life, as well as, all life on this planet. We must see that high technology is not merely nuclear weapons but what can beat swords into plowshares. We can no longer afford to allow the marketplace to be a capitalist tool for the gain of a few individuals. It must become an opportunity for all peoples to bring their material, social and spiritual goods to be shared for the gain of all. Instead of objectifying human power, industrialization could become, through the organization of our creativity, a resource which can sustain all of us on the earth. 10

How Teams Can Create High Performance Organizations

The demands of the new information technology require democratic participation. As telecommunications and other breakthroughs in information technology occur, a more flexible, responsive type of organizational structure is evolving which permits a new form of decentralized control. Large companies have become "confederations of entrepreneurs" launching countless small, quasi-independent ventures that bring the dynamic creativity of a free marketplace *inside* the large organization *itself.* Inside these organizational networks, participative leadership is on the rise. New labor-management relations involve contracts for performance, profit-sharing, collaborative decision-making, the improvement of working conditions and safeguarding employee rights.

Profit-seeking only works when large numbers of small companies compete against one another. The paradox is: this struggle for economic survival tends to concentrate corporate power, which ends the very conditions a truly free market depends upon. In America today, the largest 200 corporations own two-thirds of all industrial assets with a rising, unending wave of mergers increasing this concentration of power even more. In spite of foreign competition, the global economy will soon be dominated by massive multi-national corporations. J.P. Morgan has stated that he knows why all businessmen hate competition. It holds down prices, cuts profits, limits the market and carries within it the ever-present threat of financial ruin.

The profit-motive has been proven to be a limited goal that produces poor performance for both society and industry. CEO of Sony, Akio Morita, claims that U.S. companies offer little real competition because they have been corrupted and remain trapped by their voracious appetite for instantaneous profits. As a value to guide human behavior, the profit-motive is corrupt because an individual's slavish adherence to their self-interest harms the interests of everyone - and ultimately, those of the profit-maker. The profit motive persists because of the enormous pressures which the modern marketplace exerts on corporate executives. With the stakes so high, corporate financial analysts are forced to focus only on short-term profit because corporate boards demand it. After all, a drop of earnings, in even one quarter, poses the threat of a takeover and, it is an easily measured criteria of performance (but a superficial one). Perhaps the actual reason for the corporate focus on short-term financial gain lies with the compensation U.S. companies offer their CEOs. It is 70 times the average worker's pay compared to10 to 20 in Europe and Japan.

Economic systems are natural organisms and change through a process of social evolution. Poised on the eve of a knowledge-based society, our world is one where technological progress has superseded biological development as the principal mechanism for evolutionary change. Just as on the eve before the agricultural and industrial revolution, we are in the midst of changes in the type of work people do, the structure of institutions and the central values of our society. The information age of the future, bearing down upon us, will soon transform our reality at least as much as the industrial era transformed the agrarian age. The paradigm of the industrial age is part of our culture and forms the dimensions of our thoughts. To us it is the "truth", but paradigms are not truth, merely islands of rationality; ideological stepping stones leading in an evolutionary path from one era to another.

The industrial age fostered brutal competition and conflict because physical resources are finite. A "zero-sum game" was the norm: "I gain at your expense". However, in the imminent information age, social and information technologies increase in value when they are shared. People involved in "Positive-sum games" appear everywhere, taking an active part in collaborative problem-solving. The new capitalism of the information age does not strive to repudiate the old-style capitalism of the industrial age; it simply absorbs it into a broader synthesis in the same way that Newton's laws have been incorporated into Einstein's theories of physics. The Rand Corporation has claimed that it will soon be as easy to custom-produce a product as it was to mass-produce it, in the past, necessitating a closer involvement with clients than ever before. Management consultant, Irving Canton, has stated that management must now shift from searching for the most effective way to sell a product to trying to develop the best solution for a client's problem.

William Norris, the founder of Control Data, offers a very comprehensive description of the crisis in America today. While business ignores the major problems of society, the government tries unsuccessfully to cope with them alone. What is needed is for business to take the initiative and provide a leadership role in planning, managing and implementing programs, in cooperation with government, labor unions, universities and churches which meet the urgent need for: cheaper energy, urban renewal, environmental protection, lower food costs, inexpensive health care, high quality education, availability of technology and more jobs, especially in rural and inner city settings. What is required is to nurture the adoption of a strategy which views these urgent societal needs as profitable business opportunities. We are entering a future in which only the institutions with the self-control to place clients' needs will foremost survive.

Collaborative corporate-client relations not only serve client needs better; they provide companies the opportunity to develop new products. Studies have shown that almost all successful product innovations originate from individual customers, rather than organizations. Successful modern corporations are bringing customers into their organizations because they know that the interests of the buyer and the seller must be congruent if there is to be a sale. The goal of all modern economies should be to maximize human welfare and the purpose of all growth should be not merely physical expansion but the improvement of human well-being. Information technology is now dissolving old hierarchical organizations into flexible market networks composed of temporarily connected ventures. Institutions will no longer be collections of people working in a single place but instead, communication networks connecting people in economic and social exchanges. The vast majority of people performed labor-intensive work on the land in the agrarian age. In the industrial age, they tended machines. In the information age, they will manipulate and apply knowledge.

Information, itself, is what connects all humans within any human society; that is why information technology will accelerate the pace of social change. Computerized telecommunications networks will enable people to interact faster thus speeding up the rate of technological innovation, amplifying our ability to control events. John Naisbitt and Marilyn Ferguson, the editor of "The Leading Edge Bulletin", predict that corporate structure will be based on networks that permit changing interconnections which provide the kind of control needed by an organic organization existing in an ever transforming environment with the brief event horizon of the future. In our present society, most executives find it exceedingly difficult to allow people the freedom to do things on their own. The "macho" type manager of today feels he must maintain detailed knowledge of everything in his organization in order to feel he has the amount of control necessary to successfully manage.

Often these organizations soon find themselves fighting for survival against a rival headed by a former employee whom they had rejected as too controversial. Peter Drucker condemns American management as entirely consisting of methods which result in making it hard for people to do their work. In contrast to this, Peters and Waterman have described a "new business contract" which combines tight control over performance while maintaining an atmosphere of freedom within operations. Tasks and work assignments are based on contracts which hold business units accountable for agreed-upon goals while allowing them almost complete freedom to achieve results as they see fit; creating, in the words of Dow Corning executive, William Coggin, an organization which is psychologically attuned to achieving its goals, unhindered by bureaucracy. Modern organizations will soon discover that it is this streamlined, flexible single-mindedness which can mean the difference between economic life or death in the marketplace of the future.

Research has shown clearly that humans are actually capable of selecting work assignments appropriate to their skills (or motivated to acquire skills they will need, if given the opportunity), defining their work roles in relation to others within a team with a specified task to accomplish, as well as, hiring, supervising and training their own teammates; thus, creating "bottom-up" self-designed and self-managed organizational structures. This organizational transformation can occur if large organizations are broken up into smaller, self-governing business units conducive to nurturing a spirit of commitment and innovation. Through the use of freedom, a superior form of management evolves in which the clarification of purposes is a prominent feature, according to Professor Peter Vaill, a researcher of high-performance organizations made up of large numbers of self-managed enterprises whose mutual mission is the solution of complex problems.

Ford Personnel manager, W. James Fish, reports CEOs are giving decision-making powers to plant managers, sales people and engineers; creating work environments in which compensation depends on performance and the freedom to find ways to improve performance provides the psychic reward for the worker. Decentralized, units and individuals move freely, taking upon themselves chosen responsibilities and drawing upon the corporation's capital, facilities, personnel and information base in order to accomplish tasks which contribute to its mission. The role of management, in this organizational structure, is to establish a system for accountability and incentives consisting of methods to evaluate performance and reward it.

Management scientist, Jay Forrester, thinks that the company of the future will not assign employees to a supervisor; instead, each individual employee will negotiate a periodically changing set of relationships with other employees. Because it allows workers to choose their assignments and shop around at different divisions for capital for new ideas, 3M appears to be a loose network of laboratories. The sole responsibility of management is to support employees at Arthur D. Little, a company consisting of self-managed teams of professionals. Studies done at Digital Equipment show that employees working on several projects of their own choosing perform better than those on a single assignment because they develop wider knowledge improve inter-depart-mental coordination and are more committed.

"Network" managers focus on designing systems to measure performance, developing new technologies and providing support to operating managers. The organization of the future, consisting of networks of entrepreneurial roles, channels the energy of workers into endless HORIZONTAL outlets instead dissipating it in a climb up a company hierarchy as they struggle to empower their own lives. Author of Theory Z, William Ouchi, imagines that the efficient, perfectly integrated organization of the future will be similar to a basketball team; able to react in a swift manner on short notice, unhindered by an organizational chart. Industrial psychologist, Michael Maccoby's studies show that managers are now moving from the traditional role of boss and decision-maker to a new role as coach and teacher. Future organizational structures will not be imposed upon individuals but rather emerge as a constantly changing PATTERN evolving out of their interactions. CEO of TRW, Rubin Mettler, established a data base that enabled professionals working on many different projects to share knowledge.

As information systems rapidly connect many organizations, their boundaries become insignificant and even obstacles. The study of inter-organizational relations, coalitional structures and trans-organizational systems has grown as the number of international organizations increased from 1,000 in 1950 to 20,000 in 1982. The U.S. government study, "Work in America" found that workers want to become masters of their own environment and to feel that they and their work is important. The easiest way for companies to begin to create this is to initiate a real dialog among employees and managers and permit the company to be guided by the collective judgment of everyone. The study concluded that the human need for autonomy and the economic goal of increased productivity can be achieved by workers sharing the responsibilities of production, as well as, profits earned through such production.

In 1984, when most American steel companies lost money, the Weirton Steel Mill in Pennsylvania, the largest E.S.O.P. (Employee Stock Ownership Plan) in the U.S. increased customers, productivity and quality while LOWERING costs. This has been attributed to a vital sense of commitment generated by employees ACTIVELY involved in running THEIR company. The National Center for Employee Ownership found that companies using employee ownership grew two to four times faster than those who did not. Foremen on

Ford's Edison plant's self-managed Assembly lines serve as coaches. Problem-solving committees consisting of employees and managers working together make it hard to tell who management is and who labor at GM's Packard Electric plant is. At Prudential Insurance, employees are encouraged to redesign jobs to make assignments more interesting and productive. After completing their daily level of production, Harman International employees are free to leave for home. At TRW, skill-based pay rewards workers for learning to operate a wider range of equipment. Work sharing has eliminated layoffs and re-hiring at Motorola; retaining workers who are ready for more work-hours whenever the company needs to expand. During peak times, one can see People Express executives handling baggage and serving travelers at ticket counters. Corporate executives find that, when they give shop-floor workers control over their work, costs go down, fewer supervisors are needed and a problem-solving atmosphere is created in which better quality products are produced and higher quality services are provided.

A sense of community begins to grow which makes the organization greater than the sum of its various parts, which may include incentive systems, joint problem-solving committees, shared control, an emphasis on human values, the operational freedom to select methods to achieve goals and a commitment to excellence. A Marine Corps-like devotion is nurtured in employees by a set of corporate symbols and ceremonies which communicate a well-defined set of values creating a strong culture that makes organizational charts, policy manuals, and detailed procedures and rules obsolete. Peter Vaill reports that in these high-performing organizational systems, employees experience, what Maslow terms, "an aesthetic sense of motivation" or, "peak experiences". Sony CEO, Akio Morita has said, "Profit is generated through the cooperation - (not competition) - of all people. In Japan, we don't pay a bonus to the management; we pay the bonus to employees."

In actuality, as a recent edition of the Wall Street Journal noted, from a financial point of view, "people on the payroll have TEN TIMES as much at stake in their company's affairs as those who receive its stock dividends." Daniel Bell has stated that stockholders are owed nothing but their share in the corporation's earnings because, unlike true owners, they are not psychologically involved in its fate. Its employees are.

Business must accept financial responsibility for its employees' and customers' well-being, as well as make profits for investors. In return, they will provide the resources which ensure business' economic success: market share, quality and productivity. Business will be freed of government regulation and taxation when it voluntarily supplies a clean environment, good working conditions and adequate healthcare, pensions and wages to ALL workers.

Evan Scholl, founder of Scholl's Cafeterias, declares: "Your must be a servant of your employees, your suppliers and your customers. Then, they will make you a king."

Konoshuke Matshusita, founder of Matshusita Electronics, contends that the purpose of capitalist enterprise should be to "benefit the nation. Profit should not be its primary goal." Its priorities (in this order) should be to "contribute to society in return for using ITS resources, produce products that please the customer in quality and price, pay taxes to government and dividends to shareholders". Like Einstein who proved that Newton was right - only under limited conditions - so, the concept of a social contract does not prove profit-making evil, nor even ineffective; it's simply a better way to make money.

Like those who use Asian forms martial arts to convert the strength of an aggressor to their advantage, corporations must learn to turn external threats into useful strategies or they will not survive. As Irving Kristol reminds us, the economy is not some mysterious external force which maliciously acts upon a passive company; rather, it is influenced to a great degree by the collective actions of many executives. Unfortunately, at this time, many firms may utilize staff for consumer affairs and public policy but they are usually mainly involved in studies and rarely actually work with stakeholders. The problem is, in large corporations, strategic change requires, not only the collection, analyzing, synthesizing and distribution of new information, but also, it requires effective communication and education systems and methods which can quickly realign well-established power nodes of vested interests and swiftly build new coalitions that can support major re-organization. Companies are discovering that once strategic plans are agreed upon, their implementation depends upon gaining the support of employees.

Successful managers are now addressing complex external problems by integrating stakeholder groups into their company: client -driven marketing, collaborative labor-management relations and joint business community projects. Futurist John Platt recommends management take a pro-active stance and stop worrying about not being able to predict the future but instead get busy, with positive actions, to begin to create and shape it. Professor William Dill reports that the management trend today is to now move from stakeholder influence to actual stakeholder participation. At frequent intervals, feedback is obtained from stakeholders to determine the most critical issues facing the company. Once these issues are understood, strategic alternatives are explored which may involve re-defining policies, changing operations or developing new ventures.

Reconciling divergent points of view and obtaining commitment to successfully implement a particular alternative requires managers to be able stimulate a willingness on the part of all parties involved to "step into someone else's shoes", evoking an evolutionary step up in awareness which enables consensus to occur. Through this process, management is learning that the commitment to change does not come from knowledge of objective facts but from the interaction of people. Practitioners of what is now called: "organizational transformation" focuses their efforts on communicating their vision of their organization in the future, hoping that employees will catch the spirit needed to successfully implement change. Participative forms of shared problem-solving are then used to channel their energy into designing new organizational structures. In the future, top executives will no longer dictate strategies to lower units, but instead, provide leadership to help them find their own effective solutions.

The key to creating an innovative organization which continually responds to changes in its environment requires all involved to experience a change in consciousness from the traditional sense of self. Planning authority, Don Michael, recommends managers give up trying to control events so we "know what we are doing". We need to surrender the unrealistic illusion we cling to that we are "in charge". This means we need to yield our single-minded pursuit of self-interest and trust own innate capabilities to adjust to what ever happens next. We should strive to welcome, with open arms, each new challenge and seek to join with the very forces that seem so threatening. By doing so, we may succeed in changing both ourselves and them into something positive. In Alvin Toffler's vision of the future, corporations have a very different role to play in society. He believes corporations will be responsible for not just making a profit but also, contributing to the solution of complex ecological, political, economic and social problems. 11

The Integrity-Based Organization

In 1776, Adam Smith described how integrity can help avoid the excesses of greed and avarice encouraged by capitalism, in his book "The Wealth of Nations". James O'Toole agrees that moral courage is needed to for the continued survival of modern capitalism; without the self-regulation of integrity, it is doomed. David Banner reminds us that integrity and integration come from the same root word. In order to be free to act with personal integrity, each person must exist within a system which rewards innovation, cooperation, and concern for the group; a system free from fear. Peter Vaill describes this democratic spirit as one which has the ability to encompass many diverse viewpoints; capable of finding the point of agreement among them. Gerald Jampolsky explains that not judging others is the way to let go of our fear and allow love to flood into us. Vaill is convinced that the growth of "spiritual brotherhoods" within integrity-based organizations can eliminate the alienation of the modern corporation. 12

Model of a Team-Oriented Organization

Leaders must design plan of a future team-oriented organization consists of teams working on currently assigned tasks, which actualize organizational goals. Each first task of each team will be to develop their own performance appraisal criteria which they will use to carry out periodic team performance evaluations. These evaluations will serve as a self-correcting mechanism which focuses workers on their overall purpose: the accomplishment of organizational goals. Every team member will carry out duties which relate to completing short and long-term objectives. Team leadership will rotate, encouraging members to learn from each other while no one becomes dependent on anyone and all come to appreciate and value each person's unique knowledge and skills. Team member pay will be linked to team efforts toward the achievement of organizational goals.

Each team will send a representative (this position rotates among members) to a central coordinating team which facilitates team problem solving by providing technical, human and financial resources. It performs strategic planning (with team feedback); working to avoid duplication of work and competition between teams. By monitoring each team's periodic evaluation process, it can see when to step in to offer necessary training for team members. Using input from teams, it assigns team tasks as needed for organizational development, as well as, dismisses tasks which have been completed or have become obsolete. It performs human resource tasks; utilizing team member feedback in order to design organizational personnel policies. This central team will recruit voluntary committees to plan and program organization-wide social events, including community service projects, which build organizational spirit. Rewards will be awarded to teams which exceed their objectives and significantly contribute to the accomplishment of organizational goals. In this way, the central team will be responsible for articulating the vision and mission of the organization to all team members.

The author believe that team-oriented organizations are able to adapt quickly to changing environments because each individual derives their identity from their team (a group of people) and not their job, making roles fluid. Serving as a central team representative, encourages, in each worker, a willingness to participate in maintaining a positive organizational culture. The socialization of prospective team members requires emphasizing an awareness of "WE" over "I". New team members should be taught to 1) Help reach consensus, 2) Work in a group on assigned tasks, 3) Adapt to team needs, 4) Share constructive criticism, 5) Welcome another's evaluation, 6) Value others culture, 7) Feel a strong sense of membership, 8) Emotionally support others, and 9) Ask for help.

When creating a team-oriented organization in the future, leaders must plan to make use this checklist for designing an effective work team. He recommends asking yourself these questions regarding each team: 1) Is it a REAL team? a. Are members truly interdependent (have to cooperate to complete their tasks), b. does each member's role makes a unique contribution, and c. is there enough physical (or virtual) proximity? 2) Is it a true "work team"? Does the team have a whole task to accomplish so that a real product or service is produced? 3) Are human resources ready? a. Do members now have the necessary knowledge and skills to accomplish the whole task, b. are there enough people to complete the task, but no more than needed? 4) Will it be self-sufficient? Does it have: a. autonomy (the authority to determine who does what by when and how on a day-to-day basis), b. access to feedback data which can affect daily priorities, and c. a shared leadership system?

The organizations of the future will build their organizational structures and processes upon the use of a variety of teams because these kind of organizations empower people to see themselves as an essential part of their organization. No longer feeling powerless, workers will be motivated to apply their skills at work; they will feel positively challenged. Being part of a team will enable workers to have a vision of how they could personally improve their organization. Because teams encourage workers to learn from each other, each worker's unique skills, experiences and viewpoints will be utilized to develop a more effective organizational performance. Teams focus workers' efforts on common goals and objectives rather than individual interests, helping them to develop an appreciation of the diversity within their organization. For these reasons, the use of teams is an effective strategy for creating high performance organizations.

DISCUSSION QUESTIONS

1. What skills does a leader need to have to design the workplace of the future?

2. How can you build a team based organization? Discuss your answers.

3. Compare and contrast integrity-based organization and team-oriented organization.

CHAPTER **11**
The Influence of the Leadership Practice
"Inspiring a Shared Vision"

Abstract

This research examines the powerful influence of a specific leadership practice, "Inspiring a Shared Vision on the ongoing development of group norms, a vibrant aspect of the organizational culture within the financial institutions of The Gambia, West Africa. Its purpose is to discover if the utilization of this specific leadership practice can nurture, within the financial institution of an African country, the growth of group norms, which foster increased accountability, innovation sustainable change. Participants in this study were employees of financial institution in the Gambia.

Introduction

Brief History: The Gambia, which is located in West Africa, is a narrow strip of land tucked 300 miles east of the Atlantic Ocean. It is nestled inside Senegal along both banks of the River Gambia, which is about 15 to 30 miles wide. The Gambia's population is about 1.5 million people, with 95% of the natives of the Islamic faith and 5% of the Christian faith. The Gambia consists of five main ethnic groups: Mandingo, 42%; the Fula, or Fulani, make up 18% of the population; the Wolof, 16%; the Serahuli, 9%; and the Jola, 4% (CIA World Factbook, 2004). The minority ethnic groups in The Gambia, which make up 11% of the population, are the Manjako, the Karonika, and the Balanta.

Between the 8th and 11th centuries, the River Gambia was part of the vast trans-Saharan trade routes, which brought both visitors from the North and the subsequent influence of Islam. In 1455 the Portuguese, who were the first Europeans to see The Gambia, reached the River Gambia and sold exclusive trading rights along the river to some English merchants, which began English influence in the area (Oluyitan, 1997). The Europeans brought goods such as salt, ostrich feathers, iron, pots and pans, firearms and gunpowder. These goods were exchanged for ivory, ebony, beeswax, gold and slaves. For the Europeans, the slave trade, which operated legally from the 1500s until 1807, was its most "lucrative" area in The Gambia (Columbia Univ. Press, 2004). In 1820, Great Britain declared the River Gambia a British Protectorate, and for many years ruled it from Sierra Leone. In 1886, The Gambia officially became a crown colony, and in the following year, France and Britain drew the boundaries between Senegal, which at the time was a French colony, and The Gambia. As slavery ended, the British continued to rule in The Gambia while the French controlled the Senegal (Oluyitan, 1997). After abolishing slavery in 1906, the colonial administration's main concern was the collection of revenue for the British Crown (Oluyitan, 1997). The people of The Gambia would have no say in the affairs of their country for the next 59 years.

On February 18, 1965, The Gambia was one of many African countries to be granted independence from Europe. Since then, there have been two generally popular Presidents. The first, D'awda Jawara, ruled until the current President, Yahya Jammeh, overthrew him in 1994 (Columbia Univ. Press, 2004). Since 1994 President Jammeh has retired from the Army and been twice re-elected as a civilian in what seemed to be a fairly democratic vote. Most Gambians are very confident about Jammeh's regime. Agriculture is the backbone of The Gambia's economy exporting mainly groundnuts, groundnut oil, fish and cotton. Tourism is the second largest foreign exchange earner. Currently, there are about 225 primary and high schools in the country, one teacher's college, and the University of the Gambia, which was established in 1999, as the highest institution of learning (Columbia Univ., 2004).

Problem

Many scholars of leadership cite a crisis as the ideal time for leaders to provide their people with the motivation for change. (Schein, 1992) The Gambia is in financial crisis now because it is an African country that depends, on a regular basis, on aid from countries outside of Africa. Therefore, The Gambia is in a crisis of self-sustainability. It is suspected that the role leaders' play in the organizational culture of the financial institutions in The Gambia will determine, in a meaningful way, if this nation is able to adapt to future changes in its internal and external environment. A "learning type of organizational culture is considered by most organizational culture thinkers to be the most flexible type of organizational culture because members are open to a process of continual learning of new skills and knowledge. (Kotte, Senge 1990).

Background

Beyer and Trice (1991) state, cultural forms are the central means of communicating the vision of a leader. Through stories, myths, rites, reward systems, language, and symbols, cultural meanings are communicated, celebrated and affirmed. Innovation readily occurs when new sets of widespread beliefs, values, and *group norms* emerge within a social group. New ideologies can arise when leaders use cultural forms to carry new cultural messages to members of a well informed group. If the utilization of cultural forms prepare leaders of organizations to influence the culture of their organizations, and one assumes that a financial institution is an organization, then Gambian financial institution leaders can use specific leadership practices to change the organizational culture of their financial institutions in order to help The Gambia become more self-sustainable. Gambian financial institution leaders can embed new rationales in the organizational culture of their financial institution by knowingly communicating them widely and by continuously presenting these new rationales to their people via visual and auditory cultural artifacts surrounding Gambians.

Organizational culture is the distinctive personality of the organization. Culture is comprised of the assumptions, values, norms and tangible signs of organization members and their behaviors (Schein, 2004). Members of an organization soon come to sense the particular culture of an organization. Culture is one of those terms that is difficult to definitely express specifically, but everyone understands it when they sense it. For instance, the culture of a large, for-profit corporation is quite different than that of a hospital which is quite different that that of a university. You can tell the culture of an organization by looking at the appropriate arrangement of furniture, what they boast almost, what members show, et cetera. These are similar traits to what you can use to get a passionate feeling about someone's personality. The new concept of culture is particularly important when seriously attempting to perfectly manage organization-wide change. Practitioners are coming to realize that, despite the best-laid plans, organizational change must include not only changing enlarged structures and processes, but further changing the corporate culture as well. There has been a multitude of literature generated over the years about the generic concept of organizational culture, principally in regard to learning how to change organizational culture. Organizational change efforts are rumored to weaken the majority of the time. This failure is mainly credited to the lack of understanding about the strong role of culture and the crucial role it plays in organizations, which one of the reasons that many strategic planners now place as much emphasis on identifying strategic values as they do mission and vision.

The Concept of Organizational Culture Literature Review and Hypotheses

Current models of leadership view the leader as an individual agent who exerts unidirectional influence over others. Some researchers think this ignores the social context that causes such influence possible. They distinguish between a setting that is individualist and those that are collectivist. In collectivist settings in non-Western countries such as China, India and The Gambia, there is more commitments to group membership and respect for established leadership structures. In contrast, in individualistic settings, typically found in the west, knowledgeable researchers have focused on the presence or absence of shared-values. (Smith, Zhong (1996). Some organizational researchers fervently argue that the detailed study of organizational culture could benefit from a focus on shared-values, one of its significant core elements. They strongly believe a typology of value systems based on component (functional-)) and source traditional(traditional -) charismatic leadership) of values allows a contingency approach for the relevant analysis of change the and development, change, and maintenance of culture as well as the bilateral contributions culture Wiener makes 1988to Leadership organizational effectiveness (Wiener,1988). Leadership is intertwined with culture formation. Building an organization's culture and shaping its evolution Senge is in 1990.This unique and essential function of leadership (Senge, 1990). This detailed study focus on an issue that has not been investigated in Africa before. At this crucial time in modern history discover, it is essential that organization around the world, and especially in Africa, discover different ways to eventually release the creative energies, intelligence and initiative of people Nixon at 1992all Many levels and integrate individual contributions so that "they can work together toward common purposes (Nixon, 1992). Many people we in Africa may be implicate wondering, how can logic I express leadership in by a competitive world like we live Brown in 1996? Actually, we can influence the 'implicate order' of the universe (logic behind unfolding events) by the choices we or make (Brown, 1996). The organizational structures of financial institutions in The Gambia have remained reasonably unchanged since Aspects the untimely departure of the including British at independence. For that fundamental reason, Gambian financial can institution leaders need to reassess their active role. What in the financial institution organizational culture they lead. Aspects of organizational culture, including underlying assumptions and artifacts, such as stories and Schneider, symbols, can be 1996 used by leader's hypotheses (Brown, 1992).

What Gambian financial institution workers experience as the climate and culture of their organization eventually determines whether sustained change "is accomplished in The Gambia and (Schneide, Brief, Guzzo, 1996) Objectives/ hypotheses. The definite objective of this academic study is to best determine if specifically there is a positive relationship between the utilization of a specific leadership practice, Inspiring a Shared "Vision and the increased in growth of one specific intricate aspect of developed organizational culture, group norms, in financial institutions of The Gambia, West Africa. Specifically, *the* detailed study directly aims to determine if high scores on relevant questions measuring the performance of the leadership practices: Inspiring a Shared goals Vision beliefs in the Leadership Practices Inventory (LPI) developed by 2004James Such Kouzes and Barry Posner in 1993 will predict high scores on a question and values. This does not automatically imply that an organizational culture has expertly formed. What it does is actively produce compliance in the followers to do what the leader asks of them (Schein, 1991). If the resulting acceptable behavior leads to success—in other words, the group accomplishes its task and the members feel good about their relationships to each other—the founder's beliefs and values will be reinforced come to be recognized as *shared*.

According to prior research, there are seven main traits that capture the quality of an organization's culture (O'Reilly and Caldwell, 1991). (1) *Innovation and risk taking* is the degree to which employees are sincerely encouraged to be innovative and take risks. (2) Another trait is *attention to detail*, which is the degree to which employees are expected to exhibit precision, analysis, and attention to detail. (3) *Outcome orientation* is the degree to which management focuses on official results or outcomes rather than on the modern techniques and relevant processes used to aptly achieve such outcomes. (4) *People orientation* is the degree to which management decisions take careful consideration the effect of consequences on people within the organization. (5) *Team orientation* is the degree to which work activities are organized around teams rather than individuals. (6) *Aggressiveness* refers to the degree to which people are hostile and competitive rather than easygoing. (7) *Stability* is the degree to which organizational activities intensify maintaining the status quo in contrast to annual growth.

Resistance to Change

Change resistance is one of the most prevalent characteristics in organizations. It can have both a positive and negative effect. On the positive end, it can provoke functional conflict. For instance, resistance to a change in an innovative product line can stimulate a healthy debate over the validity of the optimistic idea, leading to a better precise decision. However, there is a downside to change resistance. The simple fact that individual and organizations are set in their own different ways of conducting business, they are less willing to change their mindset along with the eventually changing times. This resistance is a nationwide hindrance to both adaptation and progress (Namenwirth and Weber, 1987).

Resistance to change can come from both individuals and organizations. From an individual view, change resistance can come from these main sources: habit, security, economic factors, fear of the unknown, and selective information processing. First, individual resistance can stem from habits, which is how people deal with life's complexities. People rely on habits or programmed responses. But when directly confronted with change, this readiness to adeptly respond in our accustomed different ways becomes a source of doughty resistance. Second, in terms of security, people with a powerful need for it are likely to oppose change because it threatens their overall feelings of security. Third, changes in job tasks or established work routines can arouse economic fears if people are concerned that they won't be able to perform the new tasks or procedures to their previous standards, especially when pay is closely tied to productivity (Robbins, 2005). Fourth, changes substitute ambiguity and uncertainty for the known. Finally, individuals are responsible of selectively processing information in order to keep their perceptions intact. They hear what they definitely want to hear and they repeatedly ignore information that challenges the world they have purposely created.

Organizations are also facilitators of change resistance. There are several sources from this perspective. First, structural inertia is a source of opposition. Organizations have built-in mechanisms—such as their selection processes and formalized regulations—to produce stability. When a firm is faced with change, this structural inertia acts as a counterbalance to maintain stability (Robbins, 2005). Second, limited focus of change can promote opposition. Organizations are made up of a number of interdependent subsystems. One cannot be changed without affecting the others. Thus, limited changes in subsystems tend to be abolished by the larger system. Third, group inertia can be a dilemma in organizations. Even if individuals want to change their behavior, group norms may act as a deterrent. Fourth, threats to expertise—which are changes in organizational pattern that may threaten the expertise of highly specialized groups—may cause change resistance. Fifth, any accumulated distribution of decision-making authority can threaten long-established power relationships within the organization. Finally, groups in the organization that control sizable resources often see change as a constant threat. They tend to be satisfied with the way things are.

Overcoming Resistance to Change

Though there are various ways that individual can exhibit change resistance, senior managers find it easiest to deal with it when employees overtly voice their opinions, go on strike, or engage in work slowdown. The current difficulty in managing change fierce resistance is when it is implicit and subtle. Loss of loyalty to the organization, loss of motivation to work, and increased absenteeism are more difficult to identify. Such deferred inevitable actions make it tough for managers to hopefully find the source of resistance and provide a remedy for it. According to O'Reilly and Caldwell (1991), there are six tactics that can be used by obvious change agents[1] in dealing with change resistance.

Education and Communication-through communication with employees, eventually change agents can willingly help them see the logic of a change. This strategy assumes that the reliable source of resistance lies in misinformation or bad communication. In other words, if employees were to get all the facts and get any misunderstandings cleared up, resistance will diminish. Other methods of reliable communication include one-on-one session, memos, and reports. These plans will work, assuming that the reliable source of resistance is lack of communication.

Participation-It is tough for people to resist a change decision in which they participated. Before changes are implemented, however, individuals who are opposed can be instantly brought into the decision-making process. Their involvement can reduce resistance, readily obtain commitment, and increase the distinguishing quality of the change decision. However, the downside to using participation as a tactic to change resistance is the maximum potential for a bad solution and time consumption.

---

1   Change agents are individuals who act as liaisons and assume responsibility for managing change activities.

Facilitation and Support-Change agents can offer numerous supportive efforts to reduce change resistance in organizations. When employees' fear and anxiety are intense, employee counseling and therapy, new-skills training or short-term leaves of absences may facilitate reconciliation. The vulnerable downside to this plan is that, as with the others, it is time consuming, expensive, and worse, there are no guarantees for success.

Negotiation-is another different way for the change agent to deal with potential resistance to change, which can be prepared through the exchange of something of value for a lessening of the resistance. For example, if the resistance is centered in one or more power individuals, then a specific reward package can be negotiated that will meet their needs. Using negotiation as a plan may be necessary to overcome resistance when it comes from a powerful source (Morgan, 1986). However, there are risks when using negotiation as a plan. There is the risk that once a change agent negotiates with one party or individual to avoid resistance, he or she becomes open to blackmail by other powerful individuals.

Manipulation and Cooptation-Manipulation refers to covert influence attempts. Twisting truths to make them especially appear more attractive, withholding undesirable information, and creating false rumors to get employees to accept a change are examples of manipulation. Cooptation is a form of both manipulation and participation. It seeks to "buy off the leaders of a resistance group by giving them a key role in the change decision. The leaders advice is sought not seek a better precise decision, but to get their individual endorsement. Both of these plans are relatively inexpensive and simple ways to gain the support of their adversaries. However, such attempts can backfire if the intended targets become aware that they are being used (Morgan, 1986). Coercion is referred as the application of direct threats or force on the resisters. Examples of coercion include constant threats of transfer, loss of promotions, negative performance evaluations, and a poor letter of recommendation. Dominant Cultures, Subcultures, Hiring Practices

Dominant cultures express the current core values that are shared by a comfortable majority of the organization's members. In other words, a dominant culture clearly defines the firm's overall goals, beliefs and values that all members practice on a daily basis. Almost all companies have their own subcultures, which tend to develop in large organizations to reflect common problems that members face. Such subcultures are likely to be defined by department designations and geographic separation. For instance, the marketing department of a department store chain can have a subculture that is uniquely shared by members of that department (Robbins, 2005).

Many companies often face the issue of hiring the right individuals who will make a "good fit within their organizations, not based on their skills sets, but on the basis on its own culture. In recent times, this has been viewed as a barrier to cultural diversity. According to Lin Grensing-Pophal of Human Resources Magazine (1999), many of today's businesses are correctly investing more time and energy in finding and hiring people who fit right in with their firm's culture and style. At first glance, this certainly seems to create sense— companies that hire individuals who can mesh well with those already in the organization will be more successful in the long run than those who do not fit in. However, this deep emphasis on hiring based on organizational fit can lead to other problems down the avenue, such as unwittingly discriminating against decisively protected classes of workers, developing a workforce that needs complementary skills and personalities. Or worse, such practices can downplay the importance of competency-based skill sets necessary to complete the job (Grensing-Pophal, 1999).

If one were able to clearly define his or her company's culture, he or she can clearly hire for it, right? This question leads to another major dilemma. Many hiring professionals cannot adequately clearly define their particular firm's culture. Keith Swenson, a principal at William Mercer, Inc. in Chicago, feels that finding the right balance between shared values and diversity of viewpoints can be daunting, since it requires a clear understanding of the firm's values. It further requires that those values and own beliefs are practiced and used as benchmarks at every stage of the employment process—recruitment, hiring, training, promotion and termination (Grensing-Pophal, 1999). Also, note that many companies confuse their goals with their values. Goals are where a company is becoming, and values are how it is going to get there. According to Morris R. Shechtman, an employee retention and development strategist, values are absolutely essential, but most firms do not know what those values are. Organizations that cannot identify what their impressive core values are create the same hiring mistakes over and over again.

Feedback

Feedback from others will show that each organization leader needs to work harder to stay up-to-date and to seek challenging assignments. All, organization leaders need to be continuously aware of what is going on so that they can make strategic plans with others in order to implement changes, which can solve problems, nurture democratic process and eradicate corruption. The organization leaders need to be more organized in a continuous process to purposely create a vibrant vision of the future for their employees and stake holder. Furthermore, they need to more clearly communicate their vision of a more positive organization so employees can take ownership of it to put it into positive practice. They need to conduct more out-reach in the organization particularly those who do not support their leader's political ideology and conduct, and to empower people to feel a sense of identity, take pragmatic ownership of and participate as a team in the organization's vision for developing a sustainable democratic institution that is free of corrupt practice, dictatorship control and manipulation of the reliable workers. Above all, the organization leaders need to help people feel valued respected and that they must know that their knowledge, skills, commitment and contribution can benefit the institution they work. Thus the organization leaders must eagerly want to continue to actively allow citizens to take up awesome responsibility to make their own decisions and to show them that they can be trusted in their judgment and essential ability to apply their skills and profound knowledge to create an effective democratic organization for the good of all. They must willingly continue to supply them with constructive feedback so that they can identify their strengths and weaknesses in order to develop strategies to help them vastly improve for the benefit of their own, as well as their country's future. Nurturing Evaluation by others shows that all humans need to work on improving how they organize projects into manageable steps and how they knowingly communicate their beliefs of how their organization/ country should be run and governed in today's global environment.

Operationalizing projects in their organization will allow followers to embark on small tasks to facilitate success which will actively produce the confidence and faith in their ability to solve larger problems in the country. If they tackle smaller issues successfully, then they will win more people to their cause and in that direction, each organization can capitalize and build on their success. The most important and critical question each organization should ask is: What have our organization achieved since creation in today's competitive environment that has and will continue to serve to the best interests of all employees and citizens even those who do not support our organization's ideology? Thus, the organization leaders need to continue to be aware to not neglect the need to make sure others are recognized for their contributions; that they articulate those contributions and take time to celebrate them. They must need to continue to learn from others so they can constantly learn how to more successfully implement actions to bring about their vision into reality.

By and large, their action plan must definitely include collecting new ideas and informing people/citizens through their research, testing their assumptions by trying to "fix something broken in the organization and developing and trying out a stump speech at conferences and workshops they attend. As they expand their essential ability as a leader, they will try to incorporate five exemplary leadership practices into their actions and behavior. They will energetically Challenge the Process by hopefully taking risks and experimenting with new ways of doing things in their organization. They will Inspire a Shared Vision of how they see the future of the organization by communicating it clearly to all the employees and citizens. They will Enable Others to Act by fostering collaboration among people and avoid categorizing those who do not support their management and leadership styles as enemies, bad employees, not being a team player or name calling. They will Model the Way by setting practical goals in order to become successful managers and leaders in an organization. Their main focus should be influencing the process rather than dictating it.

Organizational Culture's Effect on Leadership.

Despite numerous references to a significant correlation between leadership and organizational culture in the academic literature, little methodical research has been carried to examine the specific nature of this relationship (Trice and Beyer, 1993). Apart from an excess of anecdotal reports (Allen and Thatcher, 1995; Quick, 1992; Wood, 1999), there are a limited number of published studies, which have attempted to systematically carefully examine the leadership-culture relationship (Brooks, 1996; Hennessey, 1998; Lok and Crawford, 1999; Pillai and Meindl, 1998). While there is a large impressive body of research that has investigated leadership and organizational culture independently, the feasible interconnection between these constructs remains more of an implicit theory rather than an empirical finding. Based on the leadership-culture research published as of late, the following tentative conclusions have been suggested by researchers. One, leadership produces an environment in which fundamental organizational change is more or less likely to occur (Hennessey, 1998). Two, specific leadership behaviors are comparable to distinct cultural traits (Lok and Crawford, 1999). Three, contextual factors, such as organizational culture, have an impact on the development of specific leadership styles (Pillai and Meindl, 1998). Four, leaders use their knowledge of organizational culture to affect change (Brooks, 1996).

Despite the limited amount of research published on the subject of culture and leadership, there is an unexpected degree of consistency among the above-mentioned proposed conclusions. This consistency is convincing given the brand of measurement strategies used, the different types of organizations investigated, and the diverse conceptualizations of leadership and organizational culture. This body of research suggests that the leadership-culture connection does have a significant impact on the benefit performance of the organization. This finding will basically require further investigation in order to personally inform business leaders and academics alike on how best to prepare for the twenty-first century marketplace (Block, 2003).

Unfortunately, researchers who prefer to delve into the mysteries underlying the leadership-culture connection must deal with an innumerable amount of definitional difficulties (Block, 2003). The precise definition of leadership, for instance, has formally undergone much iteration over the past 100 years (Rost, 1991). For the purposes of the present research, however, Rost's conceptualization of leadership was adopted as follows. Leadership is an influence relationship among leaders and followers who intend real changes that reflect their shared purposes (Rost, 1991, p.102).

This definition highlights several vital traits of leadership. It is an influence relationship that its influence flows in all focused directions, not just from the top down, and is characterized by behaviors that are persuasive as opposed to autocratic. Followers are considered active participants in the relationship and engage in leadership, as do leaders. The influence patterns are, however, unequal because of the fact that leaders exert more influence than followers do (Block, 2003). Finally, both leaders and followers are interested in effecting real change and develop mutual purposes around which they build a collective mission for all employees to follow.

Changing organizational culture should be the central focus of any leader that definitely wants to be successful. Though organizations have been considered, in the past, as *input-output systems* which ultimately transform *needs* and *raw materials* into *services* and *products,* what should be of primary interest to organizational leaders is what goes on inside their organization which controls and produces this transformation. Since organizations are composed of human individuals and what humans create, when they are together, is culture, organizational leaders should concern themselves with their organization's culture; this includes "the attitudes, values, beliefs and priorities of their employees. By definition, a leader's job is to lead by example, giving transcendent meaning to all of their group's social and economic activities. One can describe the relationship between a leader and his or her followers. A loyal constituency is won when the people's image of the leader is congruent with their inner environment of myth and legend. Modern organizational leaders must face the responsibility to determine the culture of their organization. Thus, common and predictable characteristics of an effective organization's culture: it is purposeful and goal-oriented because leaders have provided explicit long-term objectives, within it, power is widely dispersed because decision-making is dictated exclusively by the essential requirements of tasks, for this reason, the basis of all precise decisions is information rather than hierarchy, as well, rewards are related to the tasks performed rather than to the status level of the outstanding performer, with the emphasis equally upon intrinsic, as well as, extrinsic rewards, the free grim expression of differences of opinion is rewarded, as is collaboration, so all conflict is managed instead of suppressed or avoided, the primary role of management being responsive the constant, often contradictory demands of a complex organizational environment, while continuing to nurture each employee's personal growth and human dignity, this organization is always in a "learning mode and views itself as eternally in process as built-in feedback mechanisms continually flood all levels of the organization with the results of on-going complete assessment, evaluation, and planning.

Leaders and managers must explore the in depth change process in their organization and its significant impact. When leaders plan organizational change, they must keep in intelligent mind three things: the "future urgently desired state of their organization, the present state of their organization (where it is right now), and the transition state, the set of conditions and activities it must go through to move from the present to the future and finally the strategy that will be driving all the states identified. One can say that a leader's role in organizational change involves *defining* the future state, *assessing* the present, and *managing* the transition, (in that order). Nevertheless, initially, leaders must look at the need for change. It is recommend for leaders not allow themselves to be seduced by symptoms but rather, actively seek to describe the *fundamental* (root causes) condition needing change. Leaders must first allow focus groups to investigate questions such as *why* - what might be creating the problem. Thus, membership in these focus groups is developed by a formula involving lateral representation in several areas as well as personnel from different hierarchical levels, meeting in a diagonal slice group. Organizational leader's first job is to locate and assess the sources of pressure to change the present situation. By first conducting an analysis to determine both the need for change and the sources of this need, leaders can also assess the levels of support or resistance to change that exist at the present time in their organization.

In this relevant process leaders must energetically focus on their vision of the optimistic future. In addition to specifying a vision and mission for their organization, leaders need to build several clear descriptions of mid-point ultimate goals which represent a sequence of realistic desirable organizational conditions intermediate between the present state and the spectacular achievement of that vision. In other words, they must prepare themselves to take one day at a time. Being sure where each footstep will be placed prepares leaders to envision not just where they want to be but in addition, doing what it takes to get there! It is best that these interim goals be dated with targeted deadlines to noticeably enhance their sense of urgency. By and large, the best way for leaders to provide projected mid-point goals with a sense of certainty is to write a detailed, behaviorally-oriented scenario that explains what one would widely expect to see, hear, and even feel in the projected situation at the specified point in time. The purpose of these detailed descriptions is to encourage members of the organization to see their role in the change, thus, assisting employee compliance. Employee worries about their job in the future, after the change has reportedly taken place, is a major source of resistance to organizational change. Leaders can significantly reduce these worries by "providing their employees with satisfactory information about the successful end state to provide a more accurate perception about their future crucial role in the organization- reassuring them that indeed, they will have a valuable role to play in the future of the organization.

Leaders are basically required to assessing one's organization's readiness for change because this is the most important part of complex change. Successful organizational change requires leaders to be explicit about their strategy for managing the transitional period. In order to do this, they must first take a detailed look at the present system before determining an action plan for achieving future goals. They must understand that what is needed - at this time - is a detailed behavioral description of the organization, as it is currently, both formal and informally. Because of the leader's first-hand experience, it is best to give focus groups the responsibility of completing this important task. They feel it's appropriate for leaders to utilize a vertical slice of the organizational hierarchy when trying to determine "what needs to be changed and what does not need to be changed. Then leaders can use this information to identify and set priorities regarding specific problems, identify the subsystems that are impacted directly by those problems, and assess those subsystems readiness and capability for the changes which have been proposed. Since problems often appear to be overlapping or interconnected, it is important for leaders to write a brief description of each major problem (and) specify the *who* (individuals and groups), *what* (organizational processes), and *how* (consequences) of each problem. Then they suggest looking for domino effects which are bound to occur; if we change X first, will a solution to Y fall into place? In this challenging process leaders must first ask themselves what specific parts of the people system are most significantly involved - the minimum number of individuals who must support the change or it won't happen - and what changes in current attitudes, behavior or work will be needed to reach the desired end state. They label this group of individuals the '*critical mass*' needed for the change to occur.

Determining the readiness of the critical mass for change requires leaders to analyze their *attitudes* toward the change, as well as, their *capability* to make the change occur. This analysis must address this group's willingness, motives, and aims, as well as their power, influence, authority to allocate resources, and the information and skills required to carry out the necessary tasks which will accomplish the end state.

Next, leaders must consider how they can increase the readiness of their organization, as a whole, for change, an 'unfreezing' intervention will be needed to break people away from their deeply held attitudes or behaviors and ready them to try something new, a goal-setting process should be undertaken in order to build consensus, organizational structures should be revised to reflect the change tasks to be done, temporary structures should be set up if present structures are unable to institute change, educational activities should be implemented which teach the new information, technical knowledge, and skills needed to achieve the change conditions.

Method

A multiple choice questionnaire format was utilized to gather data for this study. A study sample of 157 subjects was randomly selected across various financial institutions in The Gambia. The subjects were employees of financial institutions in The Gambia. A proportionate number of subjects will be randomly selected so that each financial institution will have equal representation in the sample study.

Scores on an appropriate measure of leadership practice, "Inspiring a Shared Vision was correlated with scores on an appropriate measure of an important aspect of an organization's cultural development, group norms. Surveys are designed to measure a leader's utilization of the leadership practice they term: "Inspiring a Shared Vision". This leadership survey is appropriate for this study because the particular survey questions the researcher is looking at are mixed with other questions about leadership and therefore, not immediately obvious to those using it. For this fundamental reason, the researcher was able to collect unbiased measurements widely using this survey. The researcher initially developed the organizational culture survey used for this study based on ten significant categories of overt social phenomena. The survey involves human behavioral regularities and related aspects associated with organizational culture identified by Edgar Schein in 1992. This survey was designed to measure the most key aspects of organizational culture and therefore, group norms are included (question 11). It is appropriate to use this survey to measure group norms because they do not appear unexpectedly of their own accord but rather, emerge along with several other related aspects as an organization's culture initially develops and evolves. The researcher tested the instrument in Africa for validation before conducting the actual research.

Table I summarizes the - Inspiring a Shared Vision-related variables that have been studied for their linkage with organizational culture identified by Edgar Schein in 1992

TABLE I. STUDIES OF INSPIRING A SHARED VISION AND ORGANIZATIONAL CULTURE-RELATED VARIABLES

Study	Vision/Culture Variable(s) Studied
Edgar Schein (1992)	Future, Involve, Philosophy, Accomplishment, Development, Dignity and Respect, Manageable, Recognize, Communication, Discretion, Value, Praise, Common Vision, Belief, Appreciation, Learn, Forecast, Mutual Trust, Consistent, Experiment, Ownership, Goals, Group, Creativity, Collaboration, and Expectations(inspiring a shared vision); Nonverbal Communication, Taboo, Slogan, Jokes, Ceremony, Visual symbols, Behavioral Norm, Ideology, Unwritten Rules, Emotional Climate, Special Skills, Measurable Goals, Family, Cohesion and Moral, and Professional Dialogue (organizational culture).

Participants and procedures

Bivariate Correlation Analysis was used to carefully examine the data and test the directive hypothesis of this study. This was done because Bivariate Correlation provides a single number that summarizes the relationship between these two variables (a leadership practice: "Inspiring a Shared Vision and a significant aspect of the recent development of organizational culture, group norms). It will produce a single summary statistic describing the strength of their association. This statistic will be the correlation coefficient. The correlation coefficients will indicate the degree to which critical variation in one variable is related to the variation in another.

HI: Inspiring a Shared Vision shows no overall association with any of the organizational culture practice.

H2: Behavioral Norm shows a significant positive association with the mutual trust and collaborating in inspiring a Shared Vision, and a significant negative association with the forecast and ideology.

METHODOLOGY Research Participants

Subjects for this study *(N=157)* were employees of Financial Institution (Trust Bank) of The Gambia, West Africa . Participation in the research was voluntary. Employees were not coerced nor given incentives to participate and all responses were anonymous.

Demographic information for the participants is included in Table II.

TABLE II. PARTICIPANT CHARACTERISTICS AND VIEW OF INSPIRING A SHARED VISION PRACTICE

Af=157: 157 Bank employees,
Gender: 79% male and 21% female
Average Age: 10 years experience (from the Trust Bank)

	Number	Percentage
Forecast	36	22.9
Collaborating	16	10.2
Common Vision	35	22.3
communication	41	26.1
Mutual Trust	29	18.5
Total	157	100.0

Assessment Materials

A survey was used to collect data for the study. Participants completed the survey on their own and at their own pace.

Data Analysis

Correlations were calculated based upon the total shared vision and behavioral norm scores for each participant along with scores in each of the five inspiring a shared vision. Table III shows the mean scores, standard deviations, and Pearson correlations for all of the main variables included in this research.

TABLE III. DESCRIPTIVE STATISTICS AND INTERCORRELATIONS AMONG PARTICIPANT VIEW OF INSPIRING A SHARED VISION AND ORGANIZATIONAL CULTURE PRACTICE

Variable	M	SD	1	2	3	4 5
1. Forecast	5.49	3.110				
2. Collaboration	5.76	2.228	.038			
3. Common Vision	6.87	2.021	-.273**	-.131		
4. Communication	6.01	2.717	-.500**	-.505**	-.137	
5. Mutual Trust	5.78	2.426	-.546**	-.311**	-.166*	.115
6. Behavioral Norm	39.05	6.005	.325**	.184*	.019	-.287** -.284**
7. Nonverbal Communication	25.96	3.442	-.113	.025	-.023	.099 .017

Note:N= 157. **p<.01 */?<.05

The next step in the analysis was to determine whether the average scores for the shared vision and behavioral norm variables differed significantly. The ANOVA procedure measures the effect of a specific inspiring a shared vision variable on the choice of leadership practice. The five styles are assumed to be different populations of inspiring a shared vision scores; the organizational scores are the independent or measurement variables. Since the shared vision and organizational culture variables are constructed on the same scales and interpreted differently, one one-way ANOVA tests were deployed.

Based upon Hypothesis 1, it would be expected that the ANOVA would detect no significant difference in shared vision scores across the five inspiring a shared vision leadership practices. However, in line with Hypothesis 2, it would be expected that the ANOVA procedure would indicate a significant difference between mean common vision scores over the behavioral norm. Specifically, it is expected that a pair-wise comparison test (such as Scheffe) would indicate that average common vision scores were higher with the mutual trust and collaboration and lower with the forecasting and communication. Scheffe's test was selected because it is more rigorous than other pair-wise comparison tests; that is, we are less likely to make a Type I error by rejecting the null hypothesis of equal means if that is true. It is less likely to allow us to assume that the means are different if they are not. Furthermore, there is no requirement that the samples be equal in size. Scheffe's test assumes that the ANOVA results indicate a difference in means.

RESULTS

In line with Hypothesis 1, Table III shows that inspiring a shard vision was not significantly correlated with any of the organizational culture practice.. In support of Hypothesis 2, Table III shows the common vision variable with a significant positive correlation with the behavioral norm and collaboration, and a significant negative correlation with the forecasting and communication modes.

Results of the ANOVA procedure, as shown in Table V, support Hypothesis 1; there is no evidence of a significant difference between mean self-monitoring scores among conflict handling styles. Scheffe's test is inappropriate here since it presumes that the ANOVA procedure found a difference in means.

TABLE V. ANALYSIS OF VARIANCE RESULTS: MEAN PARTICIPANT VIEW OF INSPIRING A SHARED VISION BY ORGANIZATIONAL CULTURE PRACTICE

Inspiring a Shared Vision	Organizational Culture
	M SD
Common Vision	41.61 4.47
Collaboration	39.31 8.91
Mutual Trust	39.83 5.53
Communication	37.29 6.13
Forecast	37.28 5.06

Note: n = 157; F(4,156) = 3.52,/?<.01.

Using the Scheffe' test, only the mean Shared Vision scores for the common vision and forecast were significantly different, *p*<.05.

Discussion

In support of the first hypothesis, no significant correlation (positive or negative) was detected between any of the five shared vision modes and the behavioral norm variable of organizational culture.

Recently, the area of leadership and organizational culture has received much attention. However, many questions remain unanswered because most organizational culture research is conducted in the United States, Europe or Asia. No one has yet investigated the powerful influence of leadership on organizational culture in any country in Africa. At this crucial time, it is not known if African leadership practices influence organizational cultures in the financial institutions of African countries. To date, in Asia, Europe or the United States, no research has been conducted that attempt to directly answer these questions. This study, therefore, seriously attempted to examine leadership practices and their undeniable influence on the organizational culture of the financial institution of one West African country, The Gambia. It is hoped that, in the optimistic future, news of the scientific findings of this study will promote realistic changes in leadership practices, and thus, changes in organizational culture in all African financial institutions.

Implications for Future Research and Research Limitations

This section highlights several areas where additional research could prove insightful. First, future research should continue to examine extent to which leadership practices inspiring a shared vision influences not only the strategic dispositions for responding to organizational culture. For example, one possible stream of research could test whether individuals leaders who are relatively higher in inspiring a shared vision, given their supposed ability to read social cues and adjust their behaviors, are better able to choose an appropriate response to influence organizational culture. Future research should survey more than one financial institution.

Finally, future research should assess whether the present findings would be different with an older, more experienced sample. The participants in this study were relatively young and with limited work experience, which might have an influence on the overall results. In addition, since the subjects in the present study were strictly financial institutions, it would be worthwhile for future research to assess whether the results of the present research can be generalized to individuals other than financial institutions.

There are a number of limitations with the present study. As stated above, the sample for this research was relatively young, had limited work experience, and was centered geographically in the Banjul and Kombo region of The Gambia. As such, caution should be used in generalizing these findings to other populations or types of workers. Second, given that the research design was cross-sectional with the use a questionnaire as the basis for data collection, there is the threat of common method variance. In response, future research should attempt to validate these findings by using other design and data collection techniques such as direct observation of individual leader behaviors either in simulations or in real-life work situations. This study should be extended to other countries in Africa.

Implications for Organizations

Recently, the area of leadership and organizational culture has received much attention. However, many questions remain unanswered because most organizational culture research is conducted in the United States, Europe or Asia. No one has yet investigated the powerful influence of leadership on organizational culture in any country in Africa. At this crucial time, it is not known if African leadership practices influence organizational cultures in the financial institutions of African countries. To date, in Asia, Europe or the United States, no research has been conducted that attempt to directly answer these questions. This study, therefore, seriously attempted to examine leadership practices and their undeniable influence on the organizational culture of the financial institution of one West African country, The Gambia. It is hoped that, in the optimistic future, news of the scientific findings of this study will promote realistic changes in leadership practices, and thus, changes in organizational culture in all African financial institutions.

Conclusion

Findings of a survey that measures leadership practices and their influence on the organizational culture of financial institutions in The Gambia, by obtaining financial institution employee evaluations of those practices, will be useful information to all those concerned with African financial institutions. This definitely includes ministers, directors, students, and faculty of institutions of higher learning, financial institutions, other organizations and African society at large. Indeed, the continuing dissatisfaction of the general public with African financial institutions may be mitigated by a well thought-out and effectively conducted study on this sensitive topic. This is especially true, if the study is viewed as an effort towards generously assisting African financial institution leaders to achieve more accountability, innovation and self-sustainability in their countries. From the position of leaders of African financial institutions, an academic study of this nature will generously provide guidelines for the design, implementation or revision of valuable leadership training and evaluation programs in their countries. By using financial institution employees for its subjects, this study will undoubtedly thoughtfully open the questionable door for future studies of organizational culture and leadership in Africa that will use employees of African financial institutions as information sources relative to a national and even continent-wide evaluation process. Leaders of African financial institutions and financial institution employees as well, can be empowered to facilitate this urgently needed evaluation process in Africa by utilizing with consistency a survey system that is deemed valid and non-threatening.

DISCUSSION QUESTIONS

1. What is organizational culture?
2. How does organizational culture effect a leader?
3. How can a leader overcome resistance to change?

CHAPTER 12
Business Opportunity And Practice In The Gambia

Abstract

This paper addresses the business opportunities and trade policies in The Gambia. The paper provides helpful information on investment policy, economy and trade, tourism, manufacturing and telecommunication. Furthermore, the main objective of this paper is centered on business opportunity and how business is conducted effectively and efficiently in The Gambia. This paper reveals that in order to succeed one has to value and respect how Gambians view appointments and the concept of time, decision-making, negotiation, business entertaining, greetings, gestures, gifts and dress.

Introduction

Brief History: The Gambia, which is located in West Africa, is a narrow strip of land tucked 300 miles east of the Atlantic Ocean. It is nestled inside Senegal along both banks of the River Gambia, which is about 15 to 30 miles wide. The Gambia's population is about 1.5 million people, with 95% of the natives of the Islamic faith and 5% of the Christian faith. The Gambia consists of five main ethnic groups: Mandingo, 42%; the Fula, or Fulani, make up 18% of the population; the Wolof, 16%; the Serahuli, 9%; and the Jola, 4% (CIA World Factbook, 2004). The minority ethnic groups in The Gambia, which make up 11% of the population, are the Manjako, the Karonika, and the Balanta.

Between the 8th and 11th centuries, the River Gambia was part of the vast trans-Saharan trade routes, which brought both visitors from the North and the subsequent influence of Islam. In 1455 the Portuguese, who were the first Europeans to see The Gambia, reached the River Gambia and sold exclusive trading rights along the river to some English merchants, which began English influence in the area (Oluyitan, 1995). The Europeans brought goods such as salt, ostrich feathers, iron, pots and pans, firearms and gunpowder. These goods were exchanged for ivory, ebony, beeswax, gold and slaves. For the Europeans, the slave trade, which operated legally from the 1500s until 1807, was its most "lucrative" area in The Gambia (Columbia Univ. Press, 2004). In 1820, Great Britain declared the River Gambia a British Protectorate, and for many years ruled it from Sierra Leone. In 1886, The Gambia officially became a crown colony, and in the following year, France and Britain drew the boundaries between Senegal, which at the time was a French colony, and The Gambia. As slavery ended, the British continued to rule in The Gambia while the French controlled the Senegal (Oluyitan, 1995). After abolishing slavery in 1906, the colonial administration's main concern was the collection of revenue for the British Crown (Oluyitan, 1995). The people of The Gambia would have no say in the affairs of their country for the next 59 years.

On February 18, 1965, The Gambia was one of many African countries to be granted independence from Europe. Since then, there have been two generally popular Presidents. The first, D'awda Jawara, ruled until the current President, Yahya Jammeh, overthrew him in 1994 (Columbia Univ. Press, 2004). Since 1994 President Jammeh has retired from the Army and been twice re-elected as a civilian in what seemed to be a fairly democratic vote. Most Gambians are very confident about Jammeh's regime. Agriculture is the backbone of The Gambia's economy exporting mainly groundnuts, groundnut oil, fish and cotton. Tourism is the second largest foreign exchange earner. Currently, there are about 225 primary and high schools in the country, one teacher's college, and the University of the Gambia, which was established in 1999, as the highest institution of learning (Columbia Univ., 2004).

Business Opportunities and Trade Policies in The Gambia

Investment Policy: As an investment haven, The Gambia's potential for growth and prosperity is enormous. The nation's current investment policy is based on the following six premises. First, The Gambia's goal is to become a liberal, free market financial environment together with the appropriate political and social policy framework. Second, it plans to adhere to the principles of democratic governance, constitutional guarantee of rights to freedom and liberty, welfare, property ownership and protection for its citizens (Department of State, 2004). Third, it aims for full incorporation into the wider global economy through membership of and adherence to charters and principles of the Economic Community of West African States, the World Trade Organization, the African Development Bank, and a multitude of bilateral trade agreements among others.

Fourth, The Gambia plans to implement policies, economic resources, and strategies to make it a trade and investment gateway to both the Western Africa sub-region and the greater African regional market. Fifth, The Gambia will create a conducive legal and institutional framework with labor laws that support and encourage collective bargaining in line with the stipulation of the Labor Act.[2] Finally, The Gambia will articulate a national resolve and commitment to transform itself into a middle-income country by the year 2020 (Department of State, 2004).

The Economy and Trade: The Gambia's current economy is characterized by agriculture, a historic reliance on peanuts for export earnings, a re-export trade built around its ocean port, low import duties, minimal administrative procedures, a fluctuating exchange rate of its Dalasi with no exchange controls, and a significant tourism industry. Agriculture accounts for 29% of gross domestic product (GDP) and employs 75% of the labor force. Within agriculture, peanut production accounts for 6.9% of GDP, other crops 8.3%, livestock 5.3%, fishing 1.8%, and forestry 0.5%. Industry accounts for 12% of GDP and forestry 0.5%. Manufacturing accounts for 5.5% of GDP. The limited amount of manufacturing is primarily agriculturally based (e.g., peanut processing, bakeries, a brewery, and a tannery). Other manufacturing activities include soap, soft drinks, and clothing. Services account for 19% of GDP. The U.K. and other EU nations constitute 86% of The Gambia's major domestic export markets, followed by Asia at 14%. The U.K. and the other EU countries—Germany, France, Netherlands, and Belgium—were the major source of imports accounting for 60% of the total share of imports followed by Asia at 23%, and Cote d'Ivoire and other African countries at 17%. The

---

2   The Labor Act of 1990 applies to all workers except civil servants. The Act specifies that workers are free to form associations, including trade unions, and provides for their registration with the Government. Source: U.S. Department of State (http://www.state.gov).

Gambia reports 11% of its exports going to and 14.6% of its imports coming from the United States.[3]

Trade and Industrial Growth Opportunities

Tourism: In recent years employment has been a focal point in discussions on the economic advantages of tourism. Much of the debate is that, arguably, tourism has the capacity to create more jobs than any other sector of the economy. Such capacity, which is characterized by a lack of development resources, is of special interest in the context of developing nations (Dieke, 1993). There are reasons to doubt whether this job-creating ability view can be sustained, particularly in relation to some of the characteristics of the tourism jobs created. The features include conditions of employment (e.g. long hours, seasonality, labor mobility), quality of jobs (e.g. low-skill, low status level), and the issue of foreign domination. Since 1965, when The Gambia became independent of Europe's regime, tourism has been promoted, first to diversify the economic base and, second, to overcome the problems noted above and, perhaps above all, assist in the country's general development process (Dieke, 1993). Hence Erbes' (1973) suggestion that tourism is "manna from heaven," which will solve all the economic difficulties of developing countries, in terms of positive contributions to foreign exchange earnings, government revenues, regional development stimuli, and the creation of employment and income (Dieke, 1993). Nonetheless, it needs to be addressed that, for reasons advanced by Jenkins and Henry (1982), governments in developing countries have played a decisive role in the development and growth of tourism. In The Gambia's case, the support for tourism has been mainly to encourage the supply of tourism assets, which has taken numerous forms—basic infrastructure provision, manpower-training programs, and tax incentives. Other measures include direct project aid, hotel investment and management, and perhaps protecting natural, historic and cultural attractions.

Manufacturing: A key factor an international firm faces is where to locate its manufacturing activities to achieve the goals of minimizing costs and improving product quality. The Gambia is no exception. Many factors—country and technological—must be taken into consideration (Cohen and Lee, 1989). In terms of country factors, The Gambia's manufacturing is affected by its fluctuating exchange rate of the Dalasi. Adverse changes in exchange rates can quickly alter the country's attractiveness as a manufacturing base

---

3   Ibid. (http://www.state.gov)

(Hill, 1999). A steadier Dalasi, one whose value is lower relative to stronger currencies, would make The Gambia a more attractive exporting country.

The value added from the Gambian manufacturing sector has remained virtually unchanged in the past decade. In recent times, inadequate electrical supplies, limited raw materials, and low levels of managerial and technical proficiency have plagued the manufacturing industry (EIU, 2003). Manufacturing technologies have a significant effect on its exporting efficiency. Some of the ways of improving the manufacturing sector in The Gambia are to reduce setup times for complex equipment, increase the utilization of individual machines through better scheduling, and improve quality control at all stages of the manufacturing process (Nemetz and Fry, 1988). Recent research suggests that the adoption of flexible manufacturing practices may increase efficiency and lower unit costs. Apart from groundnut processing and construction, the main industrial activities are brewing, tanning, baking, and the production of fruit juices, soaps and plastic containers (Economist Intelligence Unit, 2003). Though there is room for improvement in manufacturing, particularly in strengthening its training of the workforce, the scope for development is limited by the small size of the domestic market and the country's vulnerability to illegal imports due in part to its volatile exchange rate.

Telecommunications: Many developing countries, including African nations, have seen a sharp increase in mobile telephone subscriptions since the 1980s, while landline telephone subscriptions have seen slow growth (Hamilton, 2003). According to statistics gathered by the CIA World Fact Book (2004), the telecommunications sector can be viewed as a potentially untapped market in the Gambia. Out of a population of approximately 1.5 million, there are only 38,400 landline telephones currently in use, which accounts for 2% of the general population. Most African nations have cellular access, with many of them having at least two privately owned operators, a characteristic that is evident in many developing countries (Hamilton, 2003). As a fledging market, the Gambia can be seen as a growth opportunity for popular telecommunications giants as Verizon, Cingular Wireless, and Sprint. By establishing a foothold in the Gambia, these companies can create new job opportunities for thousands of people, which will only enhance the nation's growth.

Co-Alignment: The Basic
Administrative Function in The Gambia

In a living organization such as organism, which is simply a natural system, spontaneous processes such as natural selection handle change. In an artificial organization such as a computer, or any other machine, after it is designed and manufactured, it automatically adjusts to change, given the limitations of its design. In contrast, subtle complications which face complex social organizations in The Gambia call for something more than closed-logic solutions.

Organizational survival in the Gambia depends on the co-alignment of technology and task environment with a viable domain, and of organizational design and structure appropriate to that domain. Timing is a crucial administrative matter because as environments change, the administration must deal with not just domain but also, how and how fast to redesign the structure and technology of the organization, in other words, negotiate a revised set of operational rules. Thus like any other country in the world, globalization has challenged all African countries to change so all organizations that want to succeed in business in the Gambia must adapt to this changing process in other to compete in the global market. The configuration necessary for survival of any organization in the Gambia does not come from yielding to environmental pressures but rather, from finding the strategic variables, such as organizational culture, available to be manipulated in such a way that interaction with elements in the environment will result in a viable co-alignment.

The central task of the administrative process in any organization in the Gambia is the search for flexibility. To achieve flexibility, the administrative process is not something done at one level in the organization, but spans and links all levels. The administrative process does not simply flows down from one level to the next, but informs the interaction of all levels and units of the organization. Complex organizations in the Gambia must utilize organizational culture principles to accomplish this. Organizational culture is appropriate for this task because outcome preferences are specified by the institutional level of the organization, while specification of cause/effect relationships is provided by the managerial level which controls the kinds of resources inputs obtained and the kinds of interdependence reflected in organizational structure for survival. Organizational culture can provide the managerial level with what it needs to obtain commitments from the institutional level which permit technical achievement while at the same time, obtain commitments from the technical core which provide sufficient capacity and slack to permit administrative discretion and recommitment of resources when organizational change is demanded by the environment in an organization in the Gambia.

Business Practices in The Gambia

Appointments and the concept of time: According to anthropologist Edward T. Hall (1959), cultures can be classified into time orientation. Members of *monochromic* cultures, such as the United States and Switzerland, view time as a "straight line." This linear view of time sees the past as gone, the present is here for a brief time, and the future is almost upon us (Hall, 1959). In such cultures, time is measured minute by minute, creating time pressures for action and performance, which can inflict stress on employees. On the other hand, in *polychronic* cultures, such as the Gambia and China, people hold the view that time is cyclical, and goes around and around. Time does not create pressures for immediate action or performance (Hall, 1959). Accordingly, one will have another opportunity to pass the same way again. If an opportunity is lost today—no problem, it may return again tomorrow (Hall, 1959).

A leader, manager or a businessperson can schedule appointments two months prior to arriving in The Gambia. It is advisable to make appointments between 10:00 a.m. and 12:00 p.m. and between 2:30 p.m. to 3:30p.m, Monday through Thursday. Business hours in The Gambia are usually from 8:00 a.m. to 4:00 p.m., Monday through Thursday. Unlike Western nations where time is viewed as rigid, Gambians view time as flexible. In The Gambia, late appointments are common and usually anticipated, but telephone service is poor and unreliable. It is important to note that anyone in a hurry in The Gambia is viewed with suspicion and distrust. The favorable Gambian saying, "The Gambia, no problem" sums it all. It is not advisable to have meetings on Fridays because Friday is considered a half-day and offices close at 11:00 a.m. throughout the country. Business appointments are not expected to begin on time by the Gambians but those who call for the meeting are expected to be prompt. Gambians tend not to be reasonably punctual for business meetings except in the case when an important government official or religious leader has to be present. In The Gambia, most social events do not begin on time. It is considered impolite to arrive at a party at the exact time. Also, important guests are expected to arrive much later than the less important ones, with the time ranging from thirty minutes to three hours. In the case of a wedding, all guests are expected to arrive on time, with the exception of the bride. Nevertheless, you will still have some guests come late.

Decision-making: The term "two heads are better than one" is a common premise of group decision-making in many countries' organizations. This belief has lead to many decisions being made by groups as opposed to individuals. A number of factors must be considered in decision-making. There are several advantages to group decision-making. First, groups offer a greater pool of knowledge that brings more information and experiences into the decision-making process (Kreitner, 1998). Second, Groups offer increased diversity of views, which opens up the opportunity for more approaches and alternatives to be considered (Robbins, 2005). Finally, groups lead to increased acceptance of solutions. Group members who were initially involved in the decision making process are likely to support the decision, thus encouraging others to accept it (Kreitner, 1998). On the contrary, there are a few drawbacks to group decision-making. First, they are very time-consuming, since groups typically take more time to reach a decision that would be the case if an individual were solely making the decision (Robbins, 2005). Second, there is social pressure to be accepted by the group, which can have a harmful effect on creativity. Third, groups may be dominated by a few individuals, which can cause the overall quality of the group to suffer (Kreitner, 1998). Finally, there can be ambiguous responsibility within the group—no one knows who should be held accountable for the final outcome, since the responsibility of any single member is "watered down" (Robbins, 2005).

In formal organizations in The Gambia, decision-making is based on a centralized system. It is important to note that delegation of authority is nonexistent. Gambians cling to authority and depend on supervision and direction. In the workplace, innovation is rarely tapped from the employees. A Gambian leader or manager in a high-level position is likely to help find jobs for his or her family without hesitating to do whatever it takes to succeed in hiring them. Thus, if a Gambian is very powerful, there is nothing a foreign businessperson can do to stop nepotism practice. The decision-making process in The Gambia is profoundly based on familial responsibilities. This ideology can be frustrating for European and North American business representative, who view the work environment as an opportunity for advancement and promotion if one works hard.

Negotiating: The negotiation process is both an art and a science. As a science, it requires an analysis of relative bargaining strengths of all parties involved, the different strategic options available to each party, and assessing how the other party might respond to various bargaining ploys (Bazerman, 1991). As an art, the negotiation process incorporates interpersonal skills, the ability to convince and be convinced, the ability to employ many bargaining ploys, and most importantly, the wisdom to know both when and how to use them (Raiffe, 1982). In the context of international business, the art of negotiation also includes understanding the influence of national norms, value systems, and culture on approach and negotiating tactics of the other party as well as sensitivity to such factors in shaping a firm's approach to negotiations with foreign businesses (Raiffe, 1982).

In most African cultures, including The Gambia, greetings are both habitual and centered around family. For instance, when you get lost in The Gambia, do not start off by asking the locals for the direction. Instead, greet them and ask about their family. It is considered rude and disrespectful if you start by asking directions. If you do, you will get a response like "how are you and your family," and not the answer to your question. It is important to note that the pace of negotiation in The Gambia is much slower than in Europe and the United States. Relationship building is much more important, so it will be unrealistic to complete a complicated business deal in one trip. The Gambians are open to information, but they tend to process information by going back and discussing it with their family and the elders. The most important skill for successful relationship in The Gambia is politeness and respect for elders, for they are considered to have wisdom in the society.

Protocol

Culture is the learned and shared way of thinking and acting among a group of people or society. In terms of conducting business, many executives do not take the time to learn and understand the culture, proper protocol, or language, of another society before beginning negotiations. Part of this is the fact that many managers are unaware of two main types of cultures: low-context and high-context cultures. Members of low-context cultures, such as the United States, Australia, Switzerland, and Canada, are explicit in using the spoken and written word. In such cultures, the message is largely conveyed by the words someone uses, as opposed to the context in which they are spoken (Hall, 1976). In contrast, members of high-context cultures, such as The Gambia, Asian and Middle Eastern countries, use words to convey only a limited part of the message. The rest of the message must be inferred or interpreted from the context—body language, the physical setting, and past relationships—which add meaning to what is being said (Hall, 1976).

Greetings: A good, firm handshake can easily be interpreted in a negative way by Gambians as a means of showing how strong you are as compared to the natives. This can also be interpreted as being rude, especially when dealing with elders. When talking to an elder, you must look down as a sign of respect and dignity to him or her. Be gentle and humble when shaking hands with Gambians. If you are a male and you have a woman as your Gambian partner, do not extend your hand to her unless you know that she is not a Muslim but instead greet her and nod. However, female foreign businesswomen are expected to bow when their Gambian business partner is a male and a Muslim. If you do not, this could be considered impolite and a turnoff from your Gambian business partner. As a foreign businessperson, you are expected to address your partner in The Gambia with a title and their surname. In the event the person has no title, address him or her with English titles such as Mr., Mrs., or Miss, plus their surname. It is important to learn how to pronounce Gambian names to avoid offending your business partners.

Gestures: In The Gambia, gestures are part of the culture. For example, pointing a finger at someone is considered an insult and a curse. In the case of giving a direction, use all five fingers. It is important to note that staring directly into someone's face, especially an elder's, has many negative meanings in The Gambia. Thus, foreigners must avoid staring at someone's face at all times because it can be easily mistaken as rude, disrespectful behavior and lack of home training. A final point deals with when a person is trying to get through a crowd. In The Gambia as in many African cultures, it is considered rude to walk in between two or more people that are having a conversation. In order to avoid this problem, one must constantly look down while passing through a crowd. The most acceptable way is to go around them. As a sign of respect, always remember to extend your greetings to them.

Dress: Gambian businesspersons are expected to dress formally. Men and women are allowed to wear either traditional Gambian or Western dress. It is inappropriate for both men and women to wear shorts to work. The appropriate dress for women is a long-sleeved blouse and skirt of any color of your choice. The dress must be ironed, neat, clean, and presentable. Sometimes, Gambian men wear a business suit for formal occasions such as formal dinners, parties or dinner with the family. Foreigners are expected to dress in their own traditional formal dress. Foreigners are expected to dress conservatively. This is usually done to respect the hostess. It is important to note that organizations such as banks, government, and schools may require their employees to wear uniforms.

Social contacts: In The Gambia, social contacts are highly valued and important in meeting and establishing relationships with the Gambians. No matter what you do, *never* decline an invitation to a social event, especially if one expects to see his or her Gambian business partners. Remember, in The Gambia, building a successful business relationship depends on establishing a social relationship. Thus, the Gambians use social contact to feel more comfortable and safe with the foreign businessperson, whom natives view at the beginning as a colonizer until mutual trust is established. It is important to note that if you interrupt a Gambian during a meal, he or she will ask you to join in. Gambians love to share and will like for you to join them during a meal. Even if you are full, you can taste a little bit and tell them that you have already eaten. If you fail to accept the invitation, they will feel that you have rejected them. Usually, social events in The Gambia are in the form of singing and dancing. So one should be prepared to be invited to sing and dance.

Business Entertaining: The most important thing to note is that food is part of Gambian culture and all occasions or social contacts involve food. Therefore, it is a good idea to invite your Gambian partners to your house or restaurant to celebrate the conclusion of a business deal. It is customary for the person who gives the invitation to pay for the meal, unless it was a woman. Traditionally, the man pays for the woman when they go to a restaurant, and at home the woman cooks the meal. Always remember to allow your host to order the food when invited to a restaurant, and at home expect to be served. If you have a partner or spouse, and children, you are expected to invite them. Just remember to show great appreciation and thanks afterwards. For the case of accepting an invitation to someone's home, be mindful to taste all the food prepared. At a Gambian home, show great respect for elders because you are expected to behave in this way. Gambians consider inviting their partners to their home to be a great honor. When you are invited at a Gambian home, do not be too eager to begin eating or asking what is for dinner, lunch or party otherwise this could be interpreted as greedy and rude.

Gifts: Gifts are another important part of the tradition and Gambian cultural practice. Never bring a gift when someone invites you to his or her family. Also, do not bring alcohol, especially if the family is Muslim or Christian. For that reason, alcohol is not served during meals but instead after meals. There is no drinking age in The Gambia, and children are allowed to drink.

Adults are not allowed to get drunk in the presence of their children. When you are invited to someone's home and you bring gifts, it is interpreted as the hostess not serving enough food for her guests. It is a tradition and expected in The Gambia to give their guests extra food to take home. Hence, always remember to accept some food to take home. During any special holiday, such as Christmas, you are expected to throw a party for your employees as a token of appreciation.

Conclusion

To conduct business effectively in The Gambia, one has to understand the business protocol and practices. By understanding the business practices, one will begin to find ways in which he or she can be an effective and efficient businessperson in The Gambia. In order for one to be successful in conducting business in The Gambia, he or she should conduct advanced research on the political and economic structure of the country in order to find ways to see whether they can deal with the government's rules and regulations in doing business in The Gambia. Another important factor is to have the ability to value and respect both the Gambia culture and their way of life.

DISCUSSION QUESTIONS

1. If you were to invest in the Gambia, what business will you invest in? Why? Discuss your answers.

2. How are business conducted in The Gambia? Discuss your answers.

3. Why is decision-making in formal organizations in the Gambia based on centralized system? Discuss your answers.

CHAPTER 13
Comparative Country Analysis: Ghana, The Gambia and Kenya

ABSTRACT

In this paper, I will be comparing and contrasting the countries of Ghana, The Gambia, and Kenya. The background of each country will be given in which key moments in history, education, language, religion and social stratification systems will be covered. I will also be investigating various areas of each country's economy, business, and political systems. Once those areas are examined, I will determine which country is best to do business in as a domestically-owned company and also as a foreign-owned country.

COUNTRY BACKGROUND – GHANA

History

For most of Africa below the Sahara, but north of the tropical jungles, the development up to 500 A.D. was expanding agriculture. Well-organized villages arose; many were similar to the villages that exist today. Farming began earliest on the southern tips of the Sahara. Toward the end of the classical era, important regional kingdoms were forming in West Africa, which lead to the first great state - Ghana. Ghana faced challenges such as dense vegetation, disease's impact on domesticated animals, and slow spread of agriculture southward. But the strength of the agricultural economy would have an impact on the new kingdoms to the west of the Nile. Trade brought new crops from Southeast Asia near 100 A.D. At one point Ghana was part of Nigeria the Twi tribe was located in what is now known as Benin in Nigeria, due to war they migrated to Ghana were they found resources. Formed from the merger of the British colony Gold Coast and the British Togoland trust territory by a UN Sponsored plebiscite, Ghana in 1957 became the first sub-Saharan country in colonial Africa to gain its independence.

Kwame Nkrumah was an African anti-colonial leader, founder and first president of the modern Ghanaian state. He was the 1st African head of state in the Pan-African Movement, which was an idea he appropriated during his studies at Lincoln University in the United States, at the time when Marcus Garvey was becoming famous for his "Back to Africa Movement". Nkrumah was overthrown by a CIA-assisted coup. A series of subsequent coups ended with the ascension to power of Flight Lieutenant Jerry Rawlings in 1981. His changes resulted in the suspension of the constitution in 1981 and the banning of political parties. A new constitution, restoring multiparty politics, was approved in 1992, and Rawlings was elected in free elections of that year and also in 1996. The constitution prohibited him from running for a third term. John Kufuor, the current president, is now in his second term. 2007 will mark Ghana's Golden Jubilee celebration of 50 years of independence. The population of Ghana in 2006 was 22,409,572, giving the country a population density of 97 persons per sq km (252 per sq mi). Life expectancy at birth is estimated at 58.9 years, one of the highest rates in sub-Saharan Africa. With a birth rate of 30.52 per 1,000 and a death rate of 9.72 per 1,000, the country's population growth rate is 2.07 percent (2006 estimate). While this current rate of increase is moderate compared with other West

African nations, Ghana's population almost tripled from 1960 to 2000. The rapid rise in the population reflects the advances made in the provision of medical and sanitation services in the country and has resulted in a youthful population. Family planning programs have helped reduce the nation's birth rate. Despite migrations to Ghana's urban centers, 54 percent (1998) of the population resides in rural communities. Most rural Ghanaians are farmers, herders, or fishers. In the cities, most people work in the service sector or in manufacturing.(Apt, 1996) The country's major cities are Accra, the national capital; Kumasi, the principal city of the Ashanti region; Tema, an industrial city and Ghana's major port; Sekondi and Takoradi, the coastal twin cities; Tamale, a northern trade center; and the college town of Cape Coast. LANGUAGE Over 100 linguistic and ethnic groups have been identified in Ghana, and these groups have maintained a sense of ethnic identity. However, the population is classified into two major linguistic families: the Kwa and the Gur. (Apt, 1996) The Kwa speakers, traditionally associated with the area south of the Volta, make up about 75 percent of the population.

The major Kwa linguistic subgroup is the Akan speakers, who are further subdivided into the Ashanti, Bono, Fante, Akuapem, Akyem, and Kwahu, among others. The Ashanti and Akuapem peoples speak similar Akan dialects, collectively known as Twi. Other Kwa linguistic groups include the Nzima, Ga, Gonja, Adangbe, and Ewe. Members of the Gur linguistic family live mainly in the northern regions of the country. The principal Gur language is Dagbane, and the major Gur ethnic groups are the Dagomba and Mamprusi peoples. Due to the similarities in the various dialects and to the increasing mobility of the population, a typical Ghanaian understands at least one of five major languages—Akan, Nzima, Dagbane, Ga, or Ewe—as well as English, which is the official language of the country.

Education

Christian missionaries introduced Western-style education to Ghana in the 18th century. Although some schools are still affiliated with religious groups, the state is now the main provider of education. In 1996, 20 percent of the national budget was spent on education.

Primary education is free and compulsory. In 2002–2003, 79 percent of primary school-aged children attended primary school. Attendance at the secondary school level was 39 percent and 3 percent at the university level. A greater percentage of boys attended school than girls, the gap widening above the primary school level. However, the disparity in attendance by gender was not due to any state policy. Ghana's educational system is open to all. The adult literacy rate in 2005 was recorded at 76.9 percent, with male literacy at 84.3 and female literacy at 69.8. The University of Ghana, at Legon (near Accra), was Ghana's first university, established in 1948. There are three other universities in the country, located at Cape Coast, Kumasi, and Tamale, and numerous teacher, training colleges and vocational institutions.

Religion

An estimated 69% of the population belonged to various Christian denominations, 16% were Muslims (though Muslim leaders claim the number is closer to 30%), and about 9% of the population practices other religions, including the Baha'i Faith, Buddhism, Judaism, Hinduism, Shintoism, Ninchiren Shoshu Soka Gakkai, Sri Sathya Sai Baba Sera, Sat Sang, Eckanker, the Divine Light Mission, Hare Krishna, Rastafarianism, and indigenous religions.

Christian denominations include Catholics, three branches of Methodists, Anglicans, ennonites, two branches of Presbyterians, Lutherans, the Church of Jesus Christ of Latter-Day Saints, Seventh-Day Adventists, Pentecostals, Baptists, and Society of Friends. Some Christians also include elements of indigenous religions in their own practices. There are three primary branches of Islam within the country: Ahlussuna, Tijanis, and Ahmadis. A small number of Muslims are Shi'a. Zetahil, a religion that is unique to Ghana, combines elements of both Islam and Christianity. The indigenous religions generally involve a belief in a supreme being along with lesser gods. Veneration of ancestors is also common. The Afrikan Renaissance Mission, also known as Afrikania, is an organization which actively supports recognition and practice of these traditional religions.

In many areas of the country, there is still a strong belief in witchcraft. Those suspected of being witches (usually older women) have been beaten or lynched and occasionally banished to "witch camps," which are small villages in the north primarily populated by suspected witches. The law does provide protected for alleged witches and incidents of banishment and violence against supposed offenders seems to be decreasing. Although there is no state religion, attendance at assemblies or devotional services is required in public schools, with a service that is generally Christian in nature. However, this requirement is not always enforced.

Way of Life

Ghana has long been exposed to outside influences on its society and culture. To some extent, Islam shapes the society of the north while Christianity is strong in the south. Despite the influence of these world religions, however, much of Ghanaian society continues to be traditional. Most people recognize the place of traditional practices. For example, they grant local chiefs customary rights to preside over their communities, and the young respect parents and their elders. An extended family's elders arbitrate the inheritance of the family's land, possessions, and social status. (Apt, 1996) Polygamy (the practice of having more than one wife) is legal, but as the literacy rate has risen, Ghanaians have increasingly chosen monogamy (the practice of having only one wife) as the preferred marital relation. A number of women's organizations and lobby groups were established in the 1990s. Women are not prohibited from holding public offices nor are they paid less for equal work done. Most Ghanaians throughout the country wear Western attire. Traditional clothing, which is worn usually at local ceremonies and dances, varies among ethnic groups, often taking the form of smocks for men and wraparound dresses for women.

COUNTRY BACKGROUND – THE GAMBIA

History

The first written accounts of the region come from records of Arab traders in the ninth and tenth centuries AD. In 1066, the inhabitants of Tekrur, a kingdom centered on the Sénégal River just to the north, became the first people in the region to convert to Islam. Muslim traders established the trans-Saharan trade route for slaves, gold, and ivory. At the beginning of the fourteenth century, most of what is today called The Gambia was a tributary to the Mali Empire. The Portuguese reached the area by sea in the mid-fifteenth century and began to dominate the lucrative trade.

In 1588, the claimant to the Portuguese throne, António, Prior of Crato, sold exclusive trade rights on the Gambia River to English merchants; this grant was confirmed by letters patent from Queen Elizabeth I. In 1618, James I granted a charter to a British company for trade with Gambia and the Gold Coast (now Ghana). Between 1651 and 1661, part of Gambia was (indirectly) a colony of the Polish-Lithuanian Commonwealth; it was purchased by the Courlandish prince Jakub Kettler. At that time Courland, in presentday Latvia, was a fiefdom of the Polish-Lithuanian Commonwealth. The Courlanders settled on James Island, which they called St. Andrews Island, and used it as a trade base from 1651 until it was captured by the English in 1661.

During the late seventeenth century and throughout the eighteenth, England and France struggled continually for political and commercial supremacy in the regions of the Senegal and Gambia rivers. The 1783 Treaty of Versailles gave Great Britain possession of the Gambia River, but the French retained a tiny enclave at Albreda on its north bank, which was ceded to the United Kingdom in 1857. As many as three million slaves may have been taken from the region during the three centuries of the transatlantic slave trade. In 1807, slave trading was abolished throughout the British Empire, and the British tried unsuccessfully to end the practice in Gambia. They established the military for return to democratic civilian government.

After World War II (1939-1945) Britain belatedly began to develop The Gambia and to train some Africans for administrative posts. Political parties were formed and in 1960 nationwide elections were held for members of the territory's legislative council. In the 1962 election the People's Progressive Party (PPP) gained a substantial majority, and its leader, Dawda Jawara, became the first prime minister. The Gambia became independent on February 18, 1965, with Jawara as prime minister. In a 1970 national referendum Gambians voted to form a republic, and Jawara was elected president. He and his PPP won the 1972 and 1977 elections. In 1981 a coup attempt was crushed while Jawara was visiting the United Kingdom. The coup failed because troops from Senegal intervened under a mutual defense pact, but about 1,000 people died in the conflict. A consequence of Senegal's aid in putting down the coup was the creation in 1982 of a confederation with Senegal, Senegambia, with President Abdou Diouf of Senegal as president and Jawara as vice president. The confederation resulted in closer economic cooperation, but never supplanted the political systems of the two nations and never won the full approval of Gambians. Jawara retained the presidency of The Gambia in the elections of 1982 and 1987, and the confederation with Senegal collapsed in 1989. Despite accusations of corruption and misrule, Jawara was reelected as president of The Gambia in 1992. The Gambia began to develop its own armed forces for the first time after the 1981 coup attempt, and in the early 1990s the young officers of this force grew impatient with their meager pay and with government corruption. A bloodless coup on July 22, 1994, forced Jawara into exile and led to the proclamation of Lieutenant (later Colonel) Yahya Jammeh as president. European countries and the United States objected to these maneuvers and pressed the military regime to restore democracy.

For two years the government banned political activity and prosecuted cases of official corruption. Under international pressure to hold democratic elections, Jammeh oversaw the promulgation of a new constitution that virtually guaranteed him victory in September 1996 presidential elections through candidate age limits and financial restrictions on political parties. Jammeh disbanded the Provisional Ruling Council, retired from the army, declared himself a candidate for president, and restored political activity while prohibiting three major political parties (including the PPP) from participating in the elections.

A number of countries that had provided aid to The Gambia cut off their funds after the 1994 coup. Jammeh won the 1996 elections, which were widely criticized for their unfairness. Jammeh was reelected president in October 2001. This time international observers called the elections largely free and fair. As aresult, the United States lifted sanctions it had imposed on The Gambia following the coup by Jammeh.

The return to democratic elections allowed The Gambia to again attract foreign aid, investment, and tourists. The president was praised in many quarters for improving the country's infrastructure including initiating the building of many more roads, schools, and hospitals. However, a repressive new media law introduced in 2002 led to the jailing of a number of journalists accused of libel and sedition. A prominent critic of the law, the newspaper editor Deyda Hydara, was shot dead in mysterious circumstances in 2004. Prior to 2006's presidential election the opposition candidates objected to the ruling party registering voters from outside the country. Nevertheless, in September 2006 Jammeh won a third presidential term when securing more than 67 percent of the popular vote, despite a lower turnout than in 2001. The election was described as broadly fair by international observers.

Population

The population of The Gambia (2006 estimate) is 1,641,564, making it one of the least populous countries of Africa. Still, the country has a fairly high overall population density of 164 persons per sq km (425 per sq mi), and the population is increasing at a rate of 2.8 percent a year. Banjul, formerly called Bathurst, is the capital and only seaport. The largest city is Serrekunda, a transportation hub and commercial center.

Language

In the early colonial period, education was in the colonial home language: Portuguese, Dutch, Danish or English. Christian missionaries then introduced education in the indigenous languages, and often developed a writing system to support this.

The British colonial administration took over the education system of the Gold Coast in 1925. From 1925 to 1951 the first three years of primary education were in a Ghanaian language, followed by education in English. In 1957 the colony gained independence as Ghana. The policy for the medium of instruction was varied several times in the following years, and then from 1974 to 2002 it reverted to the pattern of a Ghanaian language for the first three years followed by English. Since September 2002, the policy is for English to be used from the start of primary education, with a Ghanaian language studied as a compulsory subject up to senior secondary school level.

Education

Primary education in The Gambia is free but not compulsory. In the 2000 school year 156,800 children were enrolled in primary school (85 percent of this age group), while 56,200 were enrolled in a secondary school (34 percent of secondary school-aged children). The country's institutions of higher education include The Gambia College, in Bríkama, and several technical and training schools.

Religion

Islam, which was introduced in the 12th century, is followed by about 90%. The main Muslim branches are Tijaniyah, Qadiriyah, Muridiyah, and Ahmadiyah. Christians (9%), mostly Roman Catholics, are concentrated in the Banjul area. Protestant denominations include Anglicans, Methodists, Baptists, Seventh-Day Adventists, and Jehovah's Witnesses, along with other small evangelical groups. Some Gambians also practice traditional indigenous religions (1%). Certain Muslim and Christian holidays are officially observed.

Way of Life

A variety of ethnic groups live side by side in The Gambia while preserving individual languages and traditions. The main ethnic groups are the Mandinka (also known as Mandingo or Malinke), Fula, and Wolof. The Mandinka, the largest ethnic group, make up more than 40 percent of the country's inhabitants. The Fula (Fulani), about 18 percent of Gambians, predominate in the eastern part of the country. The Wolof, about 16 percent of the people, live mainly in Banjul and the western region. Smaller groups include the Jola, who live in the western region, and the Serahuli, whose rulers introduced Islam into the region in the 12th century. There is also a small Creole community, the Aku, who are descended from liberated slaves and from European traders who married African women. Most of The Gambia's people live in rural areas. In 2003, 26 percent of the population lived in urban areas.

COUNTRY BACKGROUND – KENYA

Inland Kenya

In the Kenya highlands, communities that produced their own food by farming and domestication of animals had taken up residence by the end of the second millennium BC. Because of the tools they used, these people—who probably came from the highlands of Ethiopia—are known as the Stone Bowl people. It was not until the last few centuries of the pre-Christian era that other food-producing and iron-working peoples began to take up residence in Kenya. These were the ancestors of the Bantu- and Nilotic-speaking groups of modern Kenya.

Bantu-speaking peoples entered Kenya from the west and south, eventually settling east of Lake Victoria, where they occupied land on the coast and in the eastern highlands. The earliest Nilotic-speaking people, ancestors of today's Highlands Nilotic speakers, entered Kenya from the northwest to take up residence in the highlands west of the Eastern Rift Valley. Later, ancestors of the Plains Nilotic speakers followed, moving into the Rift Valley and the plains to the east. Later still, ancestors of the River-Lake Nilotic speakers moved into the lower-lying regions around Lake Victoria.

Eastern Cushitic speakers ancestral to the Oromo moved into northern Kenya from lands to the northeast and were followed by Cushitic-speaking Somali. This process of migration occurred through small population movements and interactions and stretched over a period of centuries. From this process emerged the various social formations that existed in Kenya at the beginning of colonial rule in the late 19th century ad.

These groupings were fluid, representing a process of ongoing social change. For example, in the 17th century the ancestors of the Bantu-speaking Kikuyu settled in the forested hills and ridges south and west of Mount Kenya; as they did so, they borrowed customs from some peoples, absorbed other peoples, and competed with various groups for resources. Most of Kenya's people combined livestock raising with agriculture, although some, like the Nilotic-speaking Masai, were nomadic herders. Unlike nearby regions such as Ethiopia and Uganda, Kenya did not experience the emergence of large, centralized states or empires.

Coastal Kenya

The Kenyan coast developed differently from the interior due to its exposure to the Indian Ocean sphere of exploration and trade. Over the course of the first millennium, a separate Bantu language and culture, which came to be known as Swahili, developed along the East African coast. This development was strongly influenced by contact with Arabs from the Persian Gulf, who traded, settled, and intermarried with the coastal Africans. By the 9th century the Swahili-speaking people had established a number of towns between present-day Somalia and Mozambique, including Mombasa, Lamu, and Pate in what is now Kenya. These towns became important trade centers, facilitating commerce between residents of the Kenyan interior and seafaring traders from Arabia, Persia, India, and elsewhere on the Indian Ocean. The main exports from these Swahili towns were ivory, slaves, and timber and other raw materials.

By the 12th century many of the Swahili, inhabitants of the towns had adopted Islam. Some towns, such as Mombasa, grew wealthy, gaining control of coastal and inland territory and developing into city-states. A number of these Swahili city-states dotted the Kenyan coast by the time the Portuguese arrived at the start of the 16th century. After Portuguese explorer Vasco da Gama successfully sailed around Africa to India and back between 1497 and 1499, the Portuguese began actively exploring the Indian Ocean coast. At first the Portuguese were interested in dominating trade on the seas rather than controlling mainland territory in East Africa. At the end of the 16th century, however, the Portuguese constructed Fort Jesus, a massive fortress at Mombasa, in order to exercise greater control ashore. Portuguese dominance did not last long, as the Portuguese faced competition from the Arab dynastic state in Oman, which also sought to control much of the East African coast. The Swahili states, together with the Omani Arabs, succeeded in driving the Portuguese from Kenya's coast by the end of the 17th century. The Swahili states resisted Omani attempts to control the coast, but by the 1840s the Omanis had established dominance. Commerce expanded as trade in African slaves boomed.

Omani rule over the area brought further Arabic influence to Swahili language and culture. In the 19th century the East African coast also experienced greater contact with Europe, in the form of commerce and attempts by Britain to stamp out the African slave trade. British influence in the region grew, culminating in Britain's halting of the slave trade in the late 1800s and its takeover of Kenya at the end of the century.

British Colonization

In 1886 and 1890 Britain reached agreements with Germany that delineated a boundary between British territory in Kenya and German territory in Tanganyika (part of present-day Tanzania) to the south. The Imperial British East Africa Company was chartered in 1888 to administer Kenya, but the company soon found itself losing large amounts of money through its vain attempts to extend control over the interior. In 1895 the British government formally took over the territory, which was renamed the East Africa Protectorate. Its western neighbor was Britain's Uganda Protectorate, and the border between the two lay just west of the site that would become, in the late 1890s, the new city of Nairobi. Although the boundaries of the British protectorate were set, the British actually controlled little more than the Kenyan coast at the beginning of the 20th century. The British conquest of the Kenyan interior was gradual and incremental, taking second place to Britain's construction of a railway connecting Mombasa with Lake Victoria.

The railway was completed in 1901. In 1902 Britain decided to merge Uganda's Eastern Province with the East Africa Protectorate; thus the Lake Victoria basin and the western highlands became part of Kenya. By 1908 the British administration had brought the southern half of present-day Kenya under its control. Northern Kenya, then inhabited largely by nomadic peoples, did not come under British authority until well after World War I (1914-1918). (Ahluwalia, 1996) In their colonial conquest, the British followed a policy of divide and conquer, allying with some African groups against others. The Masai, who had suffered a series of 19th-century civil wars over water and grazing rights and had lost much of their livestock to disease and drought, were one group with whom the British allied in order to impose their rule. To aid colonial administration, the British divided Kenya's Bantu-, Nilotic-, and Cushitic-speaking peoples into ethnic classifications based on linguistic variations and locality. Thus, specific ethnic subgroups, called "tribes," were created in a form that had not existed previously.

The ethnic groups were assigned to live in separate areas of the colony. Within each subgroup, colonial administrators designated one "chief," who became responsible for collecting taxes levied by the colonial state. To help make the new railway profitable, the colonial government encouraged the settlement of European farmers in Kenya. After 1902 white Europeans (mostly from Britain and South Africa) took up residence in the highlands. Land for European settlement meant the loss of land for some of Kenya's peoples, most notably the highland-dwelling Kikuyu.

Many of the Kikuyu who lost land were forced to move onto European farms and estates as squatters and laborers, or to seek employment in urban areas such as Nairobi. By the time World War I ended in 1918, European settlers, desiring inexpensive farm labor, had convinced the colonial government to adopt measures that essentially forced Africans to work the farms. These included new, higher taxes on Africans, who, lacking money, were obligated to work the settlers' farms in order to pay them. By this time, the settlers had achieved considerable political influence in the territory, which was changed to a colony and renamed Kenya in 1920. The colony of Kenya was administered by a British Governor, who was advised by an elected Legislative Council. Black Africans were not allowed to vote and were denied representation in the council until the mid-1940s, when a small number of blacks were nominated to the council. The colony's small Asian and Arab populations were given several seats in the council in the 1920s. (Ahluwalia, 1996).

African Opposition to the British

Following World War I, protests against settler supremacy and the policies of the colonial government emerged among Kenyan Africans. Much of the opposition during this period came from educated Kenyans who objected to the government's high taxes, labor-control policies, and a general lack of opportunities. One of the first opposition movements to emerge was the East African Association, which was banned by colonial authorities in 1922.

In the 1920s and 1930s African protests focused on local issues and remained within the boundaries of the ethnic units recognized by colonial rule. (Ahluwalia, 1996) The Kikuyu Central Association (KCA), formed in 1924, began advocating the return of land lost to European settlement, the importance of Kikuyu cultural values, and improvement in the lot of its middle-class leadership. One of the leaders of the KCA was Jomo Kenyatta. During this period, the KCA and similar organizations in other parts of Kenya sought not the removal of colonial rule but rather improvement within it. After World War II (1939-1945), opposition increasingly took the form of nationalism, with African activists demanding self-government and independence.

A colony-wide political party, the Kenya African Union (KAU), was formed in 1944 to advocate this goal. Kenyatta became the leader of the party in 1947. KAU made little headway with its demands, however, as European settlers still enjoyed far greater influence than Africans within the colonial government. (Ahluwalia, 1996) In these postwar years, economic and political discontent mounted, particularly among the Kikuyu. Some outbreaks of violence occurred in 1951, and the following year a secret Kikuyu guerrilla organization known as Mau Mau began a campaign of violence against

Europeans. In October 1952 the colonial government declared a state of emergency and arrested Kenyatta, charging him with managing Mau Mau. Kenyatta's arrest and later conviction and imprisonment, and the banning of KAU in 1953, spurred on the Mau Mau rebellion, in which thousands of Africans—the majority of whom were Kikuyu—fought a guerrilla war against colonial rule and settler supremacy.

The rebellion proved also to be a Kikuyu civil war: Those who fought against British rule were drawn from the poorest segment of Kikuyu society, while wealthier Kikuyu, who had profited from colonial rule, fought against the rebels. After four years of fighting and thousands of deaths (mostly of Africans), the British finally suppressed the rebellion in 1956. Although the British moved to provide greater economic, educational, and political opportunities for Africans, African nationalism continued to intensify and to spread among all of Kenya's ethnic groups. In 1960 and 1961 the British rapidly took steps to end settler supremacy and establish independence for Kenya with African majority rule. Colony-wide political parties were formed, and when Kenyatta was freed from detention in 1961 he became the leader of the newly formed dominant party, the Kenya African National Union (KANU). KANU was supported by the Kikuyu and the Luo, Kenya's two largest ethnic groups at the time. In pre-independence elections held in May 1963, Kenyatta led KANU to victory over its main rival, the Kenya African Democratic Union (KADU), which was supported by a number of smaller ethnic groups.

Kenyatta became prime minister in June, and in December Kenya became an independent nation.

Kenya Under Kenyatta

As an independent country, Kenya was initially a constitutional monarchy, with the British monarch as its nominal head of state and a prime minister as head of government. In December 1964, however, Kenya became a republic with a president as both head of state and head of government. Kenyatta was chosen as the country's first president. By this time KADU had dissolved, and its members had joined KANU. The Kenyatta era, which lasted until 1978, was a period of considerable social change and economic growth for Kenya.

Kenyatta appointed members of many different ethnic groups to government positions and encouraged the people of Kenya to come together as Kenyans, rather than focus on their different ethnic alignments. Many whites had left the country when Kenya became independent, and Kenyatta divided their land among blacks. These Kenyans were encouraged to grow export crops such as coffee and tea on their new land. Aided by a steady flow of foreign investment, largely from Britain, Kenya's economy flourished.

The standard of living rose for most Kenyans, and the nation's economy became one of the fastest growing in post-colonial Africa. However, Kenyatta's capitalist economic policies and pro-Western orientation provoked division within KANU. Kenya's vice president, an ethnic Luo named Oginga Odinga, resigned from the government in 1966 and formed the Kenya People's Union (KPU), which drew a great deal of Luo support away from KANU and presented the Kenyatta government with a challenge. In 1969 Tom Mboya, an influential Luo cabinet minister, was assassinated, resulting in a further loss of Luo support for the government. Kenyatta surmounted these challenges through the use of state power: detaining opponents without trial, banning the KPU, and filling government positions with supporters. Kenyatta made appeals for ethnic solidarity among Kikuyu, and many Kikuyu achieved influence and considerable wealth under his rule. However, the president resisted attempts by Kikuyu to remove his vice president, an ethnic Kalenjin named Daniel arap Moi, from the position of successor.

Moi's Rule

Kenyatta died in 1978, and Moi assumed the presidency of Kenya. He took the Swahili word nyayo (meaning "footsteps") as his leadership motto to assure Kenyans that he was following the legacy of Kenyatta. At first, Moi adopted a populist approach, releasing political prisoners, moving to limit Kikuyu political and economic influence, and traveling among the nation's people. In the 1980s, however, Kenya's economic growth began to slow, and Moi's rule became increasingly authoritarian. In 1982 the Moi government altered the constitution to make Kenya officially a one-party state. That year Moi survived a coup attempt by air force personnel. Beginning in the 1980s, Kenya experienced several debilitating droughts and the price of coffee dropped several times.

These factors damaged the Kenyan economy; the nation fell into debt, and unemployment rose dramatically. Fueled by economic discontent, strong pressure for reform of the political system and an end to Moi's rule emerged from many sectors of Kenyan society by the end of the 1980s. Moi resisted the calls for reform, but his government came under pressure from foreign economic donors, such as the World Bank and the United States, to implement political and economic reforms. Meanwhile, in the early 1990s violent ethnic clashes rocked Kenya's Rift Valley Province, as Kalenjin people attacked Kikuyu living in traditionally Kalenjin areas. Moi finally bowed to domestic and international pressures in December 1991 and agreed to legalize other political parties. Multiparty legislative and presidential elections were held in December 1992, but the opposition to KANU split along ethnic lines; Moi was reelected in the presidential race, and KANU won the majority of seats in the assembly.

Continuing economic difficulties and calls for further reform marked Moi's new term. His administration also was accused of corruption and overspending, particularly through it's favoring of development projects in Kalenjin-dominated areas that supported him. Before the elections of 1997, opposition parties held demonstrations calling for electoral reform, and further ethnic clashes occurred. In late 1997 Moi consented to the repeal of repressive anti-opposition laws that had existed since colonial times. However, opposition to Moi's rule remained divided, and he was reelected president in December.

Recent Developments

The Kenyan economy continued to decline into the 21st century and opposition to Moi and KANU mounted. Constitutionally prohibited from seeking another term, Moi handpicked KANU's candidate to succeed him. Expressing fears that Moi would manipulate the next KANU president behind the scenes, several major opposition parties joined forces to form the National Rainbow Coalition (NARC), led by former vice president Mwai Kibaki. NARC and Kibaki swept the December 2002 elections with more than 60 percent of the vote.

Kibaki was sworn in as president of Kenya in late December, ending four decades of KANU rule. Kibaki pledged to curb corruption in the government and civil service and in 2003 established a new anticorruption senior official. However, the government's commitment to the effort was questioned. After making little progress, the anti-corruption official resigned in 2005, sparking criticism of the Kenyan government from the international economic community.

Population

Kenya's population at the time of the 1999 census was 28,686,607. In 2006 the population was estimated at 34,707,817. Kenya experienced very high population growth rates in the 1970s and 1980s, but by 2006 the rate of increase had declined to 2.6 percent. In 2006 Kenya's birth rate was estimated at 40 per 1,000 and its death rate at 14 per 1,000. The average life expectancy at birth in Kenya is 49 years. The low life expectancy and years of high birth rates have combined to give Kenya a young population: 43 percent of the people were younger than age 15 in 2006. Some 61 percent of Kenya's population lives in rural areas most concentrated in the fertile southern half of the country.

The country's largest cites are Nairobi, the capital and chief manufacturing center; Mombasa, the nation's principal seaport; and Kisumu, the chief port on Lake Victoria. Smaller cities include Nakuru, a commercial and manufacturing center in the Eastern Rift Valley; and Eldoret, an industrial center in western Kenya.

Language

Kenya's official languages are English and Swahili; both are widely used for communication between members of different ethnic groups. Nearly all of the African ethnic groups in Kenya also have their own languages, making for considerable linguistic diversity within the country. Many Kenyans thus speak three languages: the language of their particular ethnic group, Swahili, and English.

Education

Kenya's educational system, established in the 1980s to replace the system that existed under British rule, consists of eight years of primary school, four years of secondary school, and four years of higher education. Schooling is compulsory for 8 years. Primary education is nominally free in Kenya, but pupils must meet the cost of uniforms, books, supplies, and school-related fees. Examinations taken at the end of the 8th and 12th grades determine whether students will be admitted into high school and university.

Although 92 percent of school-age children attend the first years of primary school, factors such as cost, examination performance, and inadequate facilities eliminate large numbers from secondary and university education. Kenya has made great progress with adult literacy since independence. In 2005, 87 percent of the adult population was literate, although the rate was significantly higher for adult males (92 percent) than females (82 percent). Kenya has a number of public and private universities. The major public universities are the University of Nairobi (founded in 1956); Kenyatta University (1972), in Nairobi; the Jomo Kenyatta University of Agriculture and Technology (1981), near Nairobi; Egerton University (1939), near Nakuru; and Moi University (1984), outside Eldoret. The government also provides opportunities for higher education through several polytechnic institutes and teacher-training colleges.

Religion

An estimated 66% of the population is Christian with about 28% belonging to the Roman Catholic Church and 38% belonging to Protestant churches. About 10% to 20% are Muslim, with many living in the Northeast Province, the Coast Province, and the northern region of the Eastern Province. About 1% is Hindu and the remainder practice traditional religions or local branches of Christianity. As in other African states with complex religious histories and some renewal of cultural self-consciousness, it is likely that a majority of ethnic Kenyans also hold some traditional African beliefs.

Way of Life

Most Kenyans place great importance on the family and the traditional values and responsibilities associated with it. Kenyan families tend to be large, and households often include many members of the extended family. Polygamy (the practice of having multiple wives) exists to some extent among all social classes and ethnic groups. Many of Kenya's rural inhabitants live on small farms; some live in houses made of mud and wooden poles with thatched roofs, while others live in houses of brick or stone with metal roofs. A small number are nomadic livestock herders, notably some of the Masai people in the south and the Turkana in the north.

City dwellers that are wealthy or middle class typically live in modern houses and apartment buildings; however, many other city dwellers live in shantytowns or other inexpensive quarters. Kenya's most popular sport is soccer, and Kenyan runners have gained worldwide renown. Many Kenyans occupy leisure time with traditional music and dance. The overwhelming majority of the Kenyan people dress in Western-style clothing; however, some rural Kenyans wear traditional vibrantly colored or patterned garb, such as the single piece of cloth—often bright red in color—worn by the Masai.

Social Issues

The social structure that evolved in Kenya during colonial times emphasized race and class. The dominance of whites over blacks was reinforced through segregation of the races and, within the black African population, of the various ethnic groups. Within each ethnic group, status was determined largely by wealth. After Kenya gained independence in 1963, race ceased to be an important indicator of social status, but wealth and ethnic identity remained significant. Today, a number of Kenya's problems result from disparities in wealth. These problems include pervasive urban and rural poverty, overcrowded and substandard housing in urban areas, and a relatively high rate of unemployment. In the 1990s the country also witnessed periodic clashes between ethnic groups, particularly between Kalenjin and Kikuyu peoples in west central Kenya.

Tropical diseases, including malaria, have long been a public health problem in Kenya. In recent years, infection with the human immunodeficiency virus (HIV) that causes acquired immunodeficiency syndrome (AIDS) has also become a severe problem. In 2003 an estimated 1,200,000 Kenyans were infected with HIV.

ECONOMY – GHANA

Overview

Before the arrival of European colonists in the 1400s, farming, herding, and fishing were the main indigenous Ghanaian economic activities, with smaller numbers of people mining for gold. With the establishment of complete colonial control in the late 1800s, the territory's economy was drawn fully into the world capitalist system, and gold was exported in large quantities to Europe.

Ghanaian farmers produced cash crops such as cocoa for the export market. European merchants, however, dominated the export and import economy. Upon independence in 1957, the state assumed greater involvement in the national economy. From the late 1960s through the 1970s, Ghana experienced severe economic decline as a result of political instability. By the mid-1980s, however, economic recovery programs were underway to encourage and expand private sector investments.

Both the International Monetary Fund (IMF) and the International Bank for Reconstruction and Development (World Bank) supported the reform programs. In the mid-1980s the government promoted industries using local raw materials and private investment in food production. From 2000 to 2004, Ghana's economy grew an average of 4.9 percent each year. (Allman, 1996) Ghana reported a gross domestic product (GDP) of $8.9 billion, or $410 per capita, in 2004. Of the total GDP, 37.4 percent was from the service sector, 37.9 percent from agriculture, and 24.7 percent from industrial productions. (Allman, 1996) GDP is a measure of the value of all goods and services produced by a country.

The state has been responsible for the provision of infrastructure installations and facilities since colonial times. Despite efforts to increase privatization in the mid-1980s, the government funds almost all road construction and installation of new power and telephone lines.

Foreign Trade

In 2000, Ghana's total exports were valued at $1.67 billion, and its total imports at $2.93 billion. The country's chief export is gold; other major exports include cocoa, lumber, and electricity. Petroleum, consumer goods, and machinery and transport equipment are among the main imports. Ghana's major trade partners, in order of importance, are the United Kingdom, the United States, Nigeria, The Netherlands, and Germany. Ghana is a member of the Economic Community of West African States (ECOWAS).

Foreign Direct Investment

Before the 1983 Economic Recovery Program, nationalized enterprise was the cornerstone of Ghanaian investment policy. Under the supervision of the IMF and World Bank, the government styled its policies on the model of a number of Asian countries where encouragement of the private sector and foreign direct investment (FDI) are considered essential to sustained economic growth.

The principal law on FDI is the Ghana Investment Promotion Center (GIPC) Law of 1994, which governs investments in all sectors except minerals and mining (under the Minerals and Mining Act of 1986 as amended in 1994 and administered by the Minerals Commission), oil and gas (under the Petroleum Exploration and Production Law of 1984 administered by the Ghana National Petroleum Corporation— GNOC), and the free trade zones, established in 1996 (Bowditch, 1999).

The 1994 investment code guarantees the free transferability of dividends, loan repayments, licensing fees, and the repatriation of capital; provides guarantees against expropriation; and provides for dispute arbitration. Foreign investors are not subject to differential treatment on taxes, prices, or access to foreign exchange, imports, and credit. The GIPC is responsible for promoting direct investment in Ghana. The only performance requirements are that a foreign investor must have at least $10,000 in capital for joint ventures, $50,000 for wholly foreignowned ventures, and $300,000 for trading companies, and that the latter must employ at least 10 Ghanaians. (Bowditch, 1999) The free trade zone consists of land near the seaports of Tema and Takoradi and the Kotoka Airport. To qualify for free zone incentives—a year corporate tax holiday and zero duty on imports—the business must export at least

70% of its output. Small enterprises—petty trading, taxi services with less than 10-car fleets, beauty and barber shops, small scale mining, pool betting businesses, and lotteries besides soccer—are reserved for Ghanaians. Since 2000, the government has transformed its general foreign investment promotion strategy to specific firm target promotion directed at production centers of Europe and Asia.

The objectives of the program are to attract firms that seek to local and sub-regional markets and which contribute to value-added production using raw materials available in Ghana.

Because a number of different agencies are involved in the promotion and monitoring of FDI in Ghana, published statistics tend to be unreliable and unreconciled. For the period 2000 to 2002, the GIPC reported it had licensed 510 projects representing a total investment of $351.2 million, $297.9 million of which was FDI and $53.3 million local funds. Of these, 342 were joint ventures and 169 wholly foreign-owned.

From 1997 to 1999, FDI averaged $66.7 million a year (UNCTAD estimates), compared to the $100 million a year 2000 to 2002. In the first quarter of 2003, FDI was reported at a record-setting pace of $56.7 million, $49.7 million of which was for projects in the service sector. (Bowditch, 1999) The major foreign investment projects in Ghana have been in mining and manufacturing. The United Kingdom has been the largest foreign investor, with investments exceeding $750 million, primarily through Lonmin Plc's 32% stake in the Ashanti Goldfields Corporation, in 2003; Lonmin was in the process of selling its stake to Anglogold of South Africa, which was negotiating taking over the Ashanti Goldfields. (Allman, 1996) The largest firm operating in Ghana is Valco, operated by the American company, Kaiser and Reynolds Aluminum, whose guaranteed use of electric power for aluminum refining made possible the building of the Volta Dam and its hydroelectric generating plant. In early 2003, a drought caused an energy crisis in Ghana and brought Valco's operations to a near standstill. Other American companies operating in Ghana include Teberebie Golfields Limited, CMS Generation (independent power producer), Affiliated Computer Services (since 2000, involved in developing offshore business process outsourcing projects), Regimanuel-Gray Limited (construction), Coca-Cola Company, Phyto-Riker (pharmaceuticals), Westel (ICT company formed by the partnership of Western Wireless International and Ghana National Petroleum Company), Pioneer Foods (Star-Kist Tuna), Union Carbide, Amoco, ChevronTexaco, and ExxonMobile.

ECONOMY – THE GAMBIA

Overview

The Gambia has no important mineral or other natural resources and has a limited agricultural base. About 75% of the population depends on crops and livestock for its livelihood. Small-scale manufacturing activity features the processing of peanuts, fish, and hides. Re-export trade normally constitutes a major segment of economic activity, but the 50% devaluation of the CFA franc in January 1994 made Senegalese goods more competitive and hurt the re-export trade.

The Gambia has benefited from a rebound in tourism after its decline in response to the military's takeover in July 1994. (Zuboff, 2002) Current GDP per capita of The Gambia registered a peak growth of 233% in the Seventies. But this proved unsustainable and it consequently shrank by 8.30% in the Eighties and a further 5.20% in the Nineties. (Zuboff, 2002).

Tourism in this country has three major strands. There is the traditional "sun, sea and sex" holiday making use of the hot climate and wonderful beaches. The Gambia is also usually the first African destination for many European birders, in view of its easily accessed and spectacular avian fauna. There are also a significant number of African-Americans tracing their roots in this country, from which so many Africans were taken during the slave trade.

The tourist season is the dry season, during the Northern Hemisphere winter. Short-run economic progress remains highly dependent on sustained bilateral and multilateral aid and on responsible government economic management as forwarded by IMF technical help and advice. Annual GDP growth is expected to fall to less than 4% over 2000-01. The Gambia has a liberal, market-based economy characterized by traditional subsistence agriculture, a historic reliance on peanuts or groundnuts for export earnings, a re-export trade built up around its ocean port, low import duties, minimal administrative procedures, a fluctuating exchange rate with no exchange controls, and a significant tourism industry. Agriculture accounts for 23% of gross domestic product (GDP) and employs 75% of the labor force.

Within agriculture, peanut production accounts for 5.3% of GDP, other crops 8.3%, livestock 4.4%, fishing 1.8%, and forestry 0.5%. Industry accounts for

12% of GDP and forestry 0.5%. Manufacturing accounts for 6% of GDP. The limited amount of manufacturing is primarily agriculturally based (e.g., peanut processing, bakeries, a brewery, and a tannery). Other manufacturing activities include soap, soft drinks, and clothing. Services account for 19% of GDP. In FY 1999 the UK and other EU countries were The Gambia's major domestic export markets, accounting for 86% in total; followed by Asia at 14%; and the African sub-region, including Senegal, Guinea-Bissau, and Ghana at 8%. The U.K. and the other EU countries—namely, Germany, France, Netherlands, and Belgium—were the major source of imports accounting for 60% of the total share of imports followed by Asia at 23%, and Cote d'Ivoire and other African countries at 17%. The Gambia reports 11% of its exports going to and 14.6% of its imports coming from the United States.

Foreign Trade

Gambia has experienced both balance of trade deficit as well as balance of payment deficit over various years. Major exportable items of the country are fish, peanuts, and cotton. Its exports partners are Hong Kong, United Kingdom, France and Spain.

Important importable items of the country are fuel, machines and manufacturing. For imports, Gambia depends upon the countries such as France, Senegal, Hong Kong and Netherlands. In the year 1967, Gambia joined the World Bank. Since then the bank has undertaken many steps for reducing poverty and fostering economic growth.

Foreign Direct Investment

Joint ventures have been encouraged in The Gambia, but with the stipulation that a portion of the profits must be reinvested. Under an ordinance passed in 1964, developing industries are exempt from profits tax for five years. In 2002 the government embarked on a new effort to attract foreign investment, called the Gateway Project, financed by a World Bank loan. The Gambia Investment Promotion and Free Zone Agency (GIPZA) was established, with the first free zone planned for Banjui Airport. Gambia's foreign investment regime is open door and non-discriminatory, with foreign companies treated the same as local companies. Incentives for locating in the free zones include exemptions from taxes and customs duties, a ten-year tax holiday, and a reduced 10% corporate income tax rate for investments in the tourist sector. The government's priorities for foreign investment are agriculture, fisheries, tourism, light manufacture and assembly, energy, mineral exploration and exploitation, and telecommunications (Zuboff, 2002).

ECONOMY – KENYA

Overview

After independence, Kenya promoted rapid economic growth through public investment, encouragement of smallholder agricultural production, and incentives for private (often foreign) industrial investment. Gross domestic product (GDP) grew at an annual average of 6.6% from 1963 to 1973. Agricultural production grew by 4.7% annually during the same period, stimulated by redistributing estates, diffusing new crop strains, and opening new areas to cultivation. Between 1974 and 1990, however, Kenya's economic performance declined. Inappropriate agricultural policies, inadequate credit, and poor international terms of trade contributed to the decline in agriculture. Kenya's inward-looking policy of import substitution and rising oil prices made Kenya's manufacturing sector uncompetitive.

The government began a massive intrusion in the private sector. Lack of export incentives, tight import controls, and foreign exchange controls made the domestic environment for investment even less attractive. From 1991 to 1993, Kenya had its worst economic performance since independence. Growth in GDP stagnated, and agricultural production shrank at an annual rate of 3.9%. Inflation reached a record 100% in August 1993, and the government's budget deficit was over 10% of GDP. As a result of these combined problems, bilateral and multilateral donors suspended program aid to Kenya in 1991. In 1993, the Government of Kenya began a major program of economic reform and liberalization. A new minister of finance and a new governor of the central bank undertook a series of economic measures with the assistance of the World Bank and the International Monetary Fund (IMF). As part of this program, the government eliminated price controls and import licensing, removed foreign exchange controls, privatized a range of publicly owned companies, reduced the number of civil servants, and introduced conservative fiscal and monetary policies. From 1994-96, Kenya's real GDP growth rate averaged just over 4% a year. In 1997, however, the economy entered a period of slowing or stagnant growth, due in part to adverse weather conditions and reduced economic activity prior to general elections in December 1997.

In 2000, GDP growth was negative, but improved slightly in 2001 as rainfall returned closer to normal levels. Economic growth continued to improve slightly in 2002 and reached 1.4% in 2003; it was 4.3% in 2004 and 5.8% in 2005. In July 1997, the Government of Kenya refused to meet commitments made earlier to the IMF on governance reforms. As a result, the IMF suspended lending for 3 years, and the World Bank also put a $90- million structural adjustment credit on hold. Although many economic reforms put in place in 1993-94 remained, conservative economists believe that Kenya needs further reforms, particularly in governance, in order to increase GDP growth and combat the poverty that afflicts more than 57% of its population. The Government of Kenya took some positive steps on reform, including the 1999 establishment of the Kenyan Anti-Corruption Authority, and measures to improve the transparency of government procurements and reduce the government payroll. In July 2000, the IMF signed a $150 million Poverty Reduction and Growth Facility (PRGF), and the World Bank followed suit shortly after with a $157 million Economic and Public Sector Reform credit. The Anti-Corruption Authority was declared unconstitutional in December 2000, and other parts of the reform effort faltered in 2001.

The IMF and World Bank again suspended their programs. Various efforts to restart the program through mid-2002 were unsuccessful. Under the leadership of President Kibaki, who took over on December 30, 2002, the Government of Kenya began an ambitious economic reform program and has resumed its cooperation with the World Bank and the IMF. The new National Rainbow Coalition (NARC) government enacted the Anti-Corruption and Economic Crimes Act and Public Officers Ethics Act in May 2003 aimed at fighting graft in public offices. Other reforms especially in the judiciary, public procurement etc., have led to the unlocking of donor aid and a renewed hope at economic revival. In November 2003, following the adoption of key anti-corruption laws and other reforms by the new government, donors reengaged as the IMF approved a three-year $250 million Poverty Reduction and Growth Facility and donors committed $4.2 billion in support over 4 years. The renewal of donor involvement has provided a much-needed boost to investor confidence. However, the government's ability to stimulate economic demand through fiscal and monetary policy remains fairly limited while the pace at which the government is pursuing reforms in other key areas remains slow. The Privatization Bill is yet to be enacted and civil service reform has been limited despite the government's assertion that reforms would be undertaken. The main challenges include building consensus within the loosely bound NARC government, taking candid action on corruption, enacting anti-terrorism and money laundering laws, bridging budget deficits, rehabilitating and building infrastructure, maintaining sound macroeconomic policies, and addressing structural reforms needed to reverse slow economic growth. Nairobi continues to be the primary communication and financial hub of East Africa. It enjoys the region's best transportation linkages, communications infrastructure, and trained personnel, although these advantages are less prominent than in past years. A wide range of foreign firms maintain regional branch or representative offices in the city. In March 1996, the Presidents of Kenya, Tanzania, and Uganda reestablished the East African Cooperation (EAC). The EAC's objectives include harmonizing tariffs and customs regimes, free movement of people, and improving regional infrastructures. In March 2004, the three East African countries signed a Customs Union Agreement.

Foreign Trade

The country has faced a merchandise trade deficit in the recent years. The major Exportable commodities of the country are tea, coffee, horticultural products and petroleum products. The exports partners of the country are Uganda, UK, Tanzania and Germany. The major Importable commodities of the country are machinery and transportation equipment, petroleum products, motor vehicles, iron and steel, resins and plastics. The Government of Kenya has taken some virile steps on reform, including the 1999 establishment of the Kenyan Anti-Corruption Authority, and measures to improve the transparency of government procurements and reduce the government payroll. In July 2000, IMF signed a $150 million Poverty Reduction and Growth Facility, and the World Bank followed suit shortly after with a $157 million Economic and Public Sector Reform credit.

Foreign Direct Investment

In 1964, in the wake of independence, foreign investment in Kenya went down considerably. In a move to reverse this trend, the government issued a white paper in 1965 welcoming foreign investment and encouraging joint ventures. Foreign investments in 1965 totaled $30 million, rising to $52 million in 1971. The pace of investment accelerated during the 1970s, and by 1984 it was estimated that US investment alone had a value of $350 million. In 1987, tax treaties with the United Kingdom, Germany, Zambia, Denmark, Norway, and Sweden were in force, but private foreign investment stagnated. In the early 1990s, the government moved to encourage investment by liberalizing trade policies and removing impediments to the development of a free market. It was estimated in 1994 that foreign direct investment totaled more than $1 billion. The majority of foreign direct investment comes from the United Kingdom, Germany, and the United States. Regardless of the government's intentions to attract investment, as of 1999 power interruptions, poor roads, political turmoil, and rampant government corruption dissuaded most serious foreign investment.

BUSINESS ENVIRONMENT – GHANA

Overview

The economy grew 5.2 percent in 2003, compared to 4.5 percent in 2002, primarily as a result of growth in the agricultural (especially cocoa) and industrial sectors. The momentum will likely continue in the medium term, but inflationary pressures and the slow pace of government economic reforms present risks to longterm growth.

There are no laws requiring the retention of a local agent or distributor for a foreign company exporting to Ghana. However, American companies wishing to enter the Ghanaian market are strongly advised to retain a businessperson or persons resident in Ghana to market their products. An agent or distributor should possess a thorough understanding of the economy. If the exported product requires servicing, qualified personnel and a reasonable inventory of spare parts must be considered. Exporters should be aware that agents and distributors commonly represent several product lines.

Business Culture

Ghana maintains strong historical, cultural and economic links with Britain. Other major foreign investments are from Germany, China and India. However, there is an increasing demand for U.S.-made goods and a liking for things "American" in general. It is nonetheless important that U.S. companies establish and maintain a high level of personal contact within Ghana. It is generally not possible to mount a successful enterprise via telephone, email or fax contact alone. Ghanaian values are very traditional, and this tendency extends to business dealings as well. People are very polite. Culture requires an exchange of greetings and pleasantries along with handshakes before any business in transacted.

If there are several people present, handshakes are to be given beginning from your right. Ghanaians like regular, face-to-face contact and personal visits are warmly welcomed and expected. While paying personal visits may not always be the most efficient or inexpensive method, it is generally regarded as the most effective method of handling few trade initiatives. This applies whether goods are being purchased from Ghana or sold to Ghana.

Timeliness is not generally a high priority in Ghana. It is advisable that the business visitor builds flexibility into their meeting schedule and plans.

The Lebanese and Asian (primarily Indian) communities play an important role in business in Ghana. Many Lebanese businesspeople are third and fourth generation Ghanaian citizens. This group dominates much of the dry goods, furniture and fixtures, building materials and durable goods imports.

BUSINESS ENVIRONMENT – THE GAMBIA

Overview

The Gambia has no important mineral or other natural resources and has a limited agricultural base. About 75% of the population depends on crops and livestock for its livelihood. Small-scale manufacturing activity features the processing of peanuts, fish, and hides. Re-export trade normally constitutes a major segment of economic activity, but the 50% devaluation of the CFA franc in January 1994 made Senegalese goods more competitive and hurt the re-export trade.

The Gambia has benefited from a rebound in tourism after its decline in response to the military's takeover in July 1994. (Zuboff, 2002) The Gambia is an investment haven. This potential and promise is predicated upon sound and consistent macroeconomic polices constitutional guarantees against expropriation of investment and for protection of investment The Gambia has an investment policy, which is premised on six important pillars/premises. These pillars essentially include:

• Liberal, free market economic environment together with appropriate political and social policy and program framework;

• Adherence to the principles of democratic governance, constitutional guarantee of rights to freedom and liberty, welfare, property ownership and protection. In this regard, the country is constitutionally obliged to encourage, promote and protect beneficial investment as the enabler of socioeconomic change and progress. (Zuboff, 2002)

• Full integration into the wider global economy through her membership of and adherence to charters and principles of Economic Community Of West African States, organization or African unity, World Trade Organization, Multilateral Investment Guarantee Agency (MIGA), African Development Bank, The World Bank Group, ACP-EU Convention, Islamic Development Bank and a host of bilateral trade agreements among others. These testify to the national resolve at participation and integration in the global economy. (Zuboff, 2002)

• Articulation of policies and strategies to make The Gambia a trade and investment gateway to the Western Africa sub-regional and the larger African regional market. The uniqueness of the country's location on the Atlantic coast of West Africa, proximity to European and North American markets, a highly efficient port system, state-of-the-art telecommunication infrastructure, high water table and ideal climate for horticulture, unrivalled rich climate and sea resource for tourism and sea resource exploitation amongst a host of other qualities, have placed the Gambia at a comparatively advantageous position to become the sub-regional hegemony in trade and services;

• Conducive legal and institutional framework with labor laws that support and encourage collective bargaining in line with the stipulation of the Labor Act; • A national resolve and commitment to transform The Gambia into a middle income country by the year 2020. (Zuboff, 2002)

BUSINESS ENVIRONMENT – KENYA

Overview

Kenya is the logistical hub for the East African region. Through its strategic geographical location, Kenya has emerged as a significant player in regional trade, investment, infrastructure development and general economic growth. Despite many of its social and economical problems, Kenya can be described as one of Africa's post-colonial success stories: relatively prosperous, comparatively stable and host to many international organizations. Few could have imagined that Kenya would have achieved so much given the violence and terror which marked the country's struggle for independence more than 40 years ago. (Miller, 1994) Today, Kenya continues to maintain a stable government and a free-market economy with a vibrant private sector, and, through the Greater Horn of Africa Initiative, the country is in a strong position to maintain its significant role in regional trade, investment, infrastructure development and general economic co-operation for the region.

Moves to liberalize the economy taken over the last ten years have laid the groundwork for an investmentfriendly environment in Kenya. The economic recovery strategy is targeted to achieve an 8% growth rate and industrial status for Kenya by 2025, creating 500,000 jobs a year in the process. (Watson, 2000) The Central Bank of Kenya has pledged to pursue "a stable monetary policy, which accommodates the highest economic growth rate possible", while keeping inflation low and stable. Kenya is an important player in East Africa. Strategically placed, with a major port, Mombasa, and welldeveloped financial markets, the country has the makings of a regional services hub in banking, information and transportation. The country's membership in the East African Community (with Tanzania and Uganda) and the Common Market for Eastern and Southern Africa (COMESA) makes it an attractive base for foreign investors and companies looking to access the East and Central African market. Through Kenya, an investor can access the COMESA market with over 380 million people. (Watson, 2000).

Kenya and the three East African countries recently signed the protocol on the East African Customs Union creating a common external tariff to be applied to goods imported from outside the region and also harmonized the tariff rates between them. This is one of the three steps towards an eventual political union of the three East African countries. Exports from Kenya also enjoy preferential access to both the United States and the European Union. Considerable effort has been made to take advantage of opportunities offered by the African Growth and Opportunity Act (AGOA) to penetrate the US market. Analysts say AGOA is responsible for over $125 million in new investments in Kenya and the creation of over 30,000 new jobs. (Watson, 2000) Major Kenyan products that qualify for duty-free access under AGOA include textile, leather and processed agricultural products. Indeed, textile and apparel products have become Kenya's dominant export category to the United States, and more than tripled to $188 million in 2003 from $64 in 2001.

Political Environment – Ghana

Overview

Politics of Ghana takes place in a framework of a presidential representative democratic republic, whereby the President of Ghana is both head of state and head of government, and of a pluriform multi-party system. Executive power is exercised by the government. Legislative power is vested in both the government and Parliament. The Judiciary is independent of the executive and the legislature. The Constitution that established the Fourth Republic provided a basic charter for republican democratic government. (Rimmer, 1992) It declares Ghana to be a unitary republic with sovereignty residing in the Ghanaian people. Intended to prevent future coups, dictatorial government, and one-party states, it is designed to establish the concept of power-sharing. The document reflects lessons learned from the abrogated constitutions of 1957, 1960, 1969, and 1979, and incorporates provisions and institutions drawn from British and American constitutional models. (Herbst, 1993) One controversial provision of the Constitution indemnifies members and appointees of the PNDC from liability for any official act or omission during the years of PNDC rule. The Constitution calls for a system of checks and balances, with power shared between a president, a unicameral parliament, a council of state, and an independent judiciary (Herbst, 1993).

POLITICAL ENVIRONMENT – THE GAMBIA

Overview

Before the 1994 coup d'état, The Gambia was one of the oldest existing multi-party democracies in Africa. It had conducted freely contested elections every five years since independence. After the coup, politicians from deposed President Jawara's People's Progressive Party (PPP) and other senior government officials were banned from participating in politics until July 2001. (Hughes, 1999) A presidential election took place in September 1996, in which retired Col. Yahya A.J.J. Jammeh won 56% of the vote. Four registered opposition parties participated in the October 18, 2001, presidential election, which the incumbent, President Jammeh, won with almost 53% of the votes (Hughes, 1999).

The APRC maintained its strong majority in the National Assembly in legislative elections held in January 2002; particularly after the main opposition United Democratic Party (UDP) boycotted the legislative elections. On the 21st and 22nd of March 2006, amid tensions preceding the 2006 presidential elections, an alleged planned military coup was uncovered. The 1970 constitution, which divided the government into independent executive, legislative, and judicial branches, was suspended after the 1994 military coup. As part of the transition process, the AFPRC established the Constitution Review Commission (CRC) through decree in March 1995. In accordance with the timetable for the transition to a democratically elected government, the commission drafted a new constitution for The Gambia, which was approved by referendum in August 1996. The constitution provides for a strong presidential government, a unicameral legislature, an independent judiciary, and the protection of human rights (Hughes, 1999).

POLITICAL ENVIRONMENT — KENYA

Overview

Politics of Kenya takes place in a framework of a presidential representative democratic republic, whereby the President of Kenya is both head of state and head of government, and of a pluriform multi-party system. Executive power is exercised by the government. Legislative power is vested in both the government and the National Assembly. The Judiciary is independent of the executive and the legislature (Haugerud, 1995).

Since independence, Kenya has maintained remarkable stability despite changes in its political system and crises in neighboring countries. Particularly since the re-emergence of multiparty democracy, Kenyans have enjoyed an increased degree of freedom.

A cross-party parliamentary reform initiative in the fall of 1997 revised some oppressive laws inherited from the colonial era that had been used to limit freedom of speech and assembly. This improved public freedoms and contributed to generally credible national elections in December 1997. (Haugerud, 1995) In December 2002, Kenyans held democratic and open elections, which were judged free and fair by international observers. The 2002 elections marked an important turning point in Kenya's democratic evolution in that power was transferred peacefully from the single party that had ruled the country since independence to a new coalition of parties under the presidency of Mwai Kibaki, the new ruling coalition promised to focus its efforts on generating economic growth, combating corruption, improving education, and rewriting its constitution. These promises have only been partially met, however, as the new government has been preoccupied with internal wrangling and power disputes. (Haugerud, 1995) In November 2005, the Kenyan electorate resoundingly defeated a new draft constitution supported by Parliament and President Kibaki. Kibaki responded by dismissing his entire cabinet. Kibaki eventually appointed a new slate of faithful ministers. The next general elections are set to be held in December 2007. President Kibaki is expected to rerun, but has not yet confirmed or denied it.

Corruption

Political corruption in the post-colonial government of Kenya has had a history which spans the era of the Jomo Kenyatta and Daniel arap Moi's KANU governments to the Mwai Kibaki's NARC government. In the Corruption Perceptions Index 2005 Kenya is ranked 144th out of 159 countries for corruption (Countries with least corruption are rated near zero). It is estimated the average urban Kenyan pays 16 bribes per month. Most of these bribes are fairly small but large ones are also taken — bribes worth over 50,000 Kenyan shillings (€600, USD$700) account for 41% of the total value. There is also corruption on a larger scale with each of the last two regimes being criticized for their involvement.

The Best Countries to do Business With/ In Domestically-Owned Companies

Countries in Africa would be best suited to do business with Kenya. During the last two years the country has made substantial progress in stabilizing and liberalizing its economy. Inflation has been brought under control and continues to decline. The budget deficit has been reduced and interest rates have come down. The liberalization of import controls and foreign exchange rates have been major steps towards removal of trade barriers.

Mombasa, the principal seaport of Kenya, has served as a distribution hub for the lucrative East African market providing connections to landlocked neighboring countries. The port of Mombasa is linked to the world's major ports with over 200 sailings per week to ports in Europe, North and South America, Asia, Australia, Middle East and the rest of Africa. Kenya and neighboring countries - Uganda, Burundi, Rwanda, Sudan and Zaire - have established the Northern Corridor Transport Agreement which facilitates transportation of goods to and from the port of Mombasa.

Kenya is also a member of the Preferential Trade Area (PTA) agreement embracing countries in Eastern and Southern Africa which has been transformed to the Common Market for Eastern and Southern Africa (COMESA) with a population of approximately 400 million. Exports and imports within member countries enjoy preferential tariff rates. Exporters to the Preferential Trade Area (PTA) regional market (19 countries of eastern and southern Africa) receive tax advantages and have the option to trade in local currencies. The market has a total population of 190 million and a GDP of over US$50 billion. The aim of the PTA is to eventually establish a common market with no barriers across member countries' borders.

Foreign-Owned Companies

When a foreign company is looking to do business in Africa, they should also look to Kenya. Kenya has now fully liberalized its economy by removing all obstacles that previously hampered the free flow of trade and foreign private investment. Among them were exchange controls, import and export licensing, as well as restrictions on remittances of profits and dividends, all of which no longer exist. These reforms have been painstakingly undertaken by the Kenyan government in order to create the necessary environment to attract foreign investment. The President of Kenya has taken a personal interest in these reforms. The adoption of the Treaty of East African Co-operation in March 1996 has created a common market of over 80 million people providing an attractive market for commerce and industry on a vast scale. Together with the Common Market for Eastern and Southern Africa (COMESA), to which all three East African countries belong, and the recently reinvigorated Inter-Governmental Authority on Development, a dynamic market of nearly 400 million people will provide unlimited opportunities for the potential investor in Kenya and its trading partners. Last year, Kenya imported approximately $800 million worth of goods from the UAE - not to mention a substantial amount of goods that have found their way to Kenya through unofficial channels. Trade between Kenya and the UAE has been increasing every year, especially after trade restrictions and foreign exchange regulations have been lifted by the government of Kenya in order to boost foreign trade. An increasing number of Kenyan businessmen are now coming to the United Arab Emirates in search of new sources of supply and to market their goods in the lucrative Gulf market.

Conclusion

As part of their efforts to increase Kenya's competitiveness as an investment destination, the Government has also embarked on rebuilding the dilapidated infrastructure to encourage both domestic and foreign investment. Parts of these efforts have involved streamlining the operations of each of the important sectors in the economy including transport, energy, road and railway infrastructure etc. Kenya still has one of the best developed business infrastructures in the East and Central African region.

Discussion Questions

1. In what country will foreign direct investment be preferred by investors? Discuss your answers.
2. What investment opportunities does each country have?
3. How challenging is it to conduct business in Ghana, The Gambia and Kenya?

BIBLIOGRAPHY

Ahluwalia, D. P. S. Post-Colonialism and the Politics of Kenya. New York: Nova Science Publishers, 1996.

Allman, Jean Marie. The Quills of the Porcupine: Asante Nationalism in an Emergent Ghana. Madison: University of Wisconsin Press, 1993.

Apt, Nana A. Coping with Old Age in Changing Africa: Social Change and the Elderly Ghanian. Aldershot, England: Avebury, 1996.

Assensoh, A. B. African Political Leadership: Jomo Kenyatta, Kwame Nkrumah, and Julius K. Nyerere. Malabar, Fla.: Krieger Pub., 1998.

Berry, LaVerle. Ghana: A Country Study. 3d ed. Washington, D.C.: Federal Research Division, Library of Congress, 1995.

Bowditch, Nathaniel H. The Last Emerging Market: from Asian Tigers to African Lions?: The Ghana File. Westport, Conn.: Praeger, 1999.

Chenevix Trench, Charles. Men who Ruled Kenya: The Kenya Administration, 1892–1963. New York: Radcliffe Press, 1993.

Clough, Marshall S. Fighting Two Sides: Kenyan Chiefs and Politicians, 1918–1940. Niwot, Colo.: University Press of Colorado, 1990.

D and B's Export Guide to The Gambia. Parsippany, N.J.: Dun and Bradstreet, 1999.

Decalo, Samuel. The Stable Minority: Civilian Rule in Africa, 1960–1990. Gainesville, Fla.: FAP Books, 1998.

Ebron, Paulla A. Performing Africa. Princeton, N.J.: Princeton University Press, 2002.

Edgerton, Robert B. The Fall of the Asante Empire: The Hundred-year War for Africa's Gold Coast. New York: The Free Press, 1995.

Gamble, David P. The Gambia. Santa Barbara, Calif.: Clio Press, 1988.

Ghana: A Country Study. 3rd ed. W. Va.: Library of Congress, 1995.

Greene, Sandra E. Sacred Sites and the Colonial Encounter: A History of Meaning and Memory in Ghana. Bloomington: Indiana University Press, 2002.

Haugerud, Angelique. The Culture of Politics in Modern Kenya. Cambridge: Cambridge University Press, 1995.

Himbara, David. Kenyan Capitalists, the State, and Development. Boulder, Colo.: L. Rienner, 1994.

Herbst, Jeffrey Ira. The Politics of Reform in Ghana, 1982–1991. Berkeley: University of California Press, 1993.

Hughes, Arnold and Harry A. Gailey. Historical Dictionary of The Gambia. Rev. ed. Metuchen, N.J.: Scarecrow Press, 1999.

Lall, Sanjaya. Skills and Capabilities: Ghana's Industrial Competitiveness. Oxford, U.K.: Queen Elizabeth House, 1996.

Lentz, Carola and Paul Nugent (eds.). Ethnicity in Ghana: The Limits of Invention. New York: St. Martin's Press, 2000.

Mann, Kenny. Ghana, Mali, Songhay: The Western Sudan. Parsippany, N.J.: Dillon Press, 1996.

Maxon, Robert M., and Thomas P. Ofcansky. Historical Dictionary of Kenya. Lanham, Md.: Scarecrow Press, 2000.

Miller, Norman N. and Roger Yeager. Kenya: The Quest for Prosperity. Boulder, Colo.: Westview Press, 1994.

Mwakikagile, Godfrey. Ethnic Politics in Kenya and Nigeria. Huntington, N.Y.: Nova Science Publishers, 2001.

Myers, Robert A. Ghana. Santa Barbara, Calif.: Clio Press, 1991.

Newell, Stephanie. Literary Culture in Colonial Ghana. Bloomington: Indiana University Press, 2002.

Nugent, Paul. Big Men, Small Boys and Politics in Ghana: Power, Ideology and the Burden of History, 1982-1994. London: Piner, 1995.

Ogot, Bethwell A. Decolonization and Independence in Kenya, 1940–93. London: Curry, 1995.

Osei, Akwasi P. Ghana: Recurrence and Change in a Post-Independence African State. New York: P. Lang, 1999.

Owusu-Ansah, David, and Daniel M. McFarland. Historical Dictionary of Ghana. 2d ed. Metuchen, N.J.: Scarecrow Press, 1995.

Quaye, Randolph. Underdevelopment and Health Care in Africa: The Ghanaian Experience. Lewiston: Mellen University Press, 1996.

Rimmer, Douglas. Staying Poor: Ghana's Political Economy, 1950–1990. New York: Pergamon, 1992.

Salm, Steven J. Culture and Customs of Ghana. Westport, Conn.: Greenwood Press, 2002.

Shillington, Kevin. Ghana and the Rawlings Factor. New York: St. Martin's Press, 1992.

Sobania, N. W. Culture and Customs of Kenya. Westport, Ct.: Greenwood Press, 2003.

Themes in Kenyan History. Athens: Ohio University Press, 1990.

Thomas-Slayter, Barbara P. Gender, Environment, and Development in Kenya: A Grassroots Perspective. Boulder, Colo.: L. Rienner, 1995.

Watson, Mary Ann (ed.). Modern Kenya: Social Issues and Perspectives. Lanham, Md.: University Press of America, 2000.

Widner, Jennifer A. The Rise of a Party-state in Kenya: From "Harambee" to "Nyayo!". Berkeley: University of California, 1992.

Zuboff, Shoshana. The Support Economy: Why Corporations Are Failing Individuals and the Next Episode of Capitalism. New York: Viking, 2002.

Multi-Party Politics in Kenya. Athens: Ohio University Press, 1998. Historical Dictionary of Ghana. [computer file] Boulder, Colo.: netLibrary, Inc., 2000.

CHAPTER 14

Training to Change Mindsets: Think Global! By Michael Ba Banutu-Gomez, Delphine Guilmet, Ozzie Ozkok and Ryan J. Waddington

Introduction

This chapter is to be the foundation of a training module to help global managers rearrange their thinking, perception and views to their work environment and increase awareness to some problem areas in today's global business world. Globalization and technology created a new labor force where culture, cross-cultural communication, and diversity are crucial areas for a global manager. Managing culturally diverse people and creating a synergy in the system is the goal of a global leader.

As Moran (2007) says: "We don't have to convince people with any global experience that *culture counts*." In general, global leaders know that cultural competing is a requirement or diversity in the workforce is increasing. People tend to know the importance of these issues, however, without specific examples or details their perceptions stay the same. Changing a mindset is our goal. The key question is: "How to help a global leader think globally?" Related questions in our research follow as (1) how to give memorable examples, (2) how to specifically tell them how they can intervene and (3) how to go into the details of general problems like understanding cultural differences or diversity.

The data in the results part of the paper intended to show some real-world settings where multinational companies interact with these problem areas.

The search for answers led to conclusions and the appendices of this paper that may be used part of a training program for global leaders.

Training is the key solution to help a leader in the global location. In training for global leaders main focus should be in (1) identifying key mistakes that a leader/manager can make, (2) showing ways to intervene or address issues, (3) improving leader's global approach, (4) emphasizing change management skills for a cross-cultural and international setting, (5) assisting in negotiation skills, informing about doing business in different cultures and countries, and (6) supporting leaders in thinking global and building up a global human network.

To alter human behavior is not an easy task. However, with detailed visual and interactive sessions of training it is possible (1) to create attention, (2) rearrange opinion and (3) keep in mind to suspend judgment. To create more aware people in the global organization about each other is the key to an integral training and will yield to a more effective and positive work atmosphere.

Entering a New Market

Prior to entering a new market, global companies should ensure they learn about the host countries culture and its characteristics. The following ten categories are given as an aid to get started on learning about other cultures (Moran et al., 2007):

a. The space between individuals and sense of self-identity: What is an individual's comfort zone like in the other culture?

b. What is the communication system, verbal and non-verbal language like? How does the technology effect the communication?

c. Are there any different subcultures that are different in dress and appearance?

d. What is appropriate food in that country? Any forbidden or inappropriate eating habits must be researched?

e. How do people live their lives according to the time? Is there a quick pace? Sense of time and seasons vary by the culture.

f. How are relationships defined in marriages, among families or friends? The effect of age, gender and social status are all distinct in cultures.

g. The legal system of the country: What do people value most? Are there traditions that are more effective than laws?

h. How does religion affect people's attitudes in the country?

i. What are work practices for promotion, management styles, or evaluation? Some cultures have different management styles: "Live to work" vs. "Work to live"

j. How do people learn in that culture? Do they use logic or abstract thinking? What do they use as realizations?

Some of these categories are hard to find out before people actually go and interact with the host culture population. Some of them are hidden while others are obvious.

Schmitz (2003) developed a "cultural profile" that could be used as identifying some of the cultural variables:

a. Environment: Social environments can be categorized according to whether they view or relate to people, objects, and issues from the orientation of control (change environment), harmony (build balance), or constraint (external forces set parameters).

b. Time: What people value more: past, present or future?

c. Action: Are people task or relationship oriented?

d. Communication: An emphasis on implicit communication and reliance on non-verbal cues indicates high-context orientation. A low-context communication is indicated by strong value on explicit communication.

e. Space: Cultures can be categorized according to their distinction between public and private spaces.

f. Power: What is the structure of power relationships? Is there a hierarchy or an equality orientation?

g. Individualism: An emphasis on individual indicates an individualistic culture while a collectivist culture values a group, company or organization.

h. Competitiveness: Emphasis on personal achievements indicates a competitive orientation, however valuing quality of life and relationships show a cooperative orientation.

i. Structure: Some cultures minimize risk, and value rules and procedures more while others have a flexibility orientation and value innovation.

j. Thinking: There are distinct approaches in culture such as some emphasis on theory and abstract logic while others emphasis on data and experience.

Dr. Geert Hofstede (Moran, 2007, p. 17) believes that culture is very important and has identified four dimensions of national culture:

a. Power Distance
b. Uncertainty Avoidance
c. Individualism
d. Masculinity

Power distance indicates "the extent to which a society accepts that power in institutions and organizations is distributed unequally." Uncertainty avoidance indicates "the extent to which a society feels threatened by uncertain situations". Individualism refers to a loosely knit social framework in a society where people are supposed to take care of themselves and of their immediate families only. Collectivism is the opposite of the individualism and is a social framework in which people expect their in-group people (relatives, clan, organizations) to look after them and in exchange for that owe absolute loyalty to it. Masculinity indicates "the extent to which dominant values in society are assertiveness, money and material things, not caring for others, quality of life, and people".

Hofstede asked questions to employees from 40 countries and assigned an index value to each country based on the mean ratings of the employees. The United States ranked fifteenth on power distance, ninth on uncertainty avoidance (both of these are the below the average), was the most individualist country and twenty-eighth on masculinity (above average.) In France and Turkey, unlike United States, there is little concern about participative management, but great concern with who has the power. Hofstede showed that in countries with lower power distance scores than the US, such as Sweden and Germany, there is considerable acceptance of management models that are more participative than today's models. Hofstede also demonstrated in Germany there is high uncertainty avoidance and, therefore industrial democracy was brought in by legislation at first. In Sweden, where uncertainty avoidance is low, industrial democracy was started with local experiments.

Influencing people is the key to being a good leader; in a global world, as long as a leader knows more about cultures, the power of influencing people will increase. The variables associated with the cultures are researched and common themes among researchers are communication, collectivity and time.

In discussing some global companies, there are four types of corporations cited – ethnocentric, polycentric, regiocentric, and geocentric. Ethnocentric corporations are home country oriented. Corporations value host-country are called polycentric. Some global corporations focus on benefits of sharing common functions across regions – regiocentric corporations. Geocentric corporations' ultimate goal is being world-oriented and integrating the whole organization with a worldwide approach (Moran, 2007).

Problems with multinational corporations (MNC) occur when a company tries to transplant their current policies into a new culture. As stated in an article about bringing new companies to China, a direct transfer of Western business models can put foreign firms at risk (Li, 2008). It is also important not accept the local business practices, without fully understanding them. A method that should be considered is the localization method, where takes into account cultural differences and fosters a new blended corporate culture. Examples of this are McDonalds and KFC adjusting their menus based on the culture that they are ending.

The Oreo has been the best selling cookie in the United States; however the cookie was unsuccessful in China. Kraft Foods Inc, the world's second largest food company by revenue, had to reinvent Oreo taste in China to make it sell well to the most crowded country in the world. Unlike American Oreo, the Chinese one is less sweet, four-layered, longer, and thinner. Although the Chinese sales are a tiny fraction of company revenues, Chief Executive Irene Rosenfeld is trying to spread this kind of consumer-based change throughout this giant global company with $37.2 billion revenue by May 2008. Ms.Rosenfeld has been trying to tell employees all around the globe that all the product decisions shouldn't be made by the headquarters in Northfield, USA. She wants the global managers think outside the box such as Oreo may not be a round cookie for another nation's consumers. Kraft's international business now accounts for 40% of its revenues, and the company has increased spending in product research and marketing. The company is introducing dark chocolate in Germany under its Milka brand to take advantage of the European fondness for dark chocolate. Research in Russia showed that people over there like premium instant coffee, so Kraft is repositioning its freeze-dried coffee as upscale by using fashion shows and operas. Tailoring the western products to the eastern taste is not done the first time, but it is a great challenge for most of the global companies.

Wal-Mart International with nearly 3000 stores up and running globally succeeded both in mature economies such as UK and in developing nations such as Brazil, Mexico, and China. The company has a locally obsessed strategy and now uses six different store formats in nine different types, each measure to best serve a specific socio-demographic population and various shopping goals. To be successful in China, the company had to admit that the Chinese consumers shop in smaller quantities and don't have big cars as their transportations. "Everyday Low Prices" was not enough for company; Wal-Mart had to redesign its business according to cultural trends.

One of the problem areas in global management is cross-cultural communication. There are many variables to communication such as listening, thought patterns, roles, language skill, time sense, social organizations in cultures, verbal and non-verbal language differences and technology's effect in the process.

As globalization evolves throughout the world, language becomes another challenge for multinational companies. Most of them use English as a business language; however language as well as enabling communication may also act as a troublemaker in contacts. A non-native English speaker who uses English as a business communication tool is seen as communicating with its language competence, however, mostly it is forgotten that cultural backgrounds of people are diverse and affect the language (Knapp, K., & Meierkord, 2002). Research by Charles (2007) found out there were big challenges highlighted for oral interaction. Employees of one globally operating MNC emphasized the difficulties experienced in understanding each other's Englishes in oral situations. Several of the interviews identified that the problems were created by native speakers as well as by non-native speakers. Native speaker's complicated language could be difficult for non-native speakers and yield misconstrued nonverbal performance in multicultural meetings. Another challenge was identified in a merger of a Swedish and Finnish company where the official shared language (the language of management) was Swedish, that is, the mother tongue of some employees but not of all. Many Finnish employees felt they were ripped off their power. Interestingly, these same interviewees felt comforted when the official company language was changed to English, which was a foreign language to both Finnish and Swedish speakers.

Beyene (2007) made a research to identify the effects of mandating all employees use English as their common language, or *lingua franca*, in a global organization. Data show that *lingua franca* communication between native and non-native English speakers creates a socially discrediting circumstance for less fluent speakers, creating feelings of incompetence or poor standard. According to the data in the research, non-native speakers were comfortable when talking to other non-native speakers; however when an English native speaker was present non-natives felt linguistically "dominated". A non-native speaker described his experience as:

My English is not bad. It's true that I do quite well in meetings with colleagues from France, Netherlands, Poland, etc. ... [but] problems start when an English speaker is present.

Another employee said:
Working with native speakers is most stressful. Very often non-English-speaking people can share ideas using English much more easily with others like them than native English speakers.

The paper concludes those rather than competency anxiety may cause non-native speakers keep silent or withdraw from a conversation.
Cultural diversity is becoming more complex in today's companies without borders. If you go into any random US office, it is the first thing you see: diversity. Managing a multigenerational and a diverse workforce is another challenge and analysts forecast more changes to come. Adding a new HR policy will not address diversity issues. "Organizational cultures must transform in order to succeed today," says Sondra Solovay, author, law professor and employment attorney. "The interactions among employees, managers and customers illustrate an organization's priorities better than any printed policies. Unfortunately, this type of transformation is rarely organic" ("Workplace Answers," 2008). Training is the key to solve the problem, merely hiring diverse employees will not be able to bring in improved work environment or enable the organization more competitive.

Dow Chemical Company, growing rapidly in Eastern Europe, India and China, looked at its data and saw that the company had a diverse workforce and went beyond inclusive policies ("Discovering Diversity: Learn To Walk A Mile In The Other Person's Shoes," 2007). It was critical to their strategy to learn how, as leaders, Dow's executives and other people leaders could be more inclusive. "You have to find out what your personal blind spots are and dissect that," says Darlene MacKinnon, Director, Leadership Capabilities, Diversity and Inclusion for Dow. Dow started at top executives and identified the issues through workshops and interactive sessions with its people leaders. They wanted to understand their leaders and uncover potential problem areas in their thinking. "Who among us, whether majority or minority, hasn't felt excluded at some point in our lives?" MacKinnon asks. That's why it's powerful to have leaders share their personal stories and feelings about diversity.

Creating cultural synergy with a diverse workforce is a challenge most of the global companies. Synergistic management includes relaxed, supportive, and respectful atmosphere for everybody. Abraham Maslow came up with a model of characteristics of synergistic societies. Japan and Sweden are two national cultures that are high synergistically, while Serbia and Iraq would be less so.

Synergy is important inside companies in order to create a global business. The women's position is still different according to the countries. Indeed, the corporate world is still fundamentally sexist; even if some governments or some companies take some measure to fight against that. For instance, in France, only 5% of French executives are women; and in Britain, though 44% of the British workforce is female, no British woman has ever been the head of a large British company. There are still some global stereotypes towards women; such as "women lack quantitative skills", "when women become a mother, her priorities change", "women are not interesting in an international career", "women are too soft to handle ruthless managerial decision."

However, the world is changing. In Great Britain, several programs have been created to promote women: to help them to attain the necessary qualifications, career development, and guidance within an internal organization. Government quotas are bringing more women on to Norwegian boards. Some companies, in France, set also some "discrimination positive" to insert women in companies. This discrimination positive shows to other (companies, women, and men) that women are able to do as well as men. This can encourage women to move into the senior executive ranks. But some are opposed to this positive discrimination, like Katja Hall, head of employee relation for the CBI, who think that "Most people don't want to get a job simply because they are black or women" (Masters, 2008).

Women proved they make great leaders. For instance, in Citigroup Company, it is Lisa Caputo who assumes the role of Executive Vice President, Global marketing and Corporate Affairs. And according to Vikram Pandit: "Lisa brings superb judgment, strong communications experience and excellent leadership qualities to its function" ("Citigroup Inc.," 2008).

Moreover, according to a study of the US Fortune 500, having three or more women on the board correlates strongly with above-average return on shareholder equity, sales and invest capital. "Their presence could be a signal that a company was willing to rethink usual behavior and talk to a wider range of people". Beyond the financial aspect, it has been proven that "women-friendly" companies provide a more beneficial environment to men and women.

Showing genuine respect for the customs and traditions of host cultures is the key to successful international business negotiations (Watson, 2006). It is important to build synergy across cultures through highly effective interpersonal relations. This is achieved by showing an interest in, knowledge of, and genuine respect for the customs and traditions of a host culture (Watson, 2006). The problem that many companies face has to do with the time and money that must be invested in understanding a culture. This can limit the willingness of the company to accept the host culture.

As with any negotiation, the inherent balances of power between the parties are of great importance in international negotiations (Fox, 2005). It is also true that no matter whether the power balance in any given negotiation is in one's favor or not, a person needs to do justice to himself/herself when he/she approaches the negotiating table. What the negotiator says and how he/she behaves also has a big impact on the result (Fox, 2005).

National culture is perhaps social context within which negotiation can occur (Lin, 2003). Largely treating national culture as a predictor variable, existing studies focus on how cultural dimensions might exert direct influence on the preference for any given negotiation approach (Lin, 2003). The feeling throughout this article is that focusing entirely on studies is too simplistic and that companies do not look into other variables. The article also discusses the role that future relationships and the impact on the negotiations. This will alter the negotiation style as well as the overall mood of the negotiations. The article stresses the importance of understanding if the country is generally a high-context or low-context communicator.

As with the beginning stages of any venture, how a negotiator establishes a relationship with his or her counterparts is of great importance (D'Amico, 1999). Thus appropriately setting the negotiation table involves preparation in the explicit as well as implicit aspects of communication (D'Amico, 1999). The article focused on different approaches to be prepared to communicate effectively with other cultures during negotiations. The article also touched based on social identity and the source of distinctions among people. Troubles between social groups can be attributed to the past experiences of the groups as well the interpretations of the other groups. It is important to research studies and experiences of other companies when being involved in cross cultural negotiations.

Global Leader and Cultural Matters

The real world examples disclose that a global leader must take into account cultural matters. Culture affects how people communicate, listen, and act. Managers who operate globally have to be responsive to local trends that affect business. A model effective in the US is not necessarily profitable in another country. As in Oreo cookie experience in China example stated before a product taste, even its design has to be tailored to the country's preferences. This product modification experiences by MNCs is a way that shows they are able to understand the cultural differences and adapt. Global companies embrace their local talents to give them a competitive advantage in the market.

Communication is also bound with culture. As multilingual employees in global organizations travel across or work more together, the research examples show that a common official language sometimes may create less effective conversations and less fluent employees get intimidated by the superior native speakers. Language matters in communication and it affects verbal and non-verbal, formal and informal communication. Companies may have discrepancies regarding cross-cultural communication if they are not aware of the cultural backgrounds and language competencies of their employees.

Diversity is another challenge that global companies face. Diversity programs that go beyond simply increasing number of diverse employees (come from different culture, women…) or adding new written policies are not effective ways of handling diversity in global organizations. Diversity training is not a simple course that can be given to the employees and expect increased communication as a whole. Different ways of handling things are an outcome of a diverse workforce and the research shows that getting to know the workforce will help leaders to identify the problems in this area. Diversity training should also take into account that women are important in companies. They can bring something different than men cannot inevitably bring. Diversity is the strength of a company.

The studies into negotiating with different cultures reveal that being prepared is the most important step in successful negotiations. When negotiating one wants to be able to communicate smoothly and not offend or belittle anyone during the process. Cross-cultural negotiations have the same variables as inter-cultural negotiations (bargaining power, leverage) and have additional variables pertaining to the countries involved.

A major misstep in understanding the other culture is only knowing the facts and not respecting their differences. It is important to research, identify, and respect the other cultures beliefs in order to have smooth communications with this culture. Also, one must not just read one paper or talk to one person regarding another country but must research other companies' experiences as well as talk to members of the culture to understand what they value. Preparing for negotiations is not a quick process it requires a commitment from the individuals as well as the company as a whole.

Negotiations can be limited by stereotypes that each party brings to the table with them. A negotiation team must be able to drop all stereotypes about the other party in order to make the negotiations fair. This is why the multiple levels of research are important that way the negotiator does not just have one person's point of view. Different cultures have different norms, what is acceptable in social settings is not acceptable in business settings; therefore stereotypes about groups can be misleading. Stereotypes can also lead to a group feeling superior or inferior which then can cause one party to feel intimidated at the negotiation. This can lead to unwillingness to work together in the future. In order to set up a long-term relationship the countries must feel respected.

Different cultures have different negotiation styles as well as conflict resolution. It is important that each party comes together and understands the others' methods. One must have a game plan and in order to have a proper game plan a person must know the way to go about it. The negotiator does not want to come off offensive and cause the negotiations to freeze due to your tone, language, or demeanor. Many issues will come about during a negotiation, but in order to resolve these issues the negotiator must take the appropriate approach.

Negotiations involve all of the international business tools as well as all communication skills that we have learned throughout our lives. It is important to come to the negotiating table with a level of respect for the other party and an understanding of their culture. A negotiation session can only be as successful as each party has tried to make it by being prepared. They must not come to the table with no idea of whom they are dealing with. There are going to be missteps along the way the important thing is to not be stubborn, apologize and learn from the mistake. This will be experience that a person can bring with him/her for future negotiations and will be able to be better prepared. When preparing for negotiations there are several questions to consider.

a. Who am I working with?
b. Are they a high-context or low-context society?
c. How do gender, age, and race play a role within their society?
d. How does religion play a role in their society?
e. What other beliefs, cultural norms affect their day-to-day lives?

These questions will help establish a framework for preparing for negotiations. This will let the person know where to start researching and where to focus your preparation. This will help one feel confident when coming to the negotiation table and will allow him/her to focus on the task at hand, getting the best deal for one's company.

What is a Global Leader?

A good global leader is a leader who can lead anywhere in the world. With globalizations and multinationals, we need global leadership. And to become one, people have to know and be aware of some important concepts like global leadership, cross-cultural communication, culture sensitivity, and acculturation, cultural influences on management, effective intercultural performance, changing international business, cultural synergy, work culture and global culture. As all managers, a global leader has to be open and flexible towards people. He/she has to know how to manage changes while being respectful to cultural diversity. The term "cross-cultural" implies interaction with persons of different cultural, ethnic, racial, gender, sexual orientation, religious, age and class backgrounds. With "cross-cultural communication" our global manager exchanges, negotiates, and mediates one's cultural differences through language, non-verbal gestures, and space relationships. By using the "cross cultural communication" the global leader expresses their openness to an intercultural experience. By means of his/her "cultural sensitivity", our global leader is aware that cultural differences and similarities exist and that those have an effect on values, learning, and behaviour of cultures. With the phenomenon of acculturation, our global leader assimilates cultural values of a human group, in order to create a real management based on cultural influences, and people performance. Next, the global manager has to appreciate the effects of cultural differences on a standard business principle. Once the cultural integration is carefully analyzed, planned and implemented, the company can create a "cultural synergy": a harmonization of the direction and operation of separate organizations into a whole. This cultural synergy will bring a work culture inside the whole company. Thanks to media, telecommunications, Internet...a global culture will be possible, to set up trans-national strategies (Moran et al., 2007). To succeed global leaders have to set up this process.

Recommendations for Training in Global Management

This study identifies key problem areas in global management, gives real world examples of the global companies who face these challenges. An in-class or a web-based training for company employees can include the appendices put together in this paper. Appendix 1 has a presentation that will give generic guidelines to the employees of the global companies. This presentation is a power point version of the results, discussion, and conclusion parts of this paper. With this rapid movement of people around the world, today's team mate evolves into a group leader working with members from different backgrounds. The presentation keeps in mind that all the employees and colleagues today are subject to global leadership from time to time. Appendix 1 can be used in distant learning settings or put on the corporate websites as video podcasts where employees log in and view it. The goal of the training is not to tech every aspect of cultural understanding, diversity, cross-cultural communication or negotiation processes but to show the importance of these areas, increase awareness, change the way people think or perceive in their thought processes. Its aim is to ease the company employees' transition to global situations.

Following the presentation, in-class discussions of the questions in Appendix 2 may be introduced. These questions are specific examples. Moreover, they add to and support the general guidelines of the training.

Appendix 3 has different scenario settings for specific experiences. The scenarios are inspired by our experiences, readings, and in-group discussions. The class may be divided into the groups and the groups analyze and evaluate the settings. At the end, the moderator encourages feedback about the settings. The questions to the groups may include:

a. What do you think happened here?
b. What did you learn from this scenario/experience?
c. What is the best way to do in this situation?

The group is encouraged for interactive discussion or role-playing to demonstrate their best way of dealing with these situations as this kind of group activities are successful in building relationship and trust between employees.

A multinational company subject to globalization managerial challenges can use this training, because it is a non-profit project put together by graduate students by research. The training may be a stage-1 or an initial training for the whole company, since it is easy-to-follow and Appendix 1 and 2 could be portable to the web to utilize time and effort. The web portion includes authentication of the employee at the beginning and at the end of the session to ensure participation and completion. Attendance should be the only requirement. Appendix 3 - The scenarios and discussions part may be executed among top-level managers as part of a classroom setting. The design of the training assumes it is modular, customizable, portable and expandable and it increases knowledge about cultural understanding and attempts to make people think more before acting in multicultural environments.

Future Add-Ons to the training:
The scenarios in Appendix 3 may be role-played and recorded by the Rowan University College of Communication students. This recording with the questions and answers at the end of each scenario can be put on the company (who is willing to use the training for its employees) web site as a webcast. The employees log in and watch the webcast. This visualization process may be more memorable for the trainees. Another advantage of this is employees who are located at different places can reach them during their own time.

The whole training may be used as a non-profit "Global Leadership Program" for the companies in South Jersey provided by the Rohrer College of Business MBA Program/students. MBA students who are in their last semester to graduate may take this as a class project, act as consultants to the company, implement and improve this training for the companies in the area as part of their school project. These instructions can also be coordinated with Center for Innovation and Entrepreneurship (CIE) at Rowan University to make use of this training for the companies interested. According to the company's business environment, other specific modules can be introduced by the consultants – if necessary. For example if the company has employees who travel to China often, then a training module focused on Chinese business environment can be added with specific scenarios and questions such as in Appendix 2 and 3.

APPENDIX 1

Multiple Choice Questions for Group Discussions

1. The global work culture is best characterized by two words. Which are they?
A. Change and diversity
B. Change and opportunity
C. Change and technology
D. Diversity and opportunity

2. When people leave their homes generally there is a "push" factor. Which of the following is not a "push" factor?
A. War and civil strife, including religious conflicts
B. Rising unemployment
C. Safety
D. Human right violation

3. What is the "butterfly effect"?
A. Events which help to the understanding of the world
B. Events in one part of the world can significantly affect the other side of the world.
C. Events which help culture to be no longer isolated
D. Traditional concepts, like the balance of power or ideologies

4. Which of the following is not part of the Human Resource Wheel?
A. Compensation/benefits
B. Union/Labor relations
C. Selection and staffing
D. Learning and trust

5. Which of the following means Cultural Accommodation?
A. One organization is in a more powerful position than the other
B. Managers develops new solution that respect all culture
C. Managers implementing a option which tend to imitate the host culture
D. Managers work and manage as if no conflict of cultures

6. Which of the following best characterize the Mexican people?
A. Relaxed, hospitable and warm people
B. Conservative, industrious and rural
C. Emotional, affective and talkative people
D. Easygoing and friendly

7. Brazilian people are:
A. Relaxed, hospitable and warm people
B. Conservative, industrious and rural
C. Emotional, affective and talkative people
D. Easygoing and friendly

8. New Zealanders are:
A. Punctual and conscious
B. Conservative, industrious and rural
C. Emotional, affective and talkative people
D. Easygoing and friendly

9. German people are:
A. Punctual and conscious
B. Conservative, industrious and rural
C. Fatalist, competitive and formal
D. Generous, and hospitable

10. Italian people are:
A. Punctual and conscious
B. Conservative, industrious and rural
C. Fatalist, competitive and formal
D. Generous, and hospitable

11. Dr. Geert Hoftstede made a research to identify important dimensions of national character. According to this research, which country ranked fortieth (among forty countries) on individualism (the most individualist country in the sample)? (Individualism refers to a "loosely knit social framework in a society in which people distinguish them and of their immediate families only.)
A. Argentina
B. Turkey
C. China
D. USA

12. Which one of the following means: "Building upon the very differences in the world's people for mutual growth and accomplishment by cooperation"?
A. Cultural shock
B. Cultural synergy
C. Cultural assimilation
D. Cross-cultural communication

13. An American manager working with Japanese colleagues must be aware of the cultural differences between Americans and Japanese people. Japanese culture
A. is a low-context culture – where low-context refers to information is contained in explicit words or codes.
B. is a collectivist culture – where collectivist refers to a tight social framework in which people distinguish themselves in-groups or out-groups; they expect their in-group (relatives, clan, organizations) to look after them, and in exchange for that owe absolute loyalty to it.
C. is a direct culture
D. is a culture that welcomes conflict and directly attacks the conflict.

14. In conversations, _____ tend to maximize differences between persons due to gender, status, or age in contrast to North Americans who often minimize them.
A. French
B. Danish
C. Dutch
D. Mexicans

15. Which country managers use fewer gestures and words?
A. France
B. Turkey
C. USA
D. Japanese

16. Which one represents a French negotiator's selection criteria?
A. Informality
B. Age is wisdom
C. Presentability is the most important
D. Technical expertise

17. Which is an invalid argument for anyone interested in negotiating in Chinese?
A. Emphasis is placed on trust and mutual connections.
B. Long-range benefits are preferred.
C. Chinese usually keep changing their minds.
D. They respond well to foreign representatives who specialize in the Public Republic of China (PRC).

18. In which language, "Yes" may merely mean "I heard you," not agreement or intention of complying? In this language, "no" is an affront and could hurt the feelings and poor etiquette.
A. Japanese
B. Korean
C. Vietnamese
D. Turkish

19. Which one is not true about European perceptions?
A. Europeans have an inherent interest in the quality of life.
B. Europeans enjoy socialization with family and friends over beverage and meals.
C. Europeans have not lived through any ambiguities therefore they don't have the threads of ancient customs and traditions.
D. Europeans generally have an inordinate sense of reality. When one reflects on the wars and disruptions in Europe in the twentieth century alone, one can understand how Europeans know that tragedy can be just a breath away and that perhaps only this moment is real.

20. Which one is not one of the unfortunate and disturbing global stereotypes about women leaders?
A. Women are fundamentally different and too "soft" to handle ruthless managerial decisions.
B. Other men won't take women managers seriously.
C. Women cause problems by looking for love in workplace, and this will disrupt the workplace.
D. There are many women enough to promote. Most companies find difficulty in promoting these high-quality women managers.

21. When a company imitates the host culture, attempting to blend in they are displaying which of the following:
A. Cultural Accommodation
B. Cultural Compromise

C. Cultural Synergy
D. Cultural Avoidance

22. An important aspect in being a global leader is being able to put yourself in someone else's shoes. This leadership trait is called:
A. Respect
B. Empathy
C. Nonjudgmental
D. Synergy

23. The country that makes the most attempts to avoid conflict is:
A. Japan
B. United States
C. Russia
D. Germany

24. The prime example of a country that represents individualism is:
A. Sweden
B. Asia
C. United States
D. Japan

25. Which type of listening is the attempt to trap an opponent with his own words?
A. Active Listening
B. Cynical Listening
C. Hearing
D. Offensive Listening

26. Which of the following is the most spoken language in the world?
A. English
B. Spanish
C. Russian
D. Mandarin

27. Which of the following countries are not considered High-Context cultures?
A. Japan
B. Spain
C. China
D. Canada

28. The most productive organizations are ones which have which of the following?
A. Synergy
B. Conflict
C. Power
D. Anger

29. An organization that puts effort to satisfy one's own concern is which of the following?
A. Assertive
B. Unassertive
C. Compromise
D. Avoidance

30. Based on the international study on body language, the largest affect on the total impact of a message is which of the following?
A. Words Used
B. Nonverbal
C. How the words are said
D. Tone of voice

APPENDIX 2

Possible Scenarios for Group Discussions

1.

Setting:

(At the corridor of the office (in the US), while two Chinese employees are chatting in Chinese with their mugs in hands)

A native English-speaking manager/colleague:

Hey, you two! If you don't speak English, you can't improve it. Isn't this why you are here in the States? (Laughs and thinks of it as a joke and returns to his cubicle)

Chinese colleagues smile and turn to each other with puzzled faces and do not say anything. However, they are upset and an offense is taken.

Possible Interpretation:

If you are the non-native speaker who is offended in this situation by your manager, what would you do?

2.

Setting:

Group project deadline comes; a European and a Japanese team mate come together after the deadline.

European colleague: (angry)

I thought you were going to get back to the group and the leader in the same email when you submitted our work? That was what we decided at the beginning. How come you forget that? I don't understand!!!

Japanese colleague: (puzzled and shy)

I am sorry, I thought I did. (And she leaves)

However, in reality, the Japanese employee did include the group members, but the European colleague did not get it due to a technical problem.

What would you say if you were the European colleague?

3.

Setting:

At a company dinner:

A non-Muslim employee: Is alcohol forbidden in your religion?

A Muslim employee: Yes, it is.

A non-Muslim employee: But you drink, right?

A Muslim employee: That's between me and God. You can't ask me those questions.

The Muslim employee has taken an offense and thinks: "Who does he think he is?"

The non-Muslim employee thinks he asked a simple question to make conversation and he was just curious about it. He wasn't judging.

4.

Setting:

At a meeting with HR, a top executive is asked about his opinion to address diversity issues in the company:

Leader/Executive:

I suggest we first look into our demographics and try to see how diverse our organization is. This is a multinational company with thousands of employees from all over the world. A policy that will give guidelines to everybody should be published.

5.

Setting:

At lunch, two employees talking:

An American employee:

I am going to X (the name of the country, and country Y does not accept its independence) for a meeting, I think it is cool. How is it like in that country?

A Y country employee:

X is not a country; it is part of our country.

6.

Setting:

Your marketing manager – not a team player, thinks he has a team where everybody is from different backgrounds and this is being ineffective. He wants you to let him reorganize them or he will not meet the deadline for the product meeting.

Marketing manager:

This team is frustrating. I am getting nowhere with them. I think I need to reorganize this or I can't make the deadline next week.

You/leader-manager:

_____?_____

What should you say?

What is the best approach in this situation? (Hint: We may not able to change what we see, but we can always change the ways we see things.)

7.
Setting:
Two employees standing, talking about a report and looking at some charts at the office)
African employee: (Talking and walking towards the other employee) Let me tell you something, this report needs more work on this chart...
American employee: (As the African employee walks towards him, takes a few steps back): I think this is what management is looking for, nothing more... (Thinks why the other employee has to come closer as he speaks.)
African employee: Look at this chart; it reflects revenues with unmatched costs. For example, the artist fee and the contractor variable fees are not there. This analysis will lead us to the wrong decision. (He thinks his American friend doesn't have time to talk about this because he is walking backwards as he talks).
What do you think is happening here?
What should our African employee do?

8.
Setting:
A negotiation between Japanese and American people.
The American negotiator puts his business cards to the Japanese people desks before they arrive. He is in Japan for two days to cut the deal. The Japanese crowd seems to be rather quite when they are seated.
American person: Hello, I would like to explain what I have for you in your folders in front of you. (Talks about the details of the preliminary contract) Japanese crowd looks unpleased.
What is wrong with this setting?

9.
Setting:
At a negotiating table two companies, one Japanese company and one United States company, are negotiating a contract that will allow the companies to decrease operating expense.
During the negotiation the United States representative is very forceful and agitated by the wording of the contracts. The United States representative was unable to control himself and became focused on the conflict in the wording. The Japanese representative never came across as forceful which led the United States company feel their business was not important to the

Japanese company. This led to the US company backing out of the deal and continuing with their high level of expense.

10.
Setting:
At a negotiating table two companies, one Chinese company and one United States company, are negotiating a contract that will allow the U.S. company to decrease expense by purchasing parts from the Japanese company.

During the negotiation, the Chinese company is very reluctant to jump into any contract. The U.S. company is attempting to complete the deal as soon as possible. However, the Chinese company keeps stalling and this is beginning to agitate the U.S. company. This leads to conflict that eventually leads to the contract not being completed.

CHAPTER **15**
Understanding and Leading Teams in Organization

Keywords: Teamwork, Team Socialization Process, Team Social Stratification, Team Culture, Team Leader Interpersonal Skill, Team Leadership and Team Effectiveness and Efficiency.

Introduction

In today's organization that wants to succeed, it has to realize that teamwork is very important because it is the way the employees value and respect each other. Teamwork enables employees of all skills and ages to have an important role to play in organization, and it is an important aspect of maintaining the self-sustainability of organizational performance. From a very early stage, members take on responsibility for performing certain tasks.

Organizations that socialize employees to grow up within a system of teamwork, employees quickly learn how to work with other employees in a positive way. The result is that they will soon begin to value their own potential as individuals and as a member of a team. New employees soon learn that they can join their efforts with those of others to create something to benefit the whole organization rather than individual interest. This requires us to answer the following question: What is a team? A team is a contingent of two or more people who interact and positively influence each other and coordinate their work to accomplish a meaningful shared goal or purpose for the success of organization. The next question to ask and answer is: What does TEAM mean? It means Together Each Achieve More. This is why being in a team helps individuals to pave the way to a positive future in their lives that will bring them self-respect and dignity. There are three primary reasons why teams present a dilemma for people. The first reason is that when people become part of a team, they have to rely on the success of the team, which makes them dependent on how well other people perform and act. Some people are comfortable with the idea of making sacrifices; teamwork demands that we make sacrifices for the success of the group. Secondly, teams are sometimes made up of people who have different work ethics. Some individuals do their assignments early, on time or a slow starter who finishes at the last minute (Daft, 2008).

Team Responsibility

Team members take new members around and show them their responsibilities to the organization such as the things that organization expects because the employee values "we" more than "I." Teams foster a time when individuals challenge themselves and re-evaluate their skills. Team members have to learn how to work with other members and to understand that one is different, unique and that one has knowledge and energy that can be channeled in a positive way. People in a team share a goal (Daft, 2008). As a member of the team, one can contribute to the organization and can apply what is learned here to another organization. There is no end to the team, as employees participate in them until they move to another company. Teams should be part of an organization that builds upon itself. They create an organization that wants to move forward, that wants to create a positive culture, and that eradicates strangeness among employees. In an organization where teams are a right, there all employees will find freedom.

Discipline in a Team Oriented Organization

Discipline in a team oriented organization is a responsibility that belongs to the whole employees, not just to the top managers. All employees have the right to be self disciplined. Most importantly, it is the responsibility of the senior employees, in the organization, to teach new employees to have a clean heart for the organization to succeed and become profitable. Then they will say one day, "We are proud of our senior employees; we respect our seniors because they were there for us." This is the kind of discipline that needs to exist in a team oriented organization that all employees must enjoy and take pride. One must ask where has discipline with caring and understanding gone in organization? Thus, teamwork must teach all employees that to be hard-working is to show pride in one's organization. To apply one is a way to say thanks for the ability to do what one can do to make this organization the best company to work. To be hard-working brings happiness and joy because it benefits all concerned. One must be proud of oneself in a team oriented organization.

Team Members Socialization Process

Teams are very important to the socialization of employees, particularly the new ones. Teams connect employees in a strong, healthy social network within an organization. It is a way to tap into each individual's positive energy and skills to utilize it to benefit the entire organization. Teams transform individual self-interest into a valuable resource that can then be used to build and maintain the vibrant organization. Teams foster an appreciation of each individual's talents and the contribution they can make to their organization. Teams promote the philosophy that everyone's role is important and equally necessary, if the organization is to be successful and self-sustainable. Additionally, to understand outcomes at the individual and team levels, it is necessary to take into account not only team process but also some critical individual differences that provide team members a lens for interpreting other team members' behaviors (Rockmann et al., 2010).Teams must help members in any organization realize how they can contribute to their organization. In a team all employees are socialized to become hard workers in their organization. When they mature, these employees will believe hard work brings success and joy, in the future. This hard work will pay off if the organization based their promotion policy on performance.

Team Achievement and Team Pride

When a team's works hard and achieves something great, they will have a sense of pride for their team and be motivated to do it again, because they know their role will be considered important and essential by top managers as well as all employees in the organization. Teamwork, whatever the context, requires collaboration (Peters et al., 2007). The role the teams will play in an organization will be viewed as valuable and vital to the organizational success. To be a bum and depend upon others to complete organizational task is contrary to team spirit, teamwork, and team synergy and team socialization in an organization. The guidance one is given by one's team and the important role one is given to play makes one grow into a whole human being who is proud of what one can contribute at every stage of one's life.

Team Success

To help a team succeed when they face a difficult task, the highly experienced members in an organization must kicking in and serve as team mentors. Each team in an organization should have a mentor who is not necessary a manger but someone who is skillful in teamwork to mentor the team. This is how the traditional organizational teamwork social structure should work. This is how teamwork interconnects all individuals in an organization, from new employees to older employees in the organization.

Team Social Stratification

This type of social stratification teaches one, at an early stage, that each individual's role is essential. From the first day they are employed, all employees must take on their responsibilities and learn how the failure to perform certain tasks will negatively affect the whole organization. No team member or employees should want to see this happen. Failure to perform one's tasks not only negatively affects one's team, but also the goal of the organization. Employees will soon believe that those who are socialized by good organizational culture, whose managers and leaders set a good example, whose behavior one can emulate, who are proactive leaders in their organization, will contribute in a positive way and be able to work successfully with others.

Team Activity

Participating in a team activity will help members to feel a sense of responsibility to their organization. The concept behind the team is that members are able to act strategically upon what they believe to solve their own team's challenges as well as organizational problems and challenges. Teams help employees to appreciate who they are, the environment in which they work and members unique culture, and the norms and values of the organization. Teams serve as an essential commitment to organizational mechanism that successfully accomplishes the most important task of all organization stakeholder. They are a strong foundation upon which civilizations are built. When new employees are not socialized by the use of teams, they become socially isolated individuals and will not feel or have a sense of connectedness with their organization. Not only is this sad and unfortunate, it is also devastating for the entire organization because of the resultant costs for treatment and addressing high employee turnover will not be cost effective. One might ask, "What kind of self-esteem and dignity is possible for employees who have no mentors to socialize them in good organizational culture?" All organizations have a responsibility to work with employees to see that teams are supported and maintained in their organization for maximum performance. If they continue to neglect this important responsibility, they will be responsible for encouraging poor performance and high employee turnover in their organization. If teams disappear, employees will no longer have an important and meaningful role to play in their organization but instead work just to get a paycheck. They will turn their inexhaustible energy to a negative struggle in which the most individualistic among them survives and prospers. As they become senior employees, they will turn away from the challenge of finding positive answers for the difficult economic questions that face all organizations today. Each individual, as an employee, is responsible for having, in their lives and careers, a clear destination that positively contributes to the support of teams.

Team Culture

Teams teach one to respect, love, and believe in oneself. They help employees to believe in the value of their organizational culture. Teams help employees to collaborate with all members of their organization because their team provides them with a specified role to play in relation to others in their organization. Teams assist employees to deal realistically with their weaknesses and teach them how to develop their strengths. Teams help build employee self esteem. Teams contribute to the self-sustainability and the success of their organization by providing opportunities for employees to challenge themselves to face and overcome difficulties in their organization. An organization's level of self-sustainability depends on the ability of its employees to be innovative and creative in solving organizational problems. In a team, employees learn how to deal appropriately with issues and to solve problems creatively. Above all, one learns to accept failure as a way to learn how to improve oneself. Teams should teach all members to not expect that life would always be positive all the time and help them realize that failure is an opportunity for growth and development. It also prepares members to both welcome and deal with negative aspects of one-self, others, and learn ways to work effectively in the organization. Every employee needs to have a specified positive role to play in the development of a successful organization. The socialization that is provided by teams nurtures a view of the world in which the emphasis is on *we* rather than on *I*. Each senior team is responsible in assisting the next newly formed team to implement their particular team projects and to hold joint celebrations of achievement and holidays. When team members are given opportunities to contribute to their organization through participation in team activities, they no longer rely on top managers' assistance and instead rely on their productive contribution and performance.

Team Mentoring

The mentoring of teams unifies organization by creating an atmosphere in which everyone cares for one another. In this way, the mentorship process of teams flushes out individuals' visions of how they can personally benefit their organization. This form of team mentoring empowers each member a valuable and vibrant employees who can contribute to the organizational success.

Unifying an Organization

When an organization is unified by the influence of teams, it actively works to create a safe and clean place to work. Every member of the organization will be actively and positively involved with its success. The task of socialization is accomplished because senior employees and new ones are proud to pass on what they know. An organization that is unified by utilizing teams empowers its employees to become innovative and creative in finding solutions to succeed in the 21st century.

Team Effectiveness

When it comes to having an effective team process there are certain key factors to consider. Every team consists of people coming together from different backgrounds; as a result it is imperative that the process of the team is an effective one. Considerations for an effective team process are: a climate of trust and openness, open and honest communication, a sense of belonging, diversity is valued as an asset, creativity and risk-taking are encouraged, ability to self-correct, members who are interdependent, consensus decision-making and participative leadership. Once a team is created it becomes your new family, yet in a more structured way because everyone has a responsibility as a member to finish a common objective. Having a climate where there is trust and openness gives everyone included in the team the opportunity to work freely, without being hesitant about members doing things secretly that could cause fear, lack of trust and confusion. Communication is key in any relationship, if that is hindered in a team then the rest is history because the teams' effectiveness has been set up for failure.

Furthermore, in the world knowingly or unknowingly wants to belong. Belong in a family, church, team, club and so forth. It is very important that each member of a group know that they are part of a team process, they are empowered, they are appreciated and valued. Another suggestion for having an effective team process is diversity in background. Diversified teams would most likely have a well rounded approach in fixing and dealing with problems that may arise. Diversity should be something that teams appreciate as an asset to a team because everyone with their own experience brings about numerous ideas to tackle. It seems that in a team where risk-taking and creativity is encouraged people flourish and fear is limited because it is okay to be an individual within a team.

Sometimes it is necessary for one to separate from themselves and look on from the outside in to gain a better perspective of what is going on in their surroundings. Knowing your flaws is always helpful. This allows you the opportunity to work on expanding your ability to self-evaluate even more. This helps a team process because you can work on things that are more beneficial to the teams' goal as opposed to things that you are not good at and slows everyone down. Now the part of being independent within a team comes up. As much as teams are encouraged it is very important that people do not lose their identity within a group because everyone starts singing the same tune. This type of team does not prosper since everyone says yes to the same things and everyone says no to the same ideas. Sometimes controversy is beneficial within a group because it creates an environment of independent thinking. Teams are put together for the most part to accomplish certain things within a time frame and in order for this to occur there must be an environment of harmony when making decisions. Every judgment affects all members of a group and team; so making a decision that excludes certain members' opinions could be detrimental. The most important of all is having a leader who does not separate him or herself from the group but participates and influence people to be great followers by empowering them every chance he or she gets.

Table 1.1 shows there are five common dysfunctions of teams and the effective team characteristics:

Table 1.1

Dysfunction	Effective Team Characteristics
Lack of trust	*Trust*
Fear of conflict	*Healthy conflict*
Lack of commitment	*Commitment*
Avoidance of accountability	*Accountability*
Inattention to results	*Results orientation*

In order for teams to function smoothly, leaders who take specific actions to help individuals come together as a team build them. Teams do not develop overnight and therefore it takes time and patience (Team Development 101, 2009). Understanding that everyone has different personalities and different ways of doing things provides team leaders to have an open mind to the suggestions and input of others within the team. With that being said, there are stages of team development that are easily identifiable and are currently used in the workplace today, shown in Figure 1.1 (Why is team development so important, 2009):

Figure 1.1

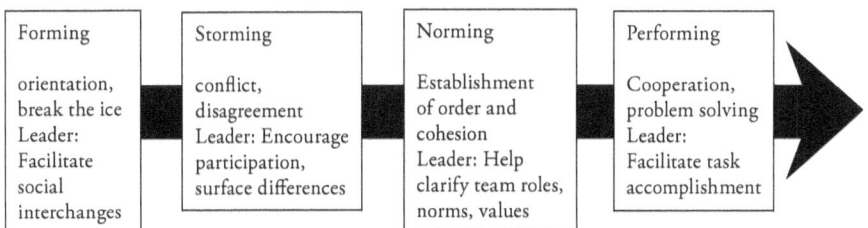

Leaders must be effective, confident, open-minded and communicative, which will bring about successful teams, in Table 1.2, provides the roles of two types of leaderships:

Table 1.2

Task-Specialist Role	Socioemotional Role
Initiate ideas	Encourage others
Give opinions	Reconcile differences
Seek information	Provide friendship and support
Pull ideas together	Go along with the team
Stimulate action	Maintain harmony

1. It is important to note that the role the team leader adopts will determine the results to be achieved in a team oriented organization because he or she is the architecture.

Team Efficiency

2. Things must line up properly to have an efficient team, setting an agenda always helps. There are a few other things that can be done to have an efficient team process like: creating a common concept, setting objectives, creating a plan, explaining functions and responsibilities, prioritizing, focusing, suggest meetings as well as phone meetings and management of time. This all makes a great and efficient team process to work within.

3. Once these are in order then the process would flow smoothly
    for the most part. Creating a common concept would organize
    everyone to start thinking in the mindset of a team and with a goal
    that is valuable to anyone involved. In order for things to get done
    setting objectives is a crucial part of making things happen within
    a group, because it gives people an idea of the plan. Planning in
    any organization is necessary, like they say "if you fail to plan you
    plan to fail." Planning gives us the ability to set things in place
    and keep us on track. If every member of a group or team in an
    organization knows their role and responsibilities then it is hopeful
    that there would be no time wasted on things that are insignificant.
    Prioritizing is something everyone must include as part of their
    method to accomplish a goal because doing so allows one to have
    control over the outcome of any situation and that would lead
    to the focus of the group or team. Whenever there are times a
    member of a team thinks that communication is lacking there
    must be an avenue for having a forum where every team member
    can participate and get things back in order to efficiently use time.
    Managing time is not always an easy task because other things
    come first and sometimes things have to be done instantaneously
    so one has to constantly remind themselves of what is going on
    around them. Team members feel that other aspects contribute to
    the success of a team such as individuals' skills and experience, and
    capability to work together as a team. Getting a group of people to
    work successfully and efficiently as a team requires communicating
    effectively, establishing trust, sharing the load, and completing
    tasks on time. This is difficult even when the team members are
    all in the same location. When team members are spread out in
    various locations, it presents new obstacles for the team leader
    (Kossler et al., 2003). For effective management of the team,
    it is required to have a virtual team charter that clearly defines
    the mission, objectives, and roles of each member. A universal
    communication etiquette defining the use of technology should be
    established (Combs et al., 2007). The phenomenon of globalization
    has resulted in supra- national organizations operating in multiple
    cultural contexts, and their educational and training programs
    should reflect this (Ahanchian, 2009). For global teams, diversity is
    always of concern.

Team Leadership

4. In the face of challenging and complex projects leaders, managers, and team leaders have to deal with a wide range of people - including sponsors, team members, clients, suppliers and internal department heads – all of whom often have conflicting goals and competing priorities. Leadership is not optional. Because of the complexity of the task, distribution of teams, communication through IT, and inherently mixed-motive goal structure, leadership is required to direct and regulate collective effort (DeChurch et al., 2010). They may also be located in different countries and speak different languages. Leaders must display interpersonal skills necessary to work in a culturally sensitive way with a variety of people and personalities.

5. Clearly, interpersonal skills are important to that of a leader in an organization and team. Is it a combination of all interpersonal skills that makes a leader effective? Are some more important than others?

6. A positive attitude is essential for boosting morale and good interaction with others is required to operate effectively and efficiently.

7. Ironically, two of the quality skills, "ability to self-evaluate" and "patient," were two skills one may perceive to be the most important to an effective team leader in an organization but Hollandsworth cited, "the most effective basic interpersonal communication skills focused on initiating conversations, listening effectively, and relationship management" (Hollandsworth, 2004). Ellis found the "ability to self-evaluate" to be necessary to the development of communication competencies both which helps leaders to gain insight into their life so they may improve upon their leadership success. Self-evaluations based on factors that determine interpersonal communication strengths and weaknesses assist leaders in improving their own level of performance. Continued self-evaluations help to add quality and value to a leader's business life and also to their personal life. Self-evaluation is essential for leaders to determine whether or not they are truly connecting with the people whom they lead (Ellis, 2002).

In addition, patience allows the leader to remain calm which translates well with team members who may be having a hard time understanding something. This gives team members a sense of understanding so they do not feel alienated.

8. Furthermore, listening is one of the top interpersonal communication skills that a team leader can master. Having a positive attitude about the listening process helps a team leader in understanding that it is an active action and requires work to master (Dance & Zak-Dance, 1996). Reserving judgment is a critical aspect for active listening if all ideas are to be given adequate consideration notes Parker (1996) who feels that "the principal listening skill is the ability to sit back, be attentive, and take in what is said while reserving judgment."Active listening includes verbal acknowledgement and paraphrasing or, what Parker calls "reflecting," and "what I hear you saying is…" (p. 39). The purpose of reflecting is to gain clarity of the message intended by the other person, and to let that individual know you care about what he/she is communicating (Parker, 1996). Good team leaders acknowledge the thoughts and ideas of team members as a way to enhance communication.

9. Stemming from good listening skills comes the ability to understand others' situations or in other words, to be able to empathize with them. "Empathy is a form of validating the thoughts and feelings of others in a way that builds trust and honesty in the relationship" (Spangle and Moorhead, 1998). This active form of listening requires leaders to be open and ready to learn. To develop this skill, Spangle and Moorhead suggest that a team leader "focus their attention on the words of others, communicate that he or she is genuinely interested in what another person has to say, and remain open to what is said, even if he or she disagrees with the message (Spangle & Moorhead, 1998). Furthermore, understanding others' situations allows team leaders to interact with people from other backgrounds, and to become more aware of their own culture. Shockley-Zalabak notes, "We have to separate our preconceptions, beliefs, and attitudes from actual behaviors, and continually open our awareness to new information and new ways of understanding others" (Shockley-Zalabak, 2002).

10. Similar to "understanding of others' situations" is "appreciating others' experiences". This is important because as a team leader you are going to work with employees of all ages, races, backgrounds, and education levels. For example, appreciating an older employee in the workplace or team setting for their experience and at the same time appreciating a younger employee's new ideas, helps to create productivity and efficiency in the workplace. Your employees or team members will appreciate your ideas more if you appreciate theirs. This interpersonal skill leads to effective workplace communication. Another important interpersonal skill was "communicating thoughts and ideas well" in a team. Being able to effectively communicate your thoughts and ideas well to your team allows them to operate effectively because they know what you want from them and what their objective is. Without proper direction nothing would get done properly.

11. Finally, the last two interpersonal skills examined, "conveys a positive self image" and "ability to gain respect" is an important attribute in team leadership. Interpersonal skills is highly important, especially the ability to gain respect. Without respect, a leader can lose the ability to effectively lead and efficiently manage their team. When team members have respect for their leader they are more willing to do what is asked of them and they are better able to communicate. It is important to note that communication is vital to effective workplace operations. Trust is the most important trait to have in a team and when leaders can trust each other and their teammates the need for power becomes obsolete. It is important to note that building trust in a team is like building a marriage. Trust must be practiced and nurtured to become part of the team's norms and culture.

Conclusion

12. To study teams in an organization and to specifically address interpersonal skills of leaders which included: active listening, patience, understanding of others' situations, appreciates others' experiences, positive attitude, interacts well with others, conveys

a positive self image, communicates thoughts and ideas well, has the ability to gain respect and the ability to self-evaluate shades new light and a whole new understanding of team leadership. All of these areas are important for a team leader to possess because interacting with people of many different backgrounds in an organization and team environment can be difficult. Many team leaders who are managers fail to be engaging or encouraging and as a result they do not see the bigger picture of being a part of a whole. This mentality of the old team leadership style of dictating is no longer the norm. People are much more receptive to team leaders who respect and value the ideas of others and encourage individuals to be better team members and leaders. A team must always have a leader and the leader is the one who determines how successful, effective, efficient, and productive a team is through the time they are working together (Avolio, Walumbwa, & Weber, 2009). Successful leadership and effective teams need five common characteristics which are trust, healthy conflict, commitment, accountability, and results orientation.

13. Trust is important because members of a team must trust each other. The leader must be able to trust his or her followers and the followers must be able to trust their leader or the team dynamic falls apart from the core. Healthy conflict is a powerful resource all effective teams must have because members of a group must be able to feel comfortable to speak their mind and challenge each other's ideas. Also, all the members of an effective group need to be committed to the group's ideas, goals, and decisions or the team will be unable to get any work done (The Importance of Leadership, 2005).

14. Accountability is important because each member needs to be accountable for their actions and work. Everyone in the group must also be able to count on the other members in the group and should always hold each member accountable for the part they are supposed to complete (Hackman, 2010). Results orientation refers to individual members setting aside their personal agendas and focusing on the team goals above their own. This is important to team success because when everyone on a team works collectively to a single goal instead of each member working towards their own goals (The Importance of Leadership, 2005). In a nutshell

teams in an organization serve as an excellent way to accelerate organizational performance and success for 21st century.

DISCUSSION QUESTIONS

1. Why are teams becoming so popular?
2. Do you like teamwork? Discuss your answers.
3. How can the understanding of this chapter help you become a good team leader? Discuss your answers.

CHAPTER 16
Act Global and Put Global Leadership Theories into Practice in your Organization

Understanding descriptive and prescriptive theories of global leadership and why both types are useful for organization success.

It is important to recognize that descriptive theories of leadership, explain global leadership processes, describe the typical activities of leaders, and explain why certain behaviors occur in particular situations. In essence, these theories describe characteristics of global leadership – what global leaders typically do or portray. For example, global leader A has behavioral characteristics of x, y, and z. Global Leaders typically act or behave in a certain manner. They will portray these particular traits that are commonplace among most other leaders. These are all characteristics common to most leaders. This theory of global leadership is useful because it illustrates *what* competencies a leader is likely to possess.

Interestingly, prescriptive theories of global leadership specify what global leaders must do to become effective, and they identify any necessary conditions for using a particular type of behavior effectively. In essence, these theories describe what makes a global leader most effective – what leaders *should* do. For example, leader B should exhibit behaviors of a, b, and c in order to be the most effective leader. In a given situation, a leader should act a certain way in order to lead in the most effective manner. This theory of leadership is useful because it illustrates *how* a global leader can demonstrate their skills most effectively. As stated, a prescriptive theory is especially useful when a wide discrepancy exists between what global leaders typically do and what they should do to be the most effective.

It is vital to be aware of the fact that descriptive theory is kind of like ingredients to a recipe for Global Leaders. While, the prescriptive theory include the actions global leaders must do to ingredients in order to make the most delicious recipe. Both the ingredients and the process are important to the end result, and they both contribute to the final product. A global leader will have certain "ingredients" or characteristics to be successful, and it is the process of implementing those ingredients that dictates how to lead the most effectively in an organization.

However global leaders have to understand that descriptive theory and the prescriptive theory are not mutually exclusive. The descriptive theory will describe more of the what, as far as what makes up typical behavior in organizations. Furthermore, the prescriptive theory will describe more of the how, as far as how do these behaviors contribute to global leadership effectiveness. Both theories are important to understand, and both provide insight and perspective on global leadership makeup.

Managerial activities and behavior affected by level of management, unit size, and lateral interdependence

One important aspect of Global Leadership is to know how Managerial activities and behavioral content are affected by level of management, size of organizational units, and lateral interdependence. Different managerial roles focus on different perspectives of management activities. For instance, a higher level manager will focus more on the big picture of management demands. They are the highest authority figure and have responsibility for the most important corporate decisions. They typically have a long-term view of company operations and manage the company on a 10 – 20 year timeline. These high-level managers are tasked with strategic making decisions, and are responsible for building more external relationships. Middle managers are also concerned with a longer term perspective, and their decisions are made in 2–5 year increments. These managers are concerned with corporate policy and program implementations. Finally, lower level managers are more focused on the company's day-to-day objectives. They are closest to the employees and manage on a much shorter timeline, typically a couple weeks to a two year time frame. These managers must manage within the confines of the policies and regulations that were formulated from those upper level managers. They lead with less autonomy and have more of a technical focus than those managers above them.

Another important aspect of global leadership is the understanding of how the size of an organization also has quite an effect on managerial activities. Managers leading much larger companies are seen to have much more demanding jobs than those leading smaller organizations. Due to the volume alone, there are significantly more decisions to be made, more knowledge a manager must possess, and more organizational subunits to deal with. Additionally, the larger the corporation, the more middle level managers you are required to deal with. It is difficult for a manger of a larger organization to structure corporate meetings with their subordinates and also. it is difficult to interact with subordinates at an individual level. The administrative workload is also significantly greater in a larger organization. As the organization gets larger, the issues within an organization are amplified. It's not just one or two issues a global leader must deal with, it is one or two issues (probably more) per subunit the global leader must face.

Finally, is the Lateral interdependence, which is the extent to which a global leader's subunit is dependent on other subunits in the same organization or on external groups." This is another component that will affect managerial activities and behavior. The more interdependence among the subunits, the more important it is to manage and coordinate that interdependence. Thus, "as lateral interdependence increases, the external activities of a leader become more important, managers spend more time in lateral interactions, and they build larger networks with contacts in other parts of the organization. The manager has a broader scope and more interaction as the interdependence grows. As the interdependence grows, more coordination and management is needed in order for the subunits to continue to run efficiently. This increases the presence of management throughout the organization and its subunits to bring maximum performance.

Planning, clarifying, and monitoring relevant for global leadership effectiveness

It is paramount to understand that effective global leadership requires specific types of task-oriented behaviors – planning work activities, clarifying roles and objectives, and monitoring operations and performance. Planning work activities includes deciding what to do, how to do it, who will do it, and when it will be done. Planning is crucial, and requires leadership direction. The leader is there to draw out the planning process in order to create an efficiently run working environment. Specific types of planning include *operational* planning, the scheduling of routine work; *action planning,* the development of detailed action steps for implementing a new policy or project; and *contingency planning,* the development of procedures for avoiding or dealing with potential problems. The planning should incorporate activities such as decision making, strategizing, assigning responsibilities, building teams, creating a vision as well as others that the global leader deem necessary to have in the organization. Time management is also extremely important during the planning process. The more thorough the leader plans, the more efficient the process and outcome will be. Some planning activities are observable via plans, budgets, schedules, and company meetings.

Clarifying roles and objectives, or more specifically communicating plans, policies, and role expectations, is also relevant for global leadership effectiveness. Subcategories for clarifying include defining job responsibilities, assigning work, and setting performance goals. In fact, "the purpose of [the] clarifying behavior is to guide and coordinate work activity and make sure people know what to do and how to do it." Clarifying includes laying out expectations and communicating these expectations clearly to all subordinates. If any confusion lies in the eyes of the employee, they will not necessarily implement their roles most efficiently and effectively. Therefore, it is imperative to clearly communicate the roles and responsibilities to your employees. Studies have found that there is a positive relationship between clarifying and managerial effectiveness. This means that the more thoroughly a role is clarified, the more effective the management will be. The employees will have a good understanding of what is expected of them in their role, and the manager will be able to devote her time to productive management.

Furthermore, monitoring operations and performance of the manager's organizational unit is also relevant for effective global leadership. This includes gathering information about the progress of work, the performance of individual subordinates, the quality of products, and the success of projects and programs. The monitoring of operations assists in the planning and problem solving initiatives. Some techniques of monitoring include observing, reviewing reports, inspecting work samples, etc. It is more likely managers will monitor more closely with inexperienced or insecure employees. The more competent the subordinate is, the less monitoring they will need. Monitoring is likely to affect performance. When monitoring is followed by praise or criticism, the effect on performance is even greater.

The potential benefits and risks of using participative global leadership

Some potential benefits of participative leadership include higher decision quality, higher decision acceptance by participants, more satisfaction with the decision process, and more development of decision-making skills. First, the decision quality will be improved when other people are involved in the process. The reason for this is because a group of people are greater than the sum of its parts. When people are able to share knowledge with each other, they typically offer more ideas. On the other hand, if goals among the group are incompatible, there is a risk that the decision quality will be negatively affected.

Another benefit of using participative leadership includes decision acceptance. When others are involved in the decision-making process, there tends to be more acceptance within the group. This is because some people may have a considerable amount of influence. It could also be because you have a shared view of some of the other ideas offered by the group. Additionally, a group atmosphere is conducive for people to express their concerns.

Participative leadership allows for more satisfaction with the decision process. It has been found that the opportunity to express opinions and preferences before a decision is made (called "voice") can have beneficial effects regardless of the amount of actual influence participants have over the final decision (called "choice"). When people have an outlet, such as a group setting, to express their ideas, they are more likely to be satisfied over the decision being implemented.

Finally, another benefit of participative leadership is the development of participant skills. The more often this type of decision making is implemented, the more developed the decision making skill set will be. Participants will be more confident and also more effective in dealing with issues.

There are some limitations to participative leadership as well. For instance, there is a lack of consistent results with this type of research. Therefore, it is not clear whether the previously mentioned benefits are, in fact, benefits at all.

Additionally, there are limitations to the experiments and studies that have been done on participative leadership. Some of these field experiments and quasi-experimental studies have been introduced by the organization, rather than the participant. Therefore, it is difficult to determine the effects of such studies. Also, these studies tend to be combined with other techniques, which inhibits whether the effects are those of participative leadership or some other technique. Finally, the measure of participation consequences in most of the studies was overall satisfaction and performance of subordinates, not satisfaction with the way a particular decision was handled or commitment to implement that decision effectively. Therefore, it is difficult to determine what was relevant to the outcome.

Discussion of Global Leadership Competencies

Global leader must encompass certain competencies in order to be effective. First, it is important for any such leader to be driven in their success. This is something that is typically portrayed prior to becoming a global leader. People who have personal drive are determined to succeed and more willing to take personal risks. These are people who, as children, were leaders in sporting activities, involved in school politics, and generally were involved and seen as authority-type figures. This goes back to the age-old question, are leaders born or made? I believe leaders can be a combination of the two. Some people are leaders in their everyday lives; it is just natural. While others have the skills to be a good leader (which I will discuss later), but they need to be developed. Either way, effective global leaders are driven toward success, and no matter how they get there, they are always willing to take risks.

Another, fairly typical, global leadership competency is to possess a certain set of cognitive skills. This includes the ability to see things in many different ways. This means that a global leader needs to be able to understand and interpret different perspectives from many different people. They must be able to assess situations from a non-biased point of view with the ability to consider all alternatives. Another important cognitive skill includes being able to manage oneself. It is not just about managing others; an effective global leader needs to be able to manage him or herself from an objective perspective. This includes monitoring your own strengths, being able to take an objective point of view, and continuing to grow as a leader. The skills one needs to have in order to become an effective and efficient leader are conceptual and interpersonal skills. Conceptual skills are a leader's ability to perceive and understand concepts and be able to recognize other events and then be able to conceptualize what is occurring. Conceptual skills are the leader's ability to convey meaning, be able to communicate with models, metaphors, and analogies, inductive and deductive reasoning, detect deviations, and be able to tell what is relevant and what is irrelevant. Interpersonal skills are the leader's ability to recognize the leader's own personality traits in relations to their workers and it also allows the leader to perceive how the workers handle their own relations within the group of workers in regards to how they interact personally with one another and how the group of workers reacts to the manager's under the leader. Conceptual, and Interpersonal skills all lead to a more effective and efficient organization if the Leader knows how to manage these skills.

These skills lead to a more effective and efficient leader and leaders who recognize and practice these skills to better their understanding and implementation of these skills do better than leaders that do not develop these skills. Effective mangers have a strong efficiency organization and always strive not to waste time and resources whether human or material hence increasing efficiency. In order to have a strong-efficiency-organization leader need to possess a high achievement of motivation, high inner work standards, and be able to build and perform task objectives to complete these objectives. A high achievement orientation is needed in order so that the organization can keep growing and profit instead of just following the beaten trail and settling for mediocre results. High inner work standards are needed in order to be able to measure performance correctly and to not settle for less, high inner work standards lead to a more efficient operation within the organization. An ability to engineer, manage, and complete task objectives are needed to keep projects on schedule and within budget, it allows the leader to correctly assess their workers and keep them within their abilities while gradually increasing their worker's abilities.

Other skills that the leader should possess in order to improve any organization's efficiency and effectiveness are the skills of initiating action, accepting responsibility, attacking obstacles, and seeking more information about events related to work of global leadership. Skills of initiating action are needed to know when it is appropriate to begin a task and when it is not, it helps managers assess the proper times to implement new processes or processes that lead to new products. A global leader's ability to attack obstacles is a great skill because obstacle cause inefficiency by stalling processes, once the obstacle is identified the global leader should take all necessary steps to turn the obstacle into a lift or leverage or destroy that obstacle, whichever is easier and more effective. A global leader's skill of wanting or needing to gather as much pertinent information related to any task or assignment they are involved in allows them to assess a more wider view of the same situation in which other leaders may have a more narrow minded approach, the narrow-minded approach will always be less efficient and effective than gathering all available information about a certain task or agenda of tasks. The global leader that possesses all of these skills and recognizes them in order to improve and maximize these skills will always be able to outperform the incompetent global leaders no matter who the incompetent global leaders know, where the incompetent global leaders went to school, or how much money the incompetent global leader has. The Competent Global Leader will always be able to lead a more efficient and effective organization and all the while pushing the bar of expectation higher from within and without the leader's sphere of influence.

Global leaders should also have a sort of emotional resilience. This means being able to maintain confidence under any kind of circumstance, particularly those that are more difficult in nature. Global Leaders must be composed in difficult situations. They will often be faced with challenges, and in the face of them, must be able to react with an emotionally stable sense of mind. It is important to lead with composure, and this requires confidence and resilience. This is one more portrayal of a global leadership competency.

In addition to competencies, there are also some skills required to be an effective global leader. A global leader, first and foremost, must be culturally sensitive. In order for a leader to truly become effective in a global context, they must be aware and sensitive to other cultures. You cannot be a global leader without awareness of the cultures that make up your organization. This is one of the main differentiators between being a good leader and being a good global leader. When entering new markets, particularly those abroad, it is imperative to have a strong understanding of the country's diversity and how it differs from your home country.

A global leader should be clear and concise with the organization's purpose. Too many times, executives and global leaders are hesitant to articulate the goals and vision of the corporation. This only inhibits the loyalty and effectiveness across the organization. Your employees need to know what they are working toward, and everyone should be working toward the same goals. There is more of a sense of trust when there is more transparency throughout the business. It provides for a more open kind of culture as well. When members of the organization are more focused on their positions and specific tasks, they are less aligned with the corporation as a whole. In order for them to feel connected to the business, they need to have full disclosure from the leader.

Effective global leaders need to be able to delegate. When leading a global organization, there are too many things to juggle on your own. Therefore, it is extremely important to have the right team in place, understanding the strengths of your team, and delegating the important decisions and tasks that are impossible to take on yourself. This responsibility is a benefit for all parties – the leader is able to focus other aspects of being a leader of a global corporation, and the delegates are able to assume an important role within the organization. Being able to take part in crucial aspects of the business is important to the success of the individual as well as the company as a whole.

The critical importance of knowledge sharing to Global Leaders

Knowledge sharing is an activity in which knowledge, such as skills, expertise or information, is exchanged among people, friends, and members of a family, community or within an organization. Global Leaders must understand that organizations have recognized that knowledge constitutes a valuable indefinable asset for creating and also sustaining some type of competitive advantages. Knowledge sharing activities are generally supported by knowledge management systems, however, technology constitutes only one of the many factors that affect the sharing of knowledge within organizations, such as organization's culture, trust, and incentives. The sharing of knowledge constitutes a major challenge in the field of knowledge management because some employees and even competitors tend to resist sharing their knowledge with the rest of the organization (Wikipedia The Free Encyclopedia, 2011).

Furthermore, Knowledge sharing extends past teamwork, even past collaboration. It's about engraining knowledge transfer into those key processes that are used for interlinking suppliers, buyers, customers and service organizations into a company's workflows. Those skillful global leaders are the ones who are able to take advantage of knowledge sharing as a competitive advantage within a global environment.

Finally, effective global leaders must be able to take ownership and responsibility of any such outcome, positive or negative. Since you should be a delegator, you are responsible for the outcome of the objectives your subordinates have implemented. When the outcome is positive, they should be credited with its success. However, when the outcome is negative, you must be willing to take the blame. The organization is ultimately in the hands of the global leader. Your team has to know you will have their back, so to speak, and in any situation will be supportive. Of course, when they do make mistakes, they must be addressed. However, they should be addressed in an appropriate manner and arena. Global leaders addressing problems and challenges in an organization should not undermine the empowerment of the employees. By and large, addressing mistakes should serve to the employees as an opportunity for growth and development.

DISCUSSION QUESTIONS

1. Discuss the importance of descriptive and prescriptive theories to global leaders. How can the understanding of each help you succeed as a leader?

2. What is knowledge sharing and how is it important in an organization?

3. Name five skills global leaders need to have and briefly explain each.

References

Casciaro, T., & Lobo, M. (2008). When Competence Is Irrelevant: The Role of Interpersonal Affect in Task-Related Ties. *Administrative Science Quarterly, 53*(4), 655-684. Retrieved from Business Source Premier database.

Daft, R. (2008). *The leadership experience.* Mason, OH: South-Western Cengage Learning.

Dance, F.E.X. & Zak-Dance, C.C. (1996). Speaking your mind: private thinking and public speaking (2nd ed.) (pp. 306-308). Dubuque, IA: Kendall/Hunt Publishing Company.

Ellis, M. (2002) Self-assessment: Knowing yourself and what you want to do. Capip News. 5(1). 1-2. Retrieved November 1, 2004. From http://www.opm.state.ok.us/CAPIPNEWS4.pdf

Hollandsworth, R. J. (2004) Asynchronous instruction of interpersonal communications.1-20. Retrieved October 15, 2004 from http://www.rhollands@vt.edu.

Hutt, Terron. "Required Interpersonal Communication Skills for Leadership Coaching." *DU Electronic Capstones, Theses, & Dissertations.* N.p., n.d. Web. 6 Dec. 2010. http://ectd.du.edu/source/uploads/3031436.pdf.

Parker, G.M. (1996). Team players and teamwork. San Francisco: Jossey-Bass Publishers.

Shockley-Zalabak, P. (2002). Fundamentals of organizational communication. (5th ed.). Boston, MA: Allyn & Bacon.

Spangle, M. & Moorhead, J. (1998). Interpersonal communication in organizational settings. Dubuque, IA: Kendall/Hunt Publishing

Wheeler, P.A. (2005, January). The importance of interpersonal skills. Healthcare Executive. 44-45. Retrieved April 14, 2005 from University of Denver, Academic Search Premier Web site: http://penlib.du.edu/findIt/Eresources/index.cfm

Achieving Effectiveness. (2009, 06 03). Retrieved 10 31, 2010, from Through Team Communication: http://www.interlinktc.com/public_html/achieving.html

Ahanchian, M.R., & McCormick, J. (2009). Culture and the processes of virtual

teaming for training. *Journal of Computer Assisted Learning, 25,* 389-396. Retrieved from Academic Source Premier database.

Avolio, B. J., Walumbwa, F. O., & Weber, T. J. (2009, 04 28). *Leadership: Current Theories, Research, and Future Directions.* Retrieved 11 08, 2010, from http://www.socsci.uci.edu/ssarc/fssp/webdocs/LeadershipCurrentTheories.pdf

Center for Creative Leadership. (2005, 04 06). *Leadership Development: Past, Present, Future.* Retrieved 12 01, 2011, from http://www.ccl.org/leadership/pdf/research/cclLeadershipDevelopment.pdf

Combs, W., & Peacocke, S. (2007). Leading virtual teams. *T+D, 61,* 27-28. Retrieved from Academic Source Premier database.

Daft, R. L. (2008). Leading Teams. In *The Leadership Experience* (pp. 294-317). Mason: South-Western CENAGE Learning.

DeChurch, L.A., Zaccaro, S.J. (2010). Perspective: teams won't solve this problem.

Human Factors, 52, 329-334. Retrieved from Academic Search Premier databse.

Foulgar, D. (2009, 06 23). *Models of the Communication Process.* Retrieved 11 25, 2010, from http://foulger.info/davis/research/unifiedModelOfCommunication.htm

Grosse, C. U. (2010, 09 05). *Managing Communication within Virtual Intercultural Teams.* Retrieved 10 31, 2010, from http://bcq.sagepub.com/content/65/4/22.short

Hackman, J. R. (2010, 12 01). *Leading Teams.* Retrieved 11 18, 2010, from Leading Teams: http://www.leadingteams.org/

Higgins, M., Young, L., Weiner, J., & Wlodarczyk, S. (2009). Leading teams of leader:

what helps team member learning? *Phi Delta Kappan, 91*, 41-45. Retrieved from Academic Search Premier database.

Kossler, M.E., & Prestridge, S. (2003). Going the distance: the challenges of leading a dispersed team. *Leadership in Action, 23*, 3-6. Retrieved from Academic Search Premier database.

Peters, L.M., & Manz, M. (2007). Identifying antecedents of virtual team collaboration. *Team Performance Management, 13*, 117–129. Retrieved from Academic Source Premier database.

Rockmann, K.W., & Northcraft, G.B. (2010). Expecting the worst? The dynamic role of competitive expectations in team member satisfaction and team performance. *Small Group Researh, 41*, 308-329. Retrieved from Academic Source Premier database.

Team Development 101. (2009, 11 29). Retrieved 11 18, 2010, from What Team Building Events Are Popular?: http://teamdevelopment101.com/team-building/team-building-events

Thamain, H.J., (2004). Leading technology-based project teams. *Engineering*

Management Journal, 2, 35-42. Retrieved from Academic Search Premier database.

The Importance of Leadership. (2005, 07 21). Retrieved 11 10, 2010, from http://www.mindedgepress.com/PDFs/htlhtl.pdf

Vivien, M. (2006). Leading in teams: part 1. *Nursing Management, 13*, 32-35. Retrieved from Academic Search Premier database.

What is team development so important. (2009, 11 29). Retrieved 11 18, 2010, from Team Development 101: http://teamdevelopment101.com/

Beyene, T. (2007) Fluency as stigma: Implications of a language mandate in global work. Ph.D. dissertation, Stanford University, United States — California. Retrieved from Dissertations & Theses: A&I database. (Publication No. AAT 3267466).

Case Study: Discovering Diversity: Learn To Walk A Mile In The Other Person's Shoes. (2007, January). *PR News*, 63(4), 1. Retrieved from ABI/INFORM Global database. (Document ID: 1204845391).

Citigroup Inc.; Citi Consolidates Global Marketing and Communications Functions Under Lisa Caputo. (2008, July). *Business & Finance Week*,

430. Retrieved from ABI/INFORM Global database. (Document ID: 1523603401).

D'Amico, L., Rubinstein, R. (1999). Cultural Considerations When "Setting" The Negotiation Table. *Negotiation Journal*, Vol. 15, Iss. 4, 389-395. Retrieved from ProQuest.

Fox, C. (2005). Talk to me. *Utility Week*, Vol. 24, iss 7, 22. Retrieved from ProQuest.

Knapp, K., & Meierkord, C. (2002). Approaching lingua franca communication. In K. Knapp& C. Meierkord (Eds.), *Lingua franca communication* (pp. 9-28). Frankfurt am Main,Germany: Peter Lang.

Li, M. (2008). When in China... *Communication World*, Vol 25, Iss 6; 34-38. Retrieved from Proquest.

Masters, B. (2008). Female directors bring added value, study claims. *Financial Times,* 17. Retrieved from ABI/INFORM Global database. (Document ID: 1501668791).

Mirjaliisa, C. (2007). Language Matters In Global Communication: Article Based on ORA Lecture, October 2006. *The Journal of Business Communication*, 44(3), 260-282. Retrieved from ABI/INFORM Global database. (Document ID: 1294713121).

Moran, R., Harris, P., & Moran, S. (2007). *Managing Cultural Differences* (7th Edition). Oxford:Elsevier.

Schmitz, J. *Cultural Orientations Guide,* Princeton, NJ: Princeton Training Press, 2003, pp10-12.

Watson, B., (2006). Culture decoded. *NZ Business*. Auckland, vol. 20, iss 8, 67. Retrieved from ProQuest.

Workplace Answers; Workplace Answers Continues Pioneer Role in Comprehensive Diversity and Inclusion Training. (2008, July). *Business & Finance Week*, 391. Retrieved from ABI/INFORM Global database. (Document ID: 1523655731).

Xiaohua, L., Miller, S. (2003). Negotiation approaches: Direct and indirect effect on national culture. *International Marketing Review*, Vol. 20, Iss. 3, 286-304. Retrieved from ProQuest. (2000). Retrieved Mar. 9, 2006, from http://en.wilkipedia.org.

United States. (2006). Retrieved Mar. 1, 2006, from http://www.cia.gov.

(n.d.). Retrieved Feb. 28, 2006, from http://www.executiveplanet.com/business-culture-in/132272346303.html.

(2000). Retrieved Mar. 9, 2006, from http://en.wilkipedia.org/w/index. php?title=Chinese_language&printable=yes.

(n.d.). Retrieved Mar. 6, 2006, from http://www.reliefweb.int/mapc/asi_ east/cnt/chn/china_mg.html.

(2000). Retrieved Mar. 6, 2006, from http://en.wikipedia.org/wiki/ Geography_of_China.

(2000). Retrieved Mar. 6, 2006, from http://en.wikipedia.org/wiki/ People's_Republic_of_China.

United States. (2006). Retrieved Feb. 6, 2006, from http://www.cia.gov/cia/ publications/factbook/print/ch.html.

United States. (2006). Retrieved Feb. 6, 2006, from http://www.cia.gov/cia/ publications/factbook/print/us.html.

(n.d.). Retrieved Mar. 9, 2006, from http://www.mtholyoke.edu/courses/ sgabriel/economics/9.html.

(n.d.). Retrieved Mar. 9, 2006, from http://www.cia.gov/cia/publications/ factbook/geos/us.html.

(n.d.). Retrieved Mar. 9, 2006, from http://gsbwww.uchicago.edu/student/ capg/recruiting/Challenges%20in%20Monetary%20Policy%20 140503%20(Deutsche).pdf.

(2004). Retrieved Mar. 9, 2006, from http://www.chinadaily.com.cn/ english/doc/2004-06/17/content_340288.htm.

(2005). Retrieved Mar. 9, 2006, from http://www.chinadaily.com.cn/ english/doc/2005-03/05/content_422086.htm.

(n.d.). Retrieved Mar. 9, 2006, from www.**china.**org.cn/e-fabuhui/ download/news/English/PressConferences/990106-2.html.

(2005). Retrieved Mar. 14, 2006, from http://usinfo.state.gov/eap/ Archive/2005/Mar/03-517799.html.

(n.d.). Retrieved Mar. 14, 2006, from http://www.odci.gov/cia/publications/ factbook/geos/ch.html#Econ.

(n.d.). Retrieved Mar. 14, 2006, from http://www.fas.org/man/ crs/980717CRSTradeRelations.htm.

(n.d.). Retrieved Mar. 14, 2006, from http://www.state.gov/r/pa/ei/ bgn/18902.htm.

(n.d.). Retrieved Mar. 14, 2006, from http://www.wto.org/english/news_e/ pres01_e/pr243_e.htm

Bazerman, M.H. (1991). Negotiating Rationally, New York: Free Press.

CIA World Fact Book (2004) http://www.odci.gov/cia/publications/ factbook/geos/ga.html (accessed 16 October 2004).

Cohen, M.A. and H.L. Lee (1989). "Resource Deployment Analysis of Global Manufacturing and Distribution Networks." Journal of Manufacturing and Operations Management, 2: 81-104.

Columbia Electronic Encyclopedia-Information about the Gambia (2004). Columbia University Press. [www document] http://www.infoplease. com/ipa/A0107560.html (accessed 15 October 2004).

Department of State for Trade Industry and Employment (DOSTIE), 2004 source of information about the Gambia, http://www.gambia.gm/ Trade.htm (accessed 20 October 2004).

Dieke, Peter U.C. (1993). "Tourism policy and employment in the Gambia." Employee Relations, Bradford, 15(2): 71-81.

The Economist Intelligence Unit, Ltd. (Oct, 2, 2003). "The Gambia: Economic Background," New York.

Erbes, R. International Tourism and the Economy of Developing Countries, OECD, Paris, 1973.

Hall, Edward T. (1976). Beyond Culture, New York: Doubleday.

Hall, Edward T. (1959). The Silent Language, New York: Anchor Books.

Hamilton, Jacqueline (Feb-Mar 2003). "Are main lines and mobile phones substitutes or complements? Evidence from Africa." Telecommunications Policy, 27(1-2): 190-133.

Hill, Charles W.L. (1999). International Business: Competing in the Global Marketplace, 2nd Edition. New York: Irwin/McGraw-Hill, Inc.

Jenkins, C.L. and Henry, B.N. (1982). "Government Involvement in Tourism in Developing Countries. Annals of Tourism Research, 9(3): 499-521.

Kreitner, R. (1998). Management7th Edition, New York: Houghton Mifflin.

Nemetz, P. and L. Fry (1988). "Flexible Manufacturing Organizations: Implications for Strategy Formulation." Academy of Management Review, 13: 627-638.

Oluyitan, Funso, Ph.D. (April 12, 1997). "Know Africa: The Gambia." The Tennessee Tribune, Nashville, 17(11): 19.

Raiffe, H. (1982). The Art and Science of Negotiation, Cambridge, MA: Harvard University Press.

Robbins, Stephen P. (2005). Organizational Behavior, 11th Edition, Upper Saddle River, NJ: Pearson Prentice Hall.

CIA World Fact Book (2004)http://www.odci.gov/cia/publications/factbook/geos/ga.html (accessed 16 October 2004).

Columbia Electronic Encyclopedia-Information about the Gambia (2004). Columbia University Press. [www document] http://www.infoplease.com/ipa/A0107560.html (accessed 15 October 2004)

Oluyitan, Funso, Ph.D. (April 12, 1997). "Know Africa: The Gambia." The Tennessee Tribune, Nashville, 17(11): 19

Namenwirth, J.Z. and Robert Philip Weber, Dynamics of Culture, Unwin Hyman Publishing, (June 1, 1987), pp. 215-7.

Schein, Edgar H. Organizational Culture and Leadership. 2004, John Wiley and Sons, Inc. San Francisco, pp.18-25.

Grensing-Pophal, Lin. "Hiring to fit your corporate culture, Human Resources Magazine, Alexandria: August 1999, Vol. 44, Issue 8, pg. 50-55.

Robbins, Stephen P. Organizational Behavior, 11th ed. 2005, Pearson Prentice Hall, Upper Saddle River, NJ, pp. 450-455.

O'Reilly III, C.A. and D.E. Caldwell, "People and Organizational Culture: A Profile Comparison Approach to Assessing Person-Organization Fit, Academy of Management Journal, September 1991, Vol. 34, Issue 3, pp. 487-516.

Becker, H.S. "Culture: A Sociological View, Yale Review, Summer 1982, Volume 75, Issue 3, pp. 513-27.

Morgan, G. Images of Organization (Beverly Hills, CA: Sage, 1986), pp. 105-110.

E.H. Schein, "What is Culture? in P.J. Frost et al., Reframing Organizational Culture (Newbury Park, CA: Sage, 1991).

Schein, E.H. 1999. The Corporate Culture Survival Guide. San Francisco: Jossey-Bass Publishers, pp. 89-92.

Schein, E.H. 1996. Culture: The missing concept in organization studies. Administrative Science Quarterly, 41(2), pp. 229-239

Schein, E.H. 1985. Organizational Culture and Leadership. San Francisco: Jossey-Bass Publishers, p.168.

REFERENCES

Quick, J.C. (1992), "Crafting an organizational culture: Herb's hand at Southwest Airlines, Organizational Dynamics, Vol. 21, Issue 2, pp. 45-57.

Trice, H.M. and Beyer, J.M. (1993), The Cultures of Work Organizations, Prentice-Hall, Englewood Cliffs, NJ

Hennessey, J.T. (1998), "Reinventing government: does leadership make the difference? Public Administration Review, Vol. 58 No. 6, pp. 522-32.

Lok, P. and Crawford, J. (1999), "The relationship between commitment and organizational culture, subculture, leadership style and job satisfaction in organizational change and development, Leadership & Organization Development Journal, Vol. 20 No. 7, pp. 365-73.

Pillai, R. and Meindl, J.R. (1998), "A meso-level examination of the relationship of organic structure, collectivism, and crisis to charismatic leadership, Journal of Management, Vol. 24 No. 5, pp. 643-72.

Brooks, I. (1996), "Leadership of a cultural change process, Leadership & Organization Development Journal, Vol. 17 No. 5, pp. 31-7.

Allen, R. and Thatcher, J. (1995), "Achieving cultural change: a practical case study", Leadership & Organization Development Journal, Vol. 16 No. 2, pp. 16-23.

Wood, J. (1999), "Establishing internal communication channels that work, Journal of Higher Education Policy & Management, Vol. 21 No. 2, pp. 135-50.

Rost, J.C. (1991), Leadership for the Twenty-first Century, Praeger, New York, NY, p. 102.

Block, Lory (2003), "The Leadership-Culture Connection: An Exploratory Investigation, Leadership and Organizational Development Journal, Bradford: Volume 24, Issue 5/6, pp. 318-335.

Beyer, Janice M., Trice, Harrision M., "Cultural Leadership In Organizations", Organizational Science, Vol. 2, No. 2, 1991.

Brown, Andrew (1992). Organizational Culture: The Key to Effective Leadership and Organizational Development. Leadership and Organization Journal, Vol. 13(2), pp 3-6.

Brown, Tom (1996). Can You Create 'Predictable Miracles'? Management Review.

Conger, Jay A. (1991). Inspiring Others: The Language of Leadership. Academy of Management Executive,Vol. 5(No. 1),31-45.

Corey, Marianne, Corey, Gerald. Groups: Process and Practice, Brooks/Cole Publishers, Pacific Grove, CA, 1992.

Demers, Russ-Forrer, Stephen E.-et al, (1996). Commitment to Change. Training & Development, 08-01-96, pp 22.

Greene, Robert J. (1995). Culturally Compatible Human Resource Strategies. Human Resources Magazine,Vol.40, pp 115(7).

Hackman, J. Richard. Groups That Work. Jossey-Bass, San Francisco, 1990.

Kouzes, James M.; Posner, Barry Z., The Leadership Challenge, Jossey-Bass,1987

Nixon, Bruce (1992). Developing a New Culture for Organizations in the 90s.

Management Education and Development,Vol.23(1),33-45.

Schein, Edgar H., Organizational Culture and Leadership, Second Edition,

Jossey-Bass Publishers, San Francisco, CA, 1992.

Schneider, Benjamin; Brief, Arthur P.; Guzzo, Richard A. (1996). Creating a Climate and Culture for Sustainable Organizational Change. Organizational Dynamics, pp 6(14).

Senge, Peter M., "The Leader's New Work: Building Learning Organizations", Sloan Management Review, 1990

Smith, Peter B.; Zhong Ming (1996). The Manager as Mediator of Alternative Meanings. Journal of International Business Studies, Vol. 27, 03-01-96, pp 115(23).

Trice, Harrison M., Beyer, Janice M., The Cultures of Work Organizations, Prentice Hall, Englewood Cliffs, N. J., 1993.

Wiener, Yoash (1988). Forms of Value Systems: A Focus on Organizational Effectiveness and Cultural Change and Maintenance

REFERENCES

1. Evolution, by A. Franklin Shull, published by McGraw-Hill, 1951.

2. Essays in Social Theory, by G.D.H. Cole, published by Macmillan, 1950.

3. Max Weber: The Theory of Social and Economic Organization by A.M. Henderson and Talcott Parsons, published by Oxford Univ. Press, 1947.

4. The Active Society, by Amitai Etzioni, published by Collier-Macmillan, 1968.

5. The Good Society, by John Freidmann, published by MIT press, 1979.

6. Postmodernity USA, by Anthony Woodiwiss, published by Sage, 1993.

7. Sociology of Social Change, by Piotr Sztompka, published by Blackwell, 1993.

8. The Changing World of the Executive, by Peter Drucker published by T. Talley, 1982.

9. Business NOT as Usual, by Ira Mitroff, published by Jossey-Bass, 1987.

10. The Future of Work, by David and Eva Gil, published by Schenkman, 1985.

11. The New Capitalism, by William Halal, published by John Wiley, 1986.

12. Designing Effective Organizations, by David K. Banner and T. Elaine Gagne, published by Sage, 1995.

13. Designing Organizations for High Performance, by David P. Hanna,

published by Addison-Wesley, 1988.

REFERENCES

Schlesinger, Jr., A.M., (1992), *The Disuniting of America: Reflections on a Multiracial Society*, W.W. Norton &Co., London and New York.

Baggett, B. 1997. Power Serve: 236 Inspiring Ideas on Servant Leadership. Saltillo Press, Germantown, TN.

Banutu-Gomez, Michael B. 2003. Leadership in the Government of The Gambia: Traditional African Leadership Practice, Shared Vision, Accountability and Willingness and Openness to Change. The Journal of American Academy of Business, Cambridge, 2, (2), 349-359.

Banutu-Gomez, Michael B. 2001. The Role African Leaders can play in Forming, Changing and Sustaining Organizational Culture. Business Research Yearbook, Vol. VIII, 496-500.

Banutu-Gomez, Michael B. 2002. Managing in Developing Countries for Twenty-First Century Organizations: The Case of Africa. Business Research Yearbook, Vol. VII, 488-492.

Bartunek, Jean M., 1984. "Changing Interpretive Schemes and Organizational Restructuring. The Example of a Religious Order",Administrative Science Quarterly, 29, 355-372.

Bass, B. 1990. Bass and Stogdill's Handbook of Leadership: Theory, Research, and Managerial Applications, 3rd ed., The Free Press, New York, NY.

Bennis, W. 1997. Managing People Is Like Herding Cats, Executive Excellence Publishing, Provo, UT.

Bennis,W. & Nanus, B. 1997. Leaders: Strategies for Taking Charge, HarperCollins New York, NY.

Block, P. 1993. Stewardship: Choosing Service over Self-Interest, Berrett-Koehler, San Francisco, CA.

Bouty, I. 2000. Interpersonal and Interaction Influences on Informal Resource Exchanges Between R&D Researchers Across Organizational Boundaries. The Academy of Management Journal, 43, (1), 50-65.

Cacioppe, R. 2000. Creating spirit at work: re-visioning organization development and leadership – Part II. The Leadership & Organizational Development Journal, 21, (2), 110-119.

Chang, A., Bordia P. & Duck J., 2003. Punctuated Equilibrium and Linear Progression: Toward a New Understanding of Group Development. The Academy of Management Journal, 46, (1), 106-117.

Coff, Russell, 2003. Bidding Wars over R&D-Intensive Firms: Knowledge, Opportunism, and the Market for Corporate Control. The Academy of Management Journal, 46, (1), 74-85.

De Pree, M. 1997. Leading without Power: Finding Hope in Service Community, Jossey-Bass, San Francisco, CA.

Deneire & Segalla, 2002. Mr. Christian Pierret, Secretary of State for Industry (1997-2002), on French perspectives on leadership and management. The Academy of Management Executive, 16, (4), 25-30.

Doh, P., 2003. Can Leadership Be Taught? Perspective From Management Educators. The Academy of Management Learning & Education, 2, (1), 54-67.

Dubrin, Andrew, J., 2001. Leadership (3rd ed.). Boston, MA, Houghton Mifflin Company.

Drucker, Peter F., 1988. "Leadership: More Doing Than Dash".

Eddelston, K.A., Kidder, D.L. & Litzky, B.E. 2002. Who's the boss?

Contending with competing expectations from customers and management. The Academy of Management Executive, 16, (4), 85-95.

Egri, P. & Herman, S. 2000. Leadership in the North American Environmental Sector: Values, Leadership Styles, and Contexts of Environmental Leaders and their Organization. The Academy of Management Journal, 43, (4), 571-604.

Fairholm, G.W. 1997. Capturing the Heart of Leadership: Spirituality and Community in the New American Workplace, Praeger, Wesport, CT.

Fairholm, G.W. 1998. Perspective on Leadership: From the Science of Management to its Spiritual Heart, Quorum Books, Westport, CT.

Fairholm, R.M. & Fairholm, G. 2000. Leadership amid the constraints of trust. The Leadership & Organizational Development Journal, 21, (2), 102-109.

Ford, L. 1991. Transforming Leadership: Jesus' Way of Creating Vision, Shaping Values, and Empowering Change, InterVasity Press, Downers Grove, IL.

Gilbert, A. & Ivancevich, M. 2000. Valuing diversity: A tale of two organizations. The Academy of Management Executive, 14, (1), 93-105.

Greenlaf, R.K. 1977. Servant Leadership: A Journey into the Nature of Legitimate Power and Greatness, Paulist Press, New York, NY.

Kelly, D. 2000. Using vision to improve organizational communication. The Leadership & Organizational Development Journal, 21, (2), 92-101.

Greenleaf, Robert K., 1991. Servant Leadership. Paulist Press, New York.

Kelly, Robert., 1992. The Power of Followership. Currency Doubleday, New York.

Kolb, David A., Rubin, Irwin M., and Osland, Joyce S., 1991. The Organizational Behavior Reader, Fifth Edition, Prentice Hall, Englewood Cliffs, New Jersey.

Kotter, John P., 1990. "What Leaders Really Do", Harvard Business Review.

Kouzes, J.M. & Posner, B.Z. 1993. Credibility: How Leaders Gain and Lose it, Why People Demand it, Jossey-Bass, San Francisco, CA.

Lam, S.S.K., & Schaubroeck, J. 2002. How similarities to peers and supervisor influences organizational advancement in different cultures. The Academy of Management Journal, 45, (6), 1120-1136.

256

Malphurs, A. 1996. Values-Driven Leadership: Discovering and Developing Your Core Values for Ministry, Baker Books, Grand Rappids, MI.

Masalin, L., 2003. Nokia Leads Change Through Continuous Learning. The Academy of Management Learning & Education, 2, (1), 68-73.

Maxwell, J.C. 1998. The 21 Irrefutable Laws of Leadership: Follow Them and People will Follow You, Thomas Nelson Publishers, Nashville, NT.

Miller, C. 1995. The Empowered Leader: 10 Keys to Servant Leadership, Broadman & Holman Publishers, Nashville, NT.

Nanus, B. 1995. Visionary Leadership: Creating a Compelling Sense of Direction for your Organization, Jossey-Bass, San Francisco, CA.

Neuschel, R.P. 1998. The Servant Leader: Unleashing the Power of Your People, Vision Sports Management, East Lansing, MI.

Osland, Kolb & Rubin2001. Organizational Behavior Reader (7th ed.). Upper Saddle River, NJ: Prentice Hall.

Perry-Smith, J.E., & Shalley C.E. 2003. The social side of creativity: A static and dynamic social network perspective. The Academy of Management Review, 28, (1), 89-106.

Robbins, S.P., 2003. Organizational Behavior (10th ed.). Upper Saddle River, NJ: Prentice Hall.

Roberts, B.D. 1987. "Power and servanthood: emerging notions of Christian leadership", Encounter, 48, (1), 83-92.

Rowden, W. 2000. The relationship between charismatic leadership behaviors and organizational commitment. The Leadership & Organizational Development Journal, 21, (1), 30-35.

Schein, E.H. 1992. Organizational Culture and Leadership, 2nd ed., Jossey-Bass, San Francisco, CA.

Senge, Peter M., 1990. "The Leader's New Work: Building Learning Organizations", Sloan Management Review.

Shaw, R.B. 1997. Trust in the Balance: Building Successful Organizations on Results, Integrity, and Concern, Jossey-Bass, San Francisco, CA.

Turner, W.B. 2000. The Learning of Love: A Journey toward Servant Leadership, Smith and Helwys Publishing, Macon, GA.

Yukl, G. & Tracey, J.B. 1992. "Consequences of influence tactics used with subordinates, peers, and the boss", Journal of Applied Psychology, 77, (4), 525-535.

Bennis, Warren, On Becoming a Leader, Addison-Wesley Publishing, 1989

Kouzes and Posner, James M. and Barry Z., The Leadership Challenge, Jossey-Bass Publishers, 1987

ORGANIZATIONAL TRANSITIONS
Managing Complex Change
by Richard Beckhard and Reuben T. Harris

Reading, Massachusetts: Addison-Wesley Publishing Company, 1987

REFERENCES

Banutu-Gomez, Michael B. (2002) leadership Practice in the Gambia. Century. Journal of Global Competitiveness, 10, 355-369.

Banutu-Gomez, Michael B. (2001). The Role African Leaders can Play in Forming, Changing, and Sustaining Organizational Culture. *Business Research Yearbook*: Vol VIII, 496-500.

Bijlsma-Frankema, Katinka., 2001. "On managing cultural integration and cultural change processes in mergers and acquisitions". Journal of European Industrial Training, 25 (2, 3, 4): 192-207.

Dubrin, 2001. Leadership (3rd ed.). Boston, MA, Houghton Mifflin Company.

Eddelston, K.A., Kidder, D.L. & Litzky, B.E. 2002. Who's the boss? Contending with competing expectations from customers and management. The Academy of Management Executive, 16, 85-95.

Frey-Ridgway, Susan., 1997. "The cultural dimension of international business". Collection Building, 16 (1): 12-23.

Jones, G.R., 2000. Organizational Theory (3rd ed.). Upper Saddle River, NJ: Prentice Hall.

Harris, Hilary and Kumra, Savita., 2000. "International manager development: Cross-cultural training in highly diverse environments". Journal of Management Development, 19 (7): 602-614.

Hill, C. 2003. International Business: Competing in the Global Marketplace (4th ed.). Burr Ridge, IL, McGraw-Hill Company.

Jeannet, Jean-Pierre, 2000. Managing with Global Mindset. NY, Prentice Hall.

Lam, S.S.K., & Schaubroeck, J. 2002. How similarities to peers and supervisor influences organizational advancement in different cultures. The Academy of Management Journal, 45, 1120-1136.

Peppas, Spero C., 2001. "Subcultural Similarities and Differences: An Examination of US Core Values" . Cross-Cultural Management, 8 (1).

Perry-Smith, J.E., & Shalley C.E. 2003. The social side of creativity: A static and dynamic social network perspective. The Academy of Management Review, 28, 89-106.

Robbins, S.P., 2003. Organizational Behavior (10th ed.). Upper Saddle River, NJ: Prentice Hall.

Rodrigues, Carl R., 1998. "Cultural Classification of Societies and How They Affect Cross-Cultural Management". Cross-Cultural Management, 5 (3).

Schneider, S.C. & Barsoux, J. 2003. Managing Across Cultures (2nd ed.). Boston, MA, Prentice Hall.

Twomey, Daniel F., 2002. Leadership, Organizational Design, and Competitiveness For the 21st Century. Journal of Global Competitiveness, 10, 31-40.

Zakaria, Norhayati., 2000. "The effects of cross-cultural training on the acculturation process of the global workforce". International Journal of Manpower, 21 (6): 492-510.

Amin, Samir, MODERN MIGRATIONS IN WESTERN AFRICA, Oxford University Press, 1974

Jackson, J.A., MIGRATION, Cambridge University Press, 1969

Jarrett, Alfred A., THE ENCROACHMENT OF RURAL-URBAN MIGRATION IN SIERRA LEONE, International Social Work, 1990

Kanter, Rosabeth Moss, COMMITMENT AND COMMUNITY, Harvard University Press, 1972

Kaunda, Kenneth, ZAMBIA SHALL BE FREE, Heinemann Books, 1962

King, Coretta Scott, THE WORDS OF MARTIN LUTHER KING, JR., Newmarket Press, 1983

Kouzes, James M. and Posner, Barry Z., THE LEADERSHIP CHALLENGE, Jossey-Bass, 1987

Mazrui, Ali A., THE AFRICAN CONDITION, Cambridge University Press, 1980

Yukl, Gary, Leadership in Organizations, Prentice Hall, Upper Saddle River, New Jersey 2010

Wikipedia, the free encyclopedia. (2011, January 31). *The definition of Lobbying*. Retrieved February 08, 2011, from Wikipedia: http://en.wikipedia.org/wiki/Lobbying

Index

developing nations 11, 18, 19, 20, 21, 63, 64, 65, 66, 67, 68, 146, 199

development xvii, 3, 11, 12, 16, 21, 31, 39, 40, 41, 42, 61, 62, 63, 64, 65, 66, 67, 68, 69, 70, 73, 81, 94, 95, 102, 106, 108, 110, 117, 120, 123, 128, 130, 134, 136, 146, 147, 156, 165, 170, 182, 185, 202, 224, 229, 237, 238, 243, 247, 252, 255, 258

Discipline in a Team Oriented Organization 220

E

Empowerment 41, 69

extended family 13, 159, 173

G

Ghana 156, 157, 158, 159, 160, 162, 174, 175, 176, 178, 182, 183, 186, 192, 193, 194

global change 89

Globalization 11, 21, 195

global leadership effectiveness 235, 236, 237

goals 1, 3, 6, 9, 10, 19, 41, 44, 49, 50, 51, 52, 58, 62, 64, 65, 66, 67, 68, 72, 74, 83, 89, 90, 96, 104, 112, 114, 117, 118, 124, 127, 128, 130, 133, 146, 200, 229, 232, 237, 238, 241

Griots 13

group 3, 4, 5, 12, 13, 17, 18, 22, 31, 42, 44, 49, 50, 52, 54, 55, 69, 76, 83, 94, 98, 107, 117, 118, 120, 122, 123, 124, 125, 127, 131, 132, 134, 136, 150, 151, 163, 166, 172, 174, 183, 197, 198, 205, 206, 207, 208, 211, 215, 220, 225, 228, 232, 238, 240

Group Development 255

group dynamics 4

Guinea-Bissau 12, 178

I

imperialism 8, 100

influence 14, 17, 22, 39, 40, 41, 47, 52, 53, 56, 65, 74, 76, 78, 86, 95, 104, 115, 120, 121, 122, 123, 127, 131, 134, 140, 141, 144, 151, 159, 166, 167, 168, 169, 170, 203, 219, 224, 226, 238, 241, 257

Innovation xvii, 44, 122, 124, 208

Inquiry 58

Inspiring Others 8, 9, 253

intimacy 1

K

Kenya 156, 164, 165, 166, 167, 168, 169, 170, 171, 172, 173, 174, 179, 180, 181, 182, 185, 186, 188, 189, 190, 191, 192, 193, 194

knowledge sharing 242

L

lateral interdependence 235, 236

leader 1, 3, 6, 8, 243, 246

Leader 10, 253, 257, 258

Leadership xvii, 1, 4, 5, 8, 9, 14, 16, 19, 31, 39, 40, 42, 47, 108, 123, 124, 130, 131, 192, 201, 208, 219, 229, 232, 235, 239, 245, 246, 247, 251, 252, 253, 254, 255, 256, 257, 258, 259, 260

leadership practices 6, 14, 17, 122, 124, 130, 138, 140, 141

leadership style 232, 252

loyalty 8, 126, 198, 211, 241

M

Managerial activities 235

Manjako 12, 120, 143

monitoring 93, 117, 139, 176, 236, 237, 239
motivation 16, 31, 43, 88, 91, 114, 121, 126, 240

N

negative experiences 9
negotiation 42, 79, 127, 143, 150, 151, 196, 203, 205, 206, 207, 217, 218
New Mission 43
non-violent 10
norms 13, 47, 89, 120, 122, 124, 126, 134, 136, 151, 205, 206, 223, 231

O

Obstacles and Risks 7
organization 1, 3, 5, 7, 8, 9, 10, 12, 13, 14, 15, 16, 17, 18, 19, 20, 31, 39, 41, 42, 44, 46, 47, 48, 49, 50, 51, 52, 53, 54, 56, 57, 68, 69, 72, 73, 74, 76, 77, 78, 79, 80, 81, 82, 83, 86, 87, 88, 89, 90, 91, 92, 93, 96, 97, 99, 104, 105, 106, 107, 108, 109, 111, 112, 113, 114, 115, 116, 117, 118, 122, 123, 124, 126, 127, 128, 129, 130, 131, 132, 133, 134, 148, 159, 168, 184, 196, 197, 199, 200, 201, 202, 209, 214, 216, 219, 220, 221, 222, 223, 224, 227, 228, 229, 231, 233, 234, 235, 236, 237, 239, 240, 241, 242, 243, 251, 255
organizational 3, 4, 5, 9, 10, 11, 12, 13, 15, 31, 41, 43, 44, 46, 47, 48, 49, 50, 51, 52, 53, 54, 56, 57, 71, 72, 73, 74, 75, 79, 80, 81, 82, 83, 85, 87, 89, 90, 91, 92, 93, 96, 101, 104, 107, 108, 109, 112, 113, 114, 116, 117, 118, 120, 121, 122, 123, 124, 126, 128, 130, 131, 132, 133, 134, 135, 136, 138, 139, 140, 141, 148, 219, 221, 222, 223, 224, 233, 235, 236, 237, 245, 252, 256, 257, 259
Organizational vii, xvii, 12, 13, 40, 46, 47, 48, 50, 74, 79, 86, 91, 92, 122, 123, 130, 132, 139, 148, 201, 251, 252, 253, 254, 255, 256, 257, 258, 259
organizational culture 12, 41, 44, 46, 48, 73, 81, 82, 92, 93, 122, 123, 124, 130, 135, 138, 140, 141, 142, 148, 223

P

participative global leadership 238
Patriotism 14
Philosophy 135
plan 6, 9, 50, 51, 53, 54, 55, 68, 77, 102, 117, 118, 127, 130, 132, 133, 205, 227, 228
planning 48, 50, 63, 72, 84, 85, 87, 97, 108, 110, 117, 132, 157, 236, 237
proceeding generations 13

R

relationship 14, 19, 20, 48, 49, 61, 78, 124, 130, 131, 136, 151, 153, 197, 203, 205, 208, 225, 229, 230, 237, 252, 257

S

Senegal 12, 120, 121, 143, 144, 160, 161, 178
skill 11, 108, 114, 128, 146, 151, 200, 230, 231, 238, 239, 240
skillful 8, 222, 242
Skillful 4
Skillful leaders 4
status quo 97, 124
Status Quo 1, 8, 10

www.ingramcontent.com/pod-product-compliance
Lightning Source LLC
Chambersburg PA
CBHW031827170526
45157CB00001B/208